Satya Sood, a third generation Indian, was born in Kenya in 1933. He was educated at Allidina Visram High School, Mombasa and the Duke of Gloucester School, Nairobi. He played cricket for Kenya Schools XI and captained Kenya Schools Hockey XI against Pakistan in 1953.

After studying medicine at Birmingham University he specialised in Obstetrics and Gynaecology. He is the first Kenyan to become a Fellow of the Royal Colleges of London, Edinburgh and Canada. He was a Professor at the University of Saskatchewan.

He is the founder President of the India-Canada Association of Saskatchewan. He has published several papers in Medical Journals and articles on Indian history and culture.

Satya Sood is married and has two children. He lives in Kent.

VICTORIA'S TIN DRAGON

A RAILWAY THAT BUILT A NATION

Satya V Sood

VICTORIA'S
TIN DRAGON

A RAILWAY THAT BUILT A NATION

Vanguard Press

A CIP catalogue record for this title is
available from the British Library.

ISBN 978 1 84386 274 1

Vanguard Press is an imprint of
Pegasus Elliot MacKenzie Publishers Ltd.
www.pegasuspublishers.com

First Published in 2007

Vanguard Press
Sheraton House Castle Park
Cambridge England

Printed & Bound in Great Britain

Dedication

For

Kusum
Sanj
Monia

And the Railway men and women who not
only built a railway but a country.

Author's Notes

With time on my hands, after years of practising Obstetrics and Gynaecology, my thoughts turned to the land of my birth. It became patently obvious that the lack of information about Indian pioneers is due to their own disinterest. The Europeans, on the other hand, curiously ignored the Indians. Their paltry writing about Indians has been full of confusion, errors and misspellings. "Most Europeans", writes the author Cynthia Salvadori, "heard the Indians only as 'gibbering' and delighted in ridiculing them by giving examples of 'babu English' although few of the authors would have been able to speak a single sentence of any Indian language". It is hoped that this informal history will redress some of this imbalance.

I wish to thank the following for their kindness in permitting me to reproduce textual material and illustrations: Mr Vishu Sharma, Mr Gurdial Singh, the late Mr Shafiq Arian, Dr Dhruv Dhupa, the late Mr Eddie Suarez, Ms Hamda Khan, Mr Joginder Bhangu, Mr Mushtaq Rajput, Mr Davinder Mayor, East African Railways Corporation, and the Victoria and Albert Museum. I also wish to thank Mr Bob Bishop for organizing and improving the old photographs.

Warmest thanks to Mrs Liane Pathak for her unflinching support and endless patience in typing and retyping the manuscript and many helpful suggestions.

To Mr Sanj Sood, my thanks for his invaluable advice and encouragement and for reading the manuscript in its final stages.

I am indebted to my mother, Lila Vati Dhupa and my father, Durga Dass Dhupa, for their vast fund of stories and anecdotes, many of which have been included.

If the readers enjoy this book even a quarter as much as I have writing it, then we shall all have fun clattering along in Victoria's Tin Dragon.

CONTENTS

1. Zinj – Ancient, Medieval and Recent Connections   19

2. Victoria's Tin Dragon   40

3. Duel of Turbans and Topees   70

4. Riding the Rails   93

5. Bwana Governor   129

6. Landies and Landiwallas   182

7. The Killing Fields   246

8. The Last Nail in Hitler's Coffin   264

9. Independence and its Aftermath   281

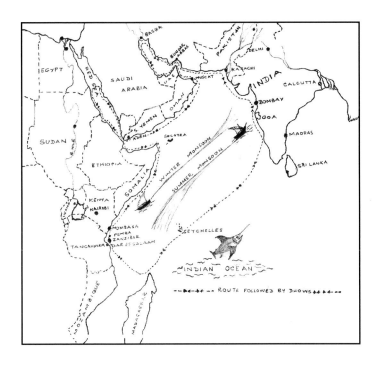

ROUTE FOLLOWED BY DHOWS

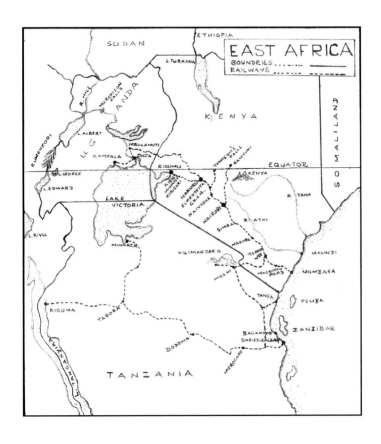

Chapter 1

Zinj – Ancient, Medieval and Recent Connections

The name Africa is perhaps derived from the Sanskrit word *aparica* meaning behind or west as one faced the sun. The ancient Indians imagined the world as a lotus flower with four large petals representing India, Europe, Siberia and China. To the south-west between the petals of Europe and India lay two smaller petals of *Sancha* (Zanzibar) and *Harina* (Madagascar)[1].

Most scholars accept that ancient Indians were a seafaring people. They traded with Egyptians and Mesopotamians before 3000 BC. This trade was carried out by Dravidians until the Aryan invasion about fifteen centuries before the birth of Christ. The Dravidians were pushed to the south and this seismic change resulted in a decline of this flourishing trade.

North India continued to be buffeted by further conquests. Persians invaded during the reign of Darius I (521-485 BC). Alexander the Great arrived in Punjab in 323 BC and conquered as far as River Beas (Hyphasis). The north was then ruled by Indian Mauryas who formed the first Indian empire with headquarters at Pataliputra. This was a period of reforms and peace. They built hospitals, schools and roads. Buddhist missionaries were sent abroad to enlighten the world. Bactrian invaders then took possession of India and they were, in turn, followed by many Scythian tribes.

Indian Guptas then repossessed the motherland and ruled for many years. They unified the north once again. This period marks the golden age of Hindu literature, arts and science. The decimal system and the use of zero evolved during this period. The theory of the rotation of the earth was postulated by Hindus and Sanskrit became the universal language.

It was then the turn of the Mongoloid Huns who disrupted the orderly Indian civilization. Once again, an Indian king, Vardhana of Gupta dynasty and his son, Harsha, recaptured India. During this period, there was a prolonged struggle for central India, especially the Royal City of Kanauji and this caused the exhaustion of the

---

[1] Ref: Pg 245-367, Wilford, Frances – *An Essay on the Sacred Isles in the West, with other Essays connected with that work,* ibid., VIII(1805)

19

major Indian kingdoms and led to the establishment of small feudal states. The Muslims conquered Sind (711 AD) during this period. The disparate Hindu princes formally accepted Barbarian Rajputs as nobles in a fire ceremony at Mount Abu and the Rajputs thus became the principal defenders of India against outsiders. Subsequently, all the invaders who crossed into India had one thing in common – ISLAM.

Meanwhile, trade with Africa continued. At the end of the first century AD, a Greek or a Greek-speaking Egyptian sailor who sailed down the East African coast, wrote in his book, *''The Periplus of the Erythraen Sea'* that there was vigorous trade between the Indians, Romans and Egyptians through the Red Sea. Indians from *Ariaca* (Kathiawar, Cutch and Gujarat) and *Bfrygaza* (Broach) were trading with *Barbica* (Somalia) and the Azania – on the East African coast south of Cape Guadafui. This trade extended as far south as Rhapta, identified by various authors as Kilwa, Dar es Salaam, Pangani and Msasani. He also mentioned Indian settlement on the island of *Discorida* (Socotra).

Periplus's account is supported by other Greek historians – Strabo and Pliny. Strabo described 120 ships sailing from Myos Hormos to India in one year and Pliny noted that India drained the Roman Empire of a hundred million sesterces every year[2]. In spite of this revelation about the benefits of trade winds and the potential for trade with Africa, these writings did not make an impact on Europeans for whom East Africa remained a neglected area.

India supplied cotton cloth, ghee, flint glass, axes, spearheads, wheat, rice, sesame oil, glass beads and sundry manufactured articles. In return it imported gold from *Ophir* (Zimbabwe), iron, ivory, silver and gum copal. Ambergris from whales found on East African beaches from Mombasa to Mogadishu, frankincense and myrrh – a fragrant gum resin from East African trees – and cinnamon, all found their way to India. The discovery of Indian Cambay beads, dating back to the third century AD, along the coast and Zimbabwe and Zanzibar lends credence to ancient contact between East Africa and India.

The trade between India and Africa was dependent on *dhows* – ancient wooden Arab lateen-rigged boats with a long overhang forward, a high poop and a low waist. These have survived over

---

[2] Ref: Strabo – *Geography,* book II, ChapV, Sec 12
Pliny – *Natural History,* XII, 18

centuries and they can still be seen bobbing up and down in the Old Mombasa harbour. Dhows were wafted to and fro by the seasonal monsoon winds. During October to March, the winds blew from the north-east towards the East African coast and were called *Kazkazi*. For the next six months, these breezes called *Kuzi* reversed their direction, cradling and pushing the same Dhows towards India. Therefore, the *Kazi* (Swahili for work) was done by the Kazkazi and Kuzi.

The *Kuzi* not only brought rich raw and rare materials to India but also delivered the very lifeblood of India – WATER. During the summer months, the Indian landmass becomes a blazing *tandoor*. The sun is hot and unrelenting. The earth becomes dry and shrinks and cracks appear. The vegetation wilts and dries. Dust storms become common and the air is hot and stifling.

During this inferno, which lasts from the end of April to the end of June, the afternoons are filled with the piercing sounds, *peeooh* – the call of the brain fever bird[3]. The cry of this hawk-cuckoo (*hierococcyx varius*) is rendered as *'brain fever, brain fever'* in English; in Punjabi and Hindustani as *peeooh* or *pi kahan* (where is my beloved). The call of this bird has a magical effect and the whole country waits anxiously for the monsoon and the rain it will bring.

The harbinger of the monsoon is the monsoon bird – pied-crested cuckoo *(clamater jacobinus)* – which fills the parched countryside with its plaintive cries. With its arrival, the air suddenly becomes cool, the rolling clouds become dark and low and soon the skies open. The rain comes down in sheets and torrents, soaking and drenching the mother earth and slaking its thirst. The land becomes moist and pleasant. New life blossoms forth and the drenching of the soil drives the cobra out of its subterranean hideout. The sound of the water, the song of the birds, the flight of the bumblebee and the dance of the peacock transform the countryside. It is the time for humans to rejoice and sing and fall in love.

While the north of India was going through political upheaval, the south remained aloof and stable and these conditions were conducive to steady progress. Insulated from external influences, the Tamil kingdoms of Pallava and Chalukya started to dominate south India. They became very strong, ambitious and adventurous thanks

---

[3] Ref: Pg 8 – Singh, Khushwant – *The History of The Sikhs,* Vol I. 1469-1839, Oxford University Press, New Delhi, 1963

to the emergence of a powerful navy. The fifth, sixth and seventh centuries have been called the period of Hindu imperialism. At the beginning of the seventh century, the South Indians colonized Pegu, Ceylon, Java, Sumatra and Cambodia. They also ventured into China, Arabia and Persia and settled there. They traded with Rome and Babylon. As Rome's power declined, India had no difficulty in substituting the lost markets with other lucrative markets. Pulakeshi II who ruled the south had a fleet of hundreds of ships and this period in the seventh century was thus the golden age of India's maritime activity.

The people of the north of India did not remain inactive. The Jats from Cutch became notorious pirates and they occupied islands in the Gulf of Bahrain. The Gupta king traded widely from Sind and Gujarat. In 603 AD, a prince from Gujarat set sail with 5,000 soldiers in six large, and hundreds of small ships and founded the kingdom of Java[4].

During the third century AD, the Kushna period in India, Indians may have introduced iron to the pre-Bantu coastal people. About the same period, it is suggested that Dravidians pushed back Hottentots and Pygmies, the original inhabitants of East Africa, and through inter-marriage, produced Bantu-speaking people. Thus, while the first seven centuries AD on the whole was a period of decline for Europe, they represented a time of enterprise and expansion for India[5]. From the seventh to the fifteenth century, Indians, Arabs and Persians influenced the East African coast. The hybrid Swahilis were emerging by 1100 AD. The Arabs named the coast Zinj or Zanj, meaning black, and the area became known as Zanzibar[6].

In the south of India, the Cholas, Pandyas and Cheras were competing for power. The seventh and eighth centuries saw the Tamil kingdoms of Pallava and Chalukya struggling for the domination of south India. By the tenth century, the Cholas, dominated southern India and reached their zenith in the eleventh century. By the twelfth century, the Pandya kingdom superseded the

---

[4] Ref: Pg 8 – Villiers, Alan – *Monsoon Seas: The Story of the Indian Ocean,* New York, 1952
Raffles, Stamford – *History of Java.* London 1817, II,87ff
[5] Ref: P110-11 – Matthew – *The East African Coast.*
Powell Price, J.C. – *History of India.* London 1955, chapters XIII & XIV
[6] Ref: Burke, E.E. – *Some Aspects of Arab Contact with South East Africa.* Unpublished paper. Leverhulme History Conference, Sept. 1960

Cholas who vanished in the thirteenth century. The Pandyas were attacked by Ala-ud-din from north India at the beginning of the fourteenth century and resulted in the Hindu kingdom of Vijyanagar becoming the independent centre of resistance to Islam.

While the south of India was becoming very powerful, the north was undergoing important changes. The Muslims invaded the Sind area as a reprisal for the attacks on Muslims in the Persian Gulf. They captured this area under Mir Kasim in 711. This was years after their peaceful arrival on the south west coast as sailors and businessmen – a fact often overlooked.

The first invasion by Muslim Afghans from the north came in 1001 when Mahmud of Ghazni descended upon India through the Khyber Pass. He was followed by other Afghans such as the Ghauris, Tugluks, Suris and Lodhis. In between, in 1398, came the Mongol Taimur the Lame.

By 1206 Kutb-ud-din Aibak had established the great Muslim empire and his influence spread south of Decca, where he usurped control from the Bahamanis. By 1347, the Bahamanis had retaken Decca and established its capital at Daulatabad. There was a large trading centre at Diu and a seaport at Dabol. The Muslim Indians who emigrated from Diu and Dabol may be the people referred to as the Dibuli and Diba in oral traditions of Zanzibar and Pemba. In 1526, India was captured by Babar who defeated Lodhi at Panipat and thus started the most powerful dynasty in India.

If the trade between India and Africa was bilateral so was the political influence. The slaves from Africa have played a significant role in Indian history. The trade goes back to time immemorial. The Ethiopians were described in the sixth century markets of Ceylon by Cosmas Indicopleustas. They were essentially free Africans who were called Sidis[7] in India and they served as soldiers in the forces of the Bahamani Kingdom. They also engaged in legitimate trade as well as piracy. They seized the island fortress of Danda-Rajpuri, 26 miles south of Bombay, and ruled it for many years.

In the thirteenth century (1236) Iltumish, the great slave king, died and he was succeeded by his daughter, Razia Sultan, who has the unique distinction of being the only woman to occupy the throne of Dehli. She fell in love with Yakut, an Abyssinian slave, and promoted him to the high office of Master of the Royal Stables. She ruled with his help until the jealous Turkish nobles murdered him.

---

[7] Ref: pp XIX-XX – Banaji, D.R. – *Bombay and the Sidis.* London 1932

Razia ruled for only three-and-a-half years when she, too, was murdered after a defeat in the battlefield.

African slaves continued to be imported in large numbers and there were 8000 slaves in the Muslim kingdom established by Rukn-ud-din Barbak in Bengal from 1459 to 1474. After Barbak's successor was murdered by the slaves, they ruled Bengal for six years until their vulnerable kingdom fell and the slaves were expelled. They eventually ended up in Gujarat and Deccan where they were absorbed into the existing slave population. In 1461, the rule of Humayan, a Bahmani king, was ended prematurely when an African slave maidservant stabbed him to death.

There is ample evidence that the connections between East Africa and India go back to ancient and medieval times and each country exerted considerable influence on the other. The only question that remains is the extent to which these connections played a part.

The period of a few centuries before Renaissance was a time of easy living and opulence for the people of the East African coast. The Zinjians enjoyed an unprecedented standard of living. They traded with the Arabs, Persians and Indians. Their ivory, gold and spices were in great demand and the profits filled their coffers to the brim. To support the extravagant Zinjian lifestyle, silks, carpets and coloured tiles came from Persia, and gold and silver jewellery, precious stones and sandalwood from India. The Arabs brought dates, swords and daggers.

The culture of the area was predominantly Arabic, influenced no doubt by the large numbers of immigrants who filtered in from the sheikdoms scattered around the Red Sea and especially from Oman. Small kingdoms sprang all along the coast at places like Kilwa, Pemba and Mombasa. The rich guarded their assets and lifestyle jealously as they feasted on the produce from fertile soil and plentiful *fruits de mer*. They hid from the sun in large palaces during the hot days and emerged during the evenings to enjoy the sea breezes, good food, and no doubt, good wines and *khat*. The women would spend their day preening themselves and applying henna and other make-up and emerge into the courtyard in the evenings and enjoy tobacco and *halwa*.

Ibn Batutta, the great fourteenth century traveller from Morocco, visited the East African coast and described the diet of a typical Mogadishu citizen: *"The food of these people is rice cooked in butter, with it they serve side dishes of stew of chicken, meat, fish and vegetables. They cook unripe bananas in fresh milk, and serve as a sauce. They put curdled milk in another vessel with peppercorns, vinegar and saffron, green ginger and mangoes*[8]. The citizens are *'fat and corpulent'*.

The ordinary citizens were no doubt thin and hardworking but the living was on the whole easy. Marco Polo was among a large number of explorers who wrote strange stories about Zinj. He described the people as large limbed and stout, with flattened noses and thick, large lips. This proved to be pure fabrication as he never visited East Africa. The coastal Swahili people and their language undoubtedly owe their origin and development to intermarriage between the locals and the visiting Arabs, Persians and Indians as their features are much finer and skin lighter in colour.

The arrival of the Europeans soon put an end to this utopia. Vasco da Gama, on his way to discovering India, arrived in East Africa after rounding the Cape of Good Hope. He was very impressed with what he saw and his reports were so favourable that the Portuguese soon made a beeline for and descended on the East African coast. They, in common with other European nations at that time, had only one thing in mind – exploitation. For the next two centuries, they wreaked havoc wherever they went. They sacked and plundered Kilwa, destroyed Pate and then turned their attention to Mombasa. The Sultan of this city kingdom refused to submit. He was therefore subjected to the full force of the Portuguese fury. The town was razed to the ground, men and women were killed and a large body of gold and silver was taken.

The defeated Sultan wrote to the King of Malindi: *"This is to inform you that a great lord has passed through the town, burning it and laying it to waste. He came to town with such strength and was of such cruelty that he spared neither man nor woman, old nor young, nay, not even the smallest child. He not only killed and burnt men but even the birds of heavens were shot down. The stench of the corpses is so great in the town that I dare not go there".* This letter must have put the fear of God into the King of Malindi who capitulated to the Portuguese invaders without a fight.

The Portuguese triumph was less destructive of Indian influence than of Arab. The Indians, although their business declined, continued to maintain significant commerce with East

---

[8] Ref: p15 – Miller, Charles – The Lunatic Express. The Macmillan Company, New York, NY 1971

Africa and they became accountants and bankers for the Portuguese as they had been for the Arabs. A rich Indian merchant, Muhammed Rukn al-Din al-Dabuli, was installed as Sultan at Kilwa[9].

The rape and pillage inflicted all along the coast made the Portuguese the most hated of all nations who came in contact with East Africa and it is perhaps because of this that all vestiges of their rule and culture were wiped out once their star began to wane. To this day, the only surviving symbols of the oppression that scars the beautiful island are Fort Jesus and the tradition of bull-fighting that continue in the offshore island of Pemba.

The first challenge to the Portuguese came from Ali Bey, a Turk who sailed into the Mombasa harbour, and with the support of the local population, inflicted a crushing defeat on the Portuguese. Being a corsair, it was not long before Ali Bey departed with his loot. The Turkish ships had hardly disappeared beyond the horizon when the Portuguese, bent on revenge, punished the city in their usual merciless manner with the help of a naval squadron which arrived from India.

Buoyed by his success three years earlier, Ali Bey returned in 1589 with the express wish to drive the Portuguese infidel out of Africa. This time, an armada of twenty Portuguese warships arrived from India to lay siege and blocked the Mombasa harbour. The Mombasans tried to get help from the Bantus on the mainland but they were double-crossed. Faced with the Portuguese on one side and the Bantu combatants on the other, Ali Bey tried to escape but he was captured, chained and shipped to Portugal. Mombasa and its people were no doubt punished once again.

In spite of this temporary success, the days of the Portuguese were numbered as other imperialist nations like England and Holland were waiting in the wings to pounce on this lucrative trade. In 1591, James Lancaster visited the East African coast and Zanzibar. He became very aware of the disdain of the locals for the Portuguese. The Portuguese who felt threatened, started a propaganda war and tried to paint the English as 'cruel man-eaters'!

In 1593, the Portuguese started building a colossal fort. This was a stone structure built by masons imported from India. This stone fort which lay at the mouth of Mombasa harbour was to protect the Portuguese from the local population and to scare off any challenge from other Europeans with similar aspirations. Fort Jesus

---

[9] Ref: p22-32 – Gray – *The Wadebuli and the Wadiba*

proved to be no more than an edifice for lulling the Portuguese into a false sense of security.

In 1631, Yusef bin Hassan was appointed the Sultan of Mombasa by the Portuguese. He was proselytized to Catholicism and named Don Geronimo bin Hassan. Hassan bided his time, and at the opportune moment, he turned on his benefactors, murdered all the Portuguese in Mombasa and became the king of the castle. By 1635, Fort Jesus was a Portuguese possession once again, but the dye was cast and for the Portuguese, the end was nigh. Various centres captured by the Portuguese to secure the passage to India began to fall like ninepins.

In 1651, the City of Muscat was captured by the Omani Arabs and a general coastal revolt began. This struggle continued for almost seventy years, culminating in the fall of Fort Jesus and the hated Portuguese being forced out of Zinj once and for all. They retreated to Mozambique to lick their wounds and to reflect on what might have been given a more human attitude and a different strategy.

The hiatus thus created was soon filled by the Omanis. These Muslim invaders did not have an easy time either. The main resistance once again came from Mombasa which became known as *Mvita*, the island of war. The Omanis appointed the Mzrui clan as administrators of Mombasa but the Mzrui had plans of their own and this resulted in constant battles between the two. Meanwhile, the feuds between various coastal cities of Zinj continued. In 1800, savage hostilities broke out among Lamu, Mombasa and Pate. Lamu, supported by the Omanis, inflicted a surprising defeat on Mombasa despite its superiority in numbers at the Battle of Sheila. However, for the Mzrui of Mombasa, this was a temporary setback and their influence in the coastal region continued to override that of the distant overlords – the Omani Imams.

It was at this juncture that distant events in India and elsewhere worked to Oman's advantage and consolidated its hold on the East African coast. This was a period of intense rivalry between the French and the British. Napoleon was very ambitious and wanted more than a toehold in India. He knew that Tippu, Sultan of Mysore, hated the British with a passion and that he had been seeking arms from the French in order to negate the British threat that was a constant thorn in his side. Napoleon decided to oblige by sharing his arsenal. Napoleon had hoped that this conflict would divert British attention to the south of India, thus affording an opportunity for the

French to move in and consolidate their position elsewhere in India. The other key factor was Imam Seyyid Said, the Sultan of Oman. If he could be won over, the French would have a secure staging post for their ships and soldiers. Tippu Sultan and Seyyid Said were thus mere pawns in the chess game being played out by the hungry super-powers who were out to grab the jewel of the east – India.

Unfortunately for Napoleon, his letters were intercepted by the British agent in Mocha who wasted no time in informing the Marquis of Wellesley, the Governor General of India, of Napoleon's designs. A crushing defeat was soon inflicted on Tippu Sultan but the Sultan of Oman was treated with kid gloves as the British also wanted his help and the use of his harbour as a staging post. A treaty was concluded with the Imam, which not only excluded the French from Oman, but also allowed a British garrison to be stationed at Bandar Abass and a full time British agent stationed at Muscat. As the Cape of Good Hope was already in British hands, since it was wrested from the Dutch in 1795, the British managed to exclude Napoleon from these important areas. The Omanis were also happy as they could now concentrate on the coastal region and put the Mzrui in their place – at least, that was their plan!

The Mzrui were constantly harassed by Oman and they were prepared to clutch at every straw. In 1823, the HMS Barracuda was put into Mombasa harbour to take on provisions while on a mission to chart the coast. The Mzrui begged for British protection and offered the island of Mombasa in return. This offer was turned down by Vidal, the ship's commander, but the Mzrui decided to fly a makeshift Union Jack on their own accord, no doubt to needle the Omani fleet that was blockading the harbour at the time. Meanwhile, Captain Owen, the commander of the sister ship HMS Levan, was putting pressure on the Imam in Oman to give up the lucrative slave trade and gave him an ultimatum of three years. Owen then sailed to Mombasa where the Mzrui again asked for British protection and offered him the island of Mombasa and 200 miles of the coastal strip. Owen decided to accept the offer on the condition that slavery would be abolished forthwith. He had no such mandate either from the Imam or the British Government. He claimed that he did not have a selfish motive and that he had acted 'in the Honour of God and my King'. Owen soon departed from the island, leaving behind a young 23 year old South African third lieutenant named James Reitz, who thus became the first Governor of British East Africa.

As soon as Owen raised anchor, the Mzrui resumed their trade in human cargo. Reitz protested but to no avail. The Mzrui gave him a large plot of land to keep him quiet. This Reitz named the English Point. Soon afterwards, Reitz contracted malaria and died in Mombasa 'in a most awful state of delirium'[10]. Today, an inner harbour of Mombasa is called Port Ritz in his memory.

The command thus fell on the shoulders of a young 16 year old midshipman named George Phillips. His days of glory were numbered because the British government had, meanwhile, made a pact with Sultan Said to limit the slave trade and Owen had inadvertently upset the apple cart. Mombasa was therefore returned to the Sultan who, as expected, made mincemeat of Mzrui.

The second quarter of the nineteenth century saw some dramatic changes. In 1828, Sultan Seyyid Said of Oman visited Zanzibar. He was very impressed with the lush green vegetation, the plethora of fruit and vegetables, the abundance of cool fresh water springs, the soft sea breezes and the richness of the soil. As well, there was an excellent large harbour in comparison with Oman, where the sands were hot, the air stifling and the land harsh, dusty and brown. So enamoured did he become with Zanzibar that he decided to loosen the grip of the coast of Oman and embrace the beauty of Zanzibar. In 1840, the Sultan quit Oman and settled in Zanzibar.

This decision was not only taken for aesthetic reasons but it made good business sense as well. With this the focus of trade shifted to the East African coast and Zanzibar became the hub of activity. The soil was ideal for clove growing which so far was the monopoly of the East Indies. The Sultan ordered the replacement of each coconut palm with three clove trees. So well did they flourish that within his lifetime, he saw Zanzibar and Pemba become the principal source of cloves in the world.

The ivory trade was booming, the slave trade was brisk, amounting to an estimated annual export of twenty to thirty thousand, and hides and gum copal were in great demand. The exports were paying for the imports of textiles, metal wares, beads, rum and other commodities. To encourage commerce, the Sultan fixed import duty at a nominal 5 per cent. There were no export duties, no harbour taxes and no monopolies. The trade with the

---

[10] Ref: p 23 – Huxley, Elspeth – *Nine Faces of Kenya.* Collins Harvill, London 1990

hinterland had new impetus. New Arab centres mushroomed in Tanganyika at Kaze (Tabora), Ujiji and Masansa.

These events also led to a revival of Indian commercial trade with East Africa. The Sultan was pro-Indian. He was impressed by them in Muscat and had developed confidence in them as he found them to be efficient, hardworking and congenial. These Muscat Indians hailed from Cutch, Porbandar and Surat and they were traders, financiers and customs collectors. They had already built a reputation as customs collectors in Zanzibar and Mombasa and thus confirmed the Sultan's impression.

The Sultan granted the Indians full religious freedom and removed all restrictions against them. He gave them responsible jobs both in his personal service and government service. As these people were an asset to Zanzibar, and as there were no immigration restrictions, their population more than doubled in just four years from the original estimate of 300 to 400 in 1840. By 1856, this number had increased sixteen-fold with the population comprised of immigrants from Cutch, Gujarat and *Konkan* (Maratha). The total population of Zanzibar also rose to 60,000 making it the biggest centre on the East African coast.

In 1866, much of the import and export trade passed through Indian traders who bought goods from French, German and American counterparts on six month credit terms. From Zanzibar merchandise was sent to the coast to Indian agents who disposed it off to buyers from the mainland. Thus the Indians had a virtual monopoly on commerce.

In 1873, Sir Bartle Frere an ex-Governor of Bombay wrote, *"wherever there is any foreign trade, it passes through the hands of some Indian traders, no produce can be collected but through him; no imports can be distributed to the natives of the country but through his agency"*, so that *"The European merchant buys and sells with the advice of a Banian"*[11]. General Rigby was also impressed and remarked that the Indian merchant had acquired this position by his reputation for 'punctuality of payment and probity'[12].

During the nineteenth century, Indians became the main bankers and provided the financial services. The Indian rupee and pice replaced the Maria Theresa dollars (*thalers*) as principal

---

[11] Ref: pp101-2 – Frere, Bartle – Memo by Sir Bartle Frere regarding Banians or Natives of India in East Africa

[12] Ref: p20 – Mangat, J. S. – A History of Asians in East Africa

currency. The principal firm in charge of trade was that of Jairam Sewji who was a Hindu belonging to the Bhattia caste. Sewji also became a partner with the American firm, R.P. Waters.While Sewji was based in Cutch, his agent Ludha Damji, was in Zanzibar. Damji spent 40 years in Zanzibar during which he was the customs agent and advisor to Sultan Seyyid Majid. Ludha Damji also financed the expeditions of Speke and Burton, and Livingstone.

In 1875, the rival firm of Tarya Topan, a Khoja Ismaili, displaced Sewji as the principal merchant and ruled the roost for five years until Jairam Sewji reclaimed his crown. Tarya Topan was a banker to the missionary and explorer Henry Morton Stanley who wrote *"I made Tarya Topan's acquaintance in 1871, and the right pious manner in which he dealt by me caused me now to proceed to him for the same purpose as before, viz. To sell me cloth, cottons..."[13]* Topan also financed the black slave gathering expeditions of a notorious Swahili slaver named Hamed bin Mahamed – better known as Tippu Tib ('one who blinks', in reference to a nervous tick). Later, Topan was instrumental in establishing the first school and the first hospital in Zanzibar in 1887. He also played a significant part in the suppression of slavery. The vast business interests of Topan and Jairam did not survive for long after their deaths. The same fate awaited the businessman, Seth Allidina Visram in Uganda, in the twentieth century. This type of calamity not uncommonly befalls a family-based business.

Other nations were not disinterested in Zanzibar. In 1833, a commercial treaty was signed with the United States of America and in 1837 a consulate was established in Zanzibar. The British consulate followed four years later in 1841. Soon afterwards, the other Europeans got a whiff of the action and descended on Zanzibar like flies. Of all the trading activities that were going on at the time, slavery was almost paramount. It had been a dastardly if lucrative trade since time immemorial – Abraham and Jacob were slave owners. In the East African context the Arabs, Europeans, the Africans and Indians – both Hindus and Muslims – contributed to it, without conscience and for pure profits, oblivious to the cruelty and inhumanity inflicted on the naive and poor victims. This trade was mostly one-sided as black peoples were herded out of Africa in the thousands. The Sudanese were ferried down the Nile, the Ethiopians

---

[13] Ref: Rigby, C. P. – 'Report on the Dominions of H. H. the Sultan of Zanzibar...' (1859), in Zanzibar Archives, Serial E. 26 of 1859

across the Red Sea to western Arabia and East African blacks through Zanzibar – this route appeared to be the best oiled assembly line of all.

The Arab and Swahili slave-gathering routes took them from Kilwa to Lake Nyasa and from Bagamoyo to Kaze (Tabora) where the slave route split and went either to Ujiji on Lake Tanganyika or northwards to Uganda up to the Ruwenzori Mountains and Victoria Nile. Kenya was mercifully spared. The white slavers took the same routes and therefore they could not be regarded as pioneers as they often claimed to be. The European *Mzungu's* (white man's) operations were closely observed by Lord Lugard and he has described their *modus operandi*. The *Mzungu*, a wolf in sheep's clothing, would arrive, pretending to be a comrade and befriend a chief by handing out guns and other goodies. Then he would find out local political and tribal weaknesses and set upon dividing and conquering. Once the slaver had the confidence of the locals, he would accept presents of women and ivory, and in time, sow the seeds of conflict and incite one side to attack the other and capture human booty. Slaves were also bought in exchange for beads, guns and Merikani – cheap American cotton cloth. The nubile young women often fetched a higher price which could vary from a hatful of corn to a few lengths of Merikani. By the time the poor woman reached Muscat, her price had escalated twenty times, giving an estimated profit of 60 per cent.

The slaves were marched towards the coast with wooden yokes or in iron chains carrying their allotted load of ivory or other material. If the slave became ill, he was simply speared in order to discourage the others from complaining or pretending. If a woman could not carry her child as well as the ivory, the child was killed to lighten her burden. The maxim was destination or death. One would trace the grizzly path of a caravan by following the vultures and the hyenas. According to Stanley Livingstone, only one out of five slaves reached the coast and for each captured slave, ten were killed during the hunt. Therefore, to sustain an annual booty of about 20,000 slaves, almost half-a-million inhabitants were lost from the area.

The human cargo then had to suffer the inhuman conditions in *dhows*. Up to 600 slaves would be packed into the hold in a knee-chest position with a ration of a bowl of rice and a cup of water per day and no sanitary facilities. There, they were forced to wallow ankle deep in the muck and filth until they reached their destination. Those who developed diseases were thrown overboard.

On arrival in Zanzibar, the survivors were made ready for sale. They were fed, watered and fattened. The men were rubbed with oil and women were dressed up with colourful cotton robes, bangles, beads. Eye make-up of kohl was applied and their hair was tinted with henna. From here, the slaves were taken to Arab states, Persia and India and perhaps further afield. Both Hindus and Muslims were party to this cruel custom and openly kept slaves. Advertisements for sale were common in Indian newspapers in the early part of the nineteenth century.

Some of the slaves, as history and records show, were cared for and looked after by their masters. The concubines and mistresses enjoyed the luxuries heaped upon them by their owners. Sometimes they or their progeny reached powerful positions as politicians and in the military, and like Yakut, left their mark on history. The Koran did not forbid slavery except for enslavement of fellow Muslims, but the institution of slavery was not regarded as evil. The Bible and the Vedas did not discourage it either.

The Arabs, unlike the Europeans, did not appear to be racists by the fact that blacks were a target only because of their ready availability and large numbers. They could just as well have taken whites and others. In fact, Indian girls were kidnapped and shipped from western India to Zanzibar where they were auctioned and no doubt suffered the same fate as black slaves. The whites, however, had a different outlook. They considered all others as inferior and specifically targeted the blacks. Their attitude and treatment of this human cargo in the West Indies and America was unmatched in cruelty and has reverberations even to the present day.

Although the extent to which the Indians contributed to the slave trade in East Africa is disputed, there is no doubt that their involvement was significant. Along with the Arabs and Europeans, they must bear the responsibilities for carrying on such a nefarious practice. Indians probably financed the Arab and Swahili caravans and slave gathering expeditions into the hinterland. As agents, bankers and money lenders they stood to gain a lot. Their abhorrence to slavery, if any, is not recorded. The Indians were also involved in the export of women in the 1840's from India to the markets in Zanzibar where they were purchased as slaves and concubines.

The Imperial Act of 1833, which provided for the eventual termination of slavery in the Empire, contained a clause expressly exempting India, in official deference to Indian customs. This clause was, however, removed the same year. In 1843, the Indian Government abolished the legal status of slavery and in 1860, owning or trading in slaves became a penal offence. Before this, the slaves were kept by Indians who were under British protection and those under the protection of Indian Native States. In 1860, C.P. Rigby, who was the British consul and political agent in East Africa, emancipated all of the 6,000 slaves owned by the Indian traders in Zanzibar and ordered the Sultan to order Indians to free all slaves held in his mainland possessions. Many Zanzibari Indians who defied this order were fined or imprisoned. The Indians, mostly Cutchees, dropped their British affiliations and sought the Sultan's protection, and with their new legal status repurchased the slaves. As a corollary to this, there was quite a surge in the number of Cutchees in Zanzibar. In 1867, another agent, H.A. Churchill, on becoming the new Consul, persuaded the Indian government to authorize him to prohibit the Cutchees from buying and selling new slaves. He received this authorization and gave the Cutchees three years to emancipate all slaves.

In 1873, Sir Bartle Frere was sent out on a special mission to East Africa to report on slavery in the Sultan's dominions. He sent back this vivid description: *"Slaves are a considerable item at most ports and everywhere are a direct and regular source of Custom's revenue, and it is not only the Indian trader who farms the Customs, but his Indian agents at the outposts who are thus directly implicated. It is their business to know of every slave landed or shipped, and thus to become accomplices in all the schemes for evading the exertions of British officials and the British Government to stop the trade. The collection and concealment of the slave cargo before shipment, the misleading of the British cruiser, the running of the cargo, and its concealment at Zanzibar or elsewhere on the way to its final destination in Arabia or other distant regions – all these are matters of everyday concern and business interest to the Indian agent of the Indian farmer of the Sultan's Customs"*[14].

The Sultan was reluctant to comply with the demand to abolish slavery and a threat of a naval blockade was necessary to press him to conform to and sign an agreement making slavery illegal between all the ports of his domain. Thus ended the notorious slave market of Zanzibar. In the same year, British Indians who were involved in the

---

[14] Ref: pp103-4 – Memo by Sir Bartle Frere regarding Banians. *Correspondence* C.820

slave trade were sent to Bombay for a trial before the High Court. Slave holding, as opposed to slave trading, was still not prohibited and it was not until 1897 that slavery was totally abolished in Zanzibar. It took another ten years, however, to achieve this on the Sultan's mainland dominions.

There is a general consensus that the Arabs were the principal people engaged in the East African slave trade and the Indians, who were undoubtedly involved, played a secondary role. This view was promulgated by Frere but contested by the missionary David Livingstone and Capt. Atkins Hamerton, the first British consul. Hamerton reported that the chiefs brought slaves to the coast carrying ivory and gum copal and the slaves, along with the goods they carried, were bartered and procured by the Banya. He wrote in 1851, *"...there is not a Banya or Indian Mussulman who has resided for any length of time in any part of the Imam's dominions, who has not purchased African females with whom they cohabit during their stay in the Imam's countries and, if they leave, they make them over or sell them clandestinely to a friend. The banyas never bring their wives with them to the Imam's dominions, either to Arabia or to Africa, nor do they take these women away with them, when they leave for their own country, but the Indian Mohammedans frequently do"[15].*

The affluence and influence of Zanzibari Indian businessmen was such that it exposed them to considerable envy and scrutiny. The Europeans did much to tarnish their image. Elton described the Indian merchant as 'crafty, moneymaking, cunning…' Sir Richard Burton referred to the Khojas pejoratively as local Jews[16] and John Hanning Speke accused them of hostility to European exploration. Livingstone accused Indians of sabotaging his explorations by fraudulent practices and called them the worst offenders in the slave trade. The accusations of both Burton and Livingstone were refuted by Speke, Rigby and Kirk. In 1873, the Frere Mission investigated this whole issue and reported that the Indians had been quite unfairly singled out for complicity in this traffic. Although Indians were accused of slave holding, it was shown that this was not so and in fact, an English firm, Fraser and Co., was the major player in Zanzibar, holding 711 slaves. Kazi Shahabudin who accompanied

---

[15] Ref: p 28 – Gregory, Robert G. – *India and East Africa. A History of Race Relations within the British Empire 1890-1939.* Clarendon Press, Oxford 1971.

[16] Ref: p22 – Mangat, J. S. – A History of the Asians in East Africa

Frere pointed out that the European and the American firms were also responsible for financing the slave traffic and that the entire supply of arms and ammunition came from the European firms.

The role of the missionaries requires some scrutiny. In the name of religion and God, they exploited the situation to further their country's commercial and political designs. They showed scant respect for the religion and feelings of others. Proselytisation was their driving force. Non-Christians suspected the motives of the missionaries and they felt that the missionaries were not above using methods foul and fair when it suited their purpose. The missionaries, while decrying slavery, were quite prepared to co-operate and take advantage of the slaves as a means to an end. The Indians, who had an ancient and well-developed religious and cultural background, and who were self-sufficient, were capable of competing and resisting all attempts at conversion. They were, therefore, often resented and treated in an uncharitable manner.

Livingstone was quite comfortable and willing to accept supplies of provisions, cloth and beads from a slaver near Lake Bangweulu. He wrote that the slave dealer 'showed the greater kindness and anxiety for my safety and success'. He approvingly said, "*I was glad to see the mode of ivory and slave-trading among these men, it formed such a perfect contrast to the ruffians from Kilwa[17]*". When Livingstone was holed up in Ujiji, he did not refuse the help and charity of the Zanzibari slavers. When faced with almost certain death, it was perhaps a matter of *'marta kya na karta'* an Indian expression meaning 'Facing death, what else could I do'.

Stanley also was quite prepared to recruit the help of Tippu Tib in order to find Livingstone. Stanley described the slaver as a 'well bred Arab'[18] and when the two caravans parted company, Stanley gave Tippu Tib a farewell party. Pragmatism I presume!

Other Europeans were equally prepared to turn a blind eye and look the other way when it suited their purpose. Captain George Sullivan who said " *I could never see a slave-dealer without a desire to hang or at least horsewhip him*" was unashamedly prepared to accept handouts from the *nakhoda* of a slave dhow when he was short of supplies. In 1858, Burton and Speke, on their way to Lake Tanganyika, received help from an Arab slaver, Snay bin

---

[17] Ref: p49 – Miller, Charles – The Lunatic Express. The Macmillan Company, New York,NY 1971

[18] Ref: p49 – Miller, Charles. The Lunatic Express

Amir. Burton acknowledged the 'open-handed hospitality and hearty goodwill of this truly noble race'[19]. In fact, it would be quite safe to say that all the 'explorers' depended on the help and hospitality of the slavers at one time or another.

In spite of their deep involvement, the abolition of slavery, an idea conceived by the British, will forever remain the greatest single act of humanitarianism this world has known. Slavery first came under attack in England in the seventeenth century. In the later years of the eighteenth century, Adam Smith spoke out against human bondage and John Wesley began to influence the populace against this outrage. In 1772, a successful test case was heard in England which was brought by a self-taught lawyer named Granville Sharp. That spelt the end of slavery in Britain. In spite of the expected opposition from the West Indian sugar planters, the movement continued to gain strength. In 1807, Wilberforce was instrumental in pushing through a bill in Parliament which outlawed all slave trade in the British Empire. The antislavery movement soon began to influence the reluctant continental nations and Portugal, Spain and France soon came on board and signed antislavery treaties with England. In 1833, slavery itself became illegal throughout the British Empire. However, it would be many years before the last of the slaves would be freed – 1907 in East Africa.

The Indian role in terminating slavery was minor in comparison. Frere was encouraged by the Zanzibari Indians and they co-operated with him to bring this trade to an end. Frere reported, *"I believe there is no class so anxious to see this question settled"*[20]. Even the Rao of Cutch sent his minister Kazi Shahabuddin to help Frere. Tarya Topan, an outstanding Indian trader and a member of the Ismaili community, was knighted in 1890 for his efforts in the suppression of slavery in Zanzibar.

The second half of the nineteenth century saw more and more attention being focused on East Africa. The Europeans were restless again and in a mood for expansion. The missionaries began to descend on the land ostensibly to save the natives and as exploration delved deep into the Dark Continent, the mainland gradually began

---

[19] Ref: p48 – Miller, Charles – The Lunatic Express. The Macmillan Company, New York,NY 1971

[20] Ref: p25 – Gregory, Robert G – India and East Africa. A History of Race Relations within the British Empire1890 – 1939. Clarendon Press, Oxford 1971

to reveal its magnificent secrets. In 1840 Johann Rebmann, a German, was recruited into the Church Missionary Society by a countryman and a missionary named Johann Ludwig Krapf. Rebmann became very enamoured with Chaggaland. He found its beauty overpowering and he repeatedly visited the area. Mamkinga, the ruler of this area, and Rebman both had ulterior motives. One had on his agenda the conversion of the natives to his beliefs and the other wanted material goods. However, Rebmann would achieve a success of a different kind. At 10 o'clock on 11 May 1848, he saw a most magnificent sight. The cloud lifted its veil of secrecy to reveal Mount Kilimanjaro in all its majesty, wearing a silver crown of what Rebmann's guide called *Beridi* (Swahili for cold).

Meanwhile, Krapf distinguished himself by continuing his exploration and proselytisation. His dedication resulted in his translating the New Testament into Swahili by 1850. He became the first European to cross the River Tsavo and to scale the Yatta escarpment. He then went on to explore River Tana. He also became the first white man to see the Embu, Meru and Kikuyu tribes. On his travels, Krapf was informed by an Embu tribesman of the presence of a large mountain covered with white matter which rolled down the sides with a great noise. He had been at the foot of the mountain but not climbed it because of the intense cold. A great thrill was in store for Krapf too. On 3 December 1849, the cloud suddenly parted and there, behind the *Ghungat* (Hindi for veil), was the shy maiden, *Kima ja Kegnia* or Mount Kenya, in all its glory with its twin peaks covered in snow.

The poor scholars at home were sceptical and unbelieving. A member of the Royal Geographic Society, in utter disbelief, attributed Rebmann's account as, 'betraying weak powers of observation, strong fancy, an eager craving for wonders and childish reasoning...' Krapf's confirmation of Rebmann's mountain and another one of his own, on the equator no less, put the critics into convulsions and drove the last nail into the coffin of their arguments.

The French were beginning to challenge British supremacy in East Africa. They had impeded the Abolitionist movement by recruiting African slaves from the Sultan's dominions, for sugar plantations in Bourbon (now Re'union), a French island possession in the Indian Ocean. This was only resolved in 1859 when the British agreed to the French recruitment of the Indian coolies instead. Other events were taking place in Europe at the same time and these were to influence the events in East Africa. The Industrial

Revolution made nations hungry for raw materials, and in turn, there was a crying need for fresh markets to disgorge the manufactured goods. Expansion was inevitable. The French, having been mauled by Germany in the Franco-Prussian war of 1870, were chomping at the bit to expand in order to capture their lost pride. Germany, buoyed with fresh confidence, was also seeking to expand. The British wanted to protect and preserve their gains and possessions. So the stage was set for an unholy scramble for East Africa.

Chapter 2

Victoria's Tin Dragon

The opening of the Uganda Railway was the most important single event in the history of Eastern Africa. It opened the country from the coast to the great lake thus exposing the hinterland to new influences from abroad. It touched every aspect of life in the whole country and affected the Asians, Africans and Europeans alike. It speeded up the development of Kenya, Uganda and the areas beyond. It provided a new area for the emigration of Indians and Europeans and much needed jobs for everyone. It helped in social intercourse between the three races and by exposing the Africans to new ways and new technology; it had a major impact on civilising them.

Events in Africa had moved in such a way that the construction of a railway was inevitable. In 1890, an approach was made by members of the Imperial British East Africa Company (IBEA) to its directors for a 60-mile railway from the coast to upcountry, and in response, the directors sent materials for a 60-mile narrow gauge railway. Only seven miles of the track was laid before aborting the project in favour of a more substantial railway once it was confirmed that help from the British Government was forthcoming.

The original track was dismantled and re-laid along the existing roads in Mombasa, stretching from Kilindini to the Old Port and around the European areas of the island. The *thelas* (Hindi for trolley) were individually owned by Europeans and the motive force was provided by the barefoot Africans who, dressed in *kanzus*, pushed the *Mzungus* from place to place. These contraptions consisted of a wooden platform on four steel wheels with a bench seating two persons abreast and a curved canopy for shade. They were light enough to be lifted off the rails and easily stored until the *bwana* was ready to take off again. It would not be long before this Mickey Mouse mode of transportation would become obsolete and condemned to the scrap heap.

Old Trolley lines, Mombasa

Appeals for financial aid were made to the British Government by Sir William MacKinnon, who was a very influential and well-respected individual with friends in high places. His opinion carried a lot of weight. He founded and organised the British East Africa Association a pre-cursor to the IBEA and obtained from the Sultan a 50-year concession to administer a ten-mile coastal strip of land. He was also the founder of the British India Steam Navigation Company in 1872. In 1888, the Association became the IBEA under a Royal Charter.

.

Sir William Mackinnon, the founder of the Imperial British East Africa Company. Statue at Mombasa.

The IBEA's resources were over-stretched due to its efforts to counteract the aggressive policies of the German Government and because of the need to protect the Imperial 'sphere of influence' which covered 75,000 square miles. A good railway was considered essential to protect the territory and the headwaters of the Nile and the presence of a steamer on the great lake would go a long way to putting an end to the slave trade. Lord Salisbury, the Tory Prime Minister, was impressed by these arguments and he supported the IBEA's case to the Treasury in spite of bitter opposition in the country and in the House of Commons. The opposition of Liberals, Radicals and Irish Nationalists fought tooth and nail to scuttle the project. They had gross reservations in the first place to the unjustifiable occupation of vast African lands. The area was unknown to most English people and it appeared to have no commercial or other potential. Henry Labouchere, a Radical Parliamentarian, called the Government's position 'vague general claptrap'. He objected to the use of public funds on Uganda's religious conflicts 'to prevent these very remarkable Christians from cutting each other's throats'. [21]He called the occupied area Britain's *'demnosa heriditas'*. In spite of all the opposition, in January 1891, the British Government informed the IBEA of its willingness to give financial aid of £1,250,000 and that was precisely the impetus that was needed to set the ball rolling.

The IBEA consulted three eminent engineers who all estimated the final cost to be higher than the Treasury 'grant'. One of the engineers, Sir Gilford Molesworth, in his report in 1891, pointed out that no accurate estimate could be made in view of the paucity of information, and intangible and formidable hurdles like the Kinangop and Mau escarpments. It was decided that the railway would have to be a telescopic type much like the one built in Balauchistan.

On 24 November 1891, a survey party under Capt. J.R.L. MacDonald, who had been appointed the Chief Engineer, arrived in Mombasa from Aden aboard S.S. Madura. They set out of Mombasa in earnest on 18 December to survey the route and they were back in Mombasa on 23 September 1892. The total length of the survey was 2,700 miles at a cost of £19,710. The length of the projected three-foot six-inch gauge railway from Mombasa to Berkley Bay on the lake in Uganda was 657 miles, at an estimated cost of £3,409 per mile. It was proposed to build a station every 30 miles and to power the trains by locally available wood, at the speed of about twelve miles per hour. The estimated traffic would rise to 11,000 tons, instead of 50 tons, of mostly ivory, and 11,000 passengers per year.

---

[21] Ref: p256 – Miller, Charles – The Lunatic Express. The Macmillan Company, New York, NY 1971

The gross earnings of £61,000 per year would cover all the operating costs. This was thus deemed to be the cheapest possible link from the salt water of the sea to the sweet water of Lake Victoria.

On 11 December 1895, S.S. Ethiopia, a 2,000 ton steam ship belonging to the British India Steam Navigation Company, chugged into the old Mombasa harbour carrying George Whitehouse who had been appointed Chief Engineer to the Uganda Railways. He had impeccable credentials and vast experience, having built railways in South America, Mexico, India and South Africa. The maps and surveys prepared so far were incomplete and did not fully denote the natural geographical hurdles that had to be surmounted. Meanwhile, the coolies were on their way from India and the supplies of tools, rolling stock and locomotives, and 100 miles of rails had been ordered. The estimated completion time was four years but the impatient Railway Committee hoped that this could be achieved even sooner!

The arrival of Whitehouse was the green flag for the railway construction to begin, but it took him six months to organise the infrastructure. The first rail of the Uganda Railway was laid in Mombasa on 30 May 1896. A commemorative photograph of the event shows that it was as grand an affair as the circumstances would allow. Present for the occasion were a hundred or so men with half-a-dozen English ladies. The railway officials wore immaculate white uniforms and thick white pith helmets. The VIPs wore blazers, bow ties and straw boaters and carried walking sticks. The ladies wore long white flowing dresses with hats and carried parasols. A dozen or so Indians were present. One wore a white *achkan,* tight trousers and a large coloured turban and the rest – perhaps soldiers or police – wore uniforms of khaki shorts and shirts with calf-length puttee and khaki turbans.

Laying the first railway line, Mombasa
1986

The surveyors staked out the line, following MacDonald's route, but changed it wherever necessary. The ground for the tracks was then prepared by earthwork gangs which cleared the bush and trees and made banks and cuttings ready for the plate-laying gangs that followed. The first lines of the metre gauge railway were laid on 5 August 1896. The rails, each 30-foot long and weighing 500 pounds, were carried by teams of men. The rails were laid across creosoted pine sleepers because it was mistakenly thought that salts in the soil would corrode the steel. Yet another gang joined the rails with rectangular steel fishplates and bolts. The rails were attached to the sleepers with bolts and lugs and finally secured with steel keys which were driven home with long keying hammers. The section was then aligned with *trembos* (Swahili for crowbars). This process had to be repeated *ad nauseum* and *ad infinitum*.

From the very onset the railway was beset with a large number of serious problems. The first of the many physical hurdles lay at the very doorstep. Crossing the Makupa creek, a natural moat around the ramparts of Mombasa Island, was a formidable challenge. It was decided that a bridge was the only feasible option in order to allow a passage for sea-craft. A wooden bridge was only a temporary solution, because the waters were infested with *Teredo Navalis* and the timber would not last long. Again no suitable wood of adequate strength and dimensions was available in Africa and it had to be imported. This caused a delay of eight months before a 1,732-foot Salisbury Bridge was in place.

**Salisbury Bridge which once linked
Mombasa Island to the mainland.**

On the opposite side of the creek lay the Rabai Hills. These hills had steeply sloping sides covered with thick scrub and creepers and massive Baobab trees. Cutting these was no mean task. In addition, some of the cuttings were 40-foot deep and in the course of fifteen miles the land rose by 560 feet. The earthworks were therefore a formidable undertaking and took all of two months to complete. The unlucky mile thirteen brought the gangs against a formidable 400-foot-wide gully called the Mazeras Ravine and this needed a wooden viaduct, which again delayed progress by 25 days. Another problem that hampered progress was the shortage of rolling stock in March 1897 due to a peculiar English disease, the strike of workers in England. Then there were numerous washouts of the track due to flash floods and occasionally the crossing of game which destroyed the embankments. In April 1897 Bubonic plague in India put a brake

46

on the emigration of coolies and construction was crippled for several months.

The Indians who worked at the railhead came from the hardy tribes of Punjab. They were housed in tents with very few belongings of their own. The camps were moved ahead of the rails every ten to fifteen miles. This was not a great personal hardship once the routine was mastered and was reminiscent of the departure of a village circus. All the tents and the railway paraphernalia were loaded onto the open carriages and the workers clambered all over the train and the engine wherever there was an inch of space to spare. An occasional *jamadar* (headman) had the luxury of a *charpai*. This not only confirmed his status but on one occasion proved to be a life-saver. In this instance, there was trouble with the natives and the occupants of the tent had just taken refuge under the *charpai* when a spear came through the canvas and landed on this rickety fortification.

Of what the Indians did possess included clothes, some trinkets and amulets, medicines against the ravages of *pardes* (Hindi for foreign lands) and of course, candy. The candy was in the form of a *kuja* formed from sugar that was crystallized on a skeleton of wood and string forming a small bowl-like structure. Sugar in this form sweetened tea, was a substitute for sweetmeats and mysteriously kept disease and the devil away! Churanjilal, a surveyor, recalled that it was such a precious commodity that the men would break it off and place a piece in the cheek while sipping tea and, once the cup was empty, the candy was carefully saved for the next time. On one occasion Churangilal gave a piece of the *kuja* to an African who was so thrilled that he came back with a gift of an elephant tusk. This adorned the tent entrance for a few days until it was time to move on.

The 'medicine chest' included Ayurvedic medicines like *Amritdhara* – oils extracted from cloves and many other spices, *Gulkund* – rose petals in sugar and *Chavanprash*. These 'drugs' had the power to cure chest congestion, dysentery, constipation, haemorrhoids and other such afflictions. Like most remedies of the time they did not do any good but were harmless concoctions containing a 'feel good' factor.

Surgery was mercifully confined to digging out thorns, slivers of wood and *dudus* (Swahili for giggers) that burrowed under the skin causing intense itching and pain. The 'camp surgeon' sat on the ground with the patient's foot in his lap and exposed a sac of eggs with a sewing needle. He teased out the egg sac and then filled the tiny cavity with the universal cure for all evil – salt.

Health, or lack of it, was a major problem faced by all. Some of the workers were not in great shape to start with. This was compounded by the poor working conditions, lack of water and inadequate nutrition. The lower limbs were constantly exposed to sharp objects and thorns, and footwear, if any, was of poor quality. The scratches on the grime-covered skin became infected and turned into large throbbing volcanic boils which would burst, pour out thick pus and blood and often turn into chronic ulcers. Sometimes the infection would spread and make the limbs stiff and streaky as they swelled and eventually caused blood poisoning and death. Alas! If only the two physicians, Gerhard Domagk and Sir Alexander Fleming, had been born half a century earlier.

Malaria spared no one. Abnormally high rainfall at Mazeras and at Maji Chumvi filled all the ponds and hollows providing ideal conditions for mosquito larvae. The females of the species descended on the unsuspecting victims as they lay in their tents and infected them with the deadly plasmodium. Many who survived fell prey to 'griping of the gut' as amoebic dysentery and food poisoning took hold and caused diarrhoea, dehydration and death. As if this was not enough there was the fly that introduced a microscopic worm under the skin which in time developed into a boil containing a maggot that had to be squeezed out to get relief. By December 1896, 500 of the labourers were in hospital and a month later this number rose to 1,000, which was half of the total workforce. About one hundred of these had to be buried or cremated in the foreign land[22].

The age of communication was just dawning in Africa and until telegraph lines were strung, the mail service was dependent on human runners. The mail carriers who worked in relays were remarkable in their speed, endurance, regularity and reliability. Between 1896 to 1897, not one package was lost between Mombasa and Eldama Ravine. The first stage of 110 miles which ended at Ndi, and the second stage to Kikuyu, was covered by Wakamba runners. The Masai cut in for the rest of the 150 miles to Eldama Ravine where mail was taken over by the Uganda Protectorate Authorities and carried on to Kisumu. The total journey took twenty

---

[22] Ref: p294 – Miller, Charles – *The Lunatic Express.* The Macmillan Company, New York, NY 1971

days, which meant a daily marathon of 25 miles. The Railway Company decided to install a telegraph line along the railway and this began in 1896. It soon caught up with the railhead at mile 70 and overtook it, reaching Eldama Ravine on 25 March 1896. Here a delay occurred while the best route to Uganda was being decided. The route eventually adopted followed the railway to Kisumu and then on to Jinja, Kampala and Entebbe where it reached on 18 May 1900, a total distance of 800 miles. The Commissioner in Entebbe could now communicate with London in eight hours instead of the customary eight months.

Within a month of laying the first lines the trains started to roll. They were all construction trains supplying men and materials to the railhead. Beyond this the only available transport were animals and human porters. Large numbers of camels, mules, bullocks and donkeys were imported. The poor beasts were up against three formidable adversaries – temperature, thirst and trypanosomes. Camels from India and horses died within months. The bullocks succumbed to the tsetse fly. Mules and donkeys from Cyprus fared better but there too were a large number of deaths. In the theatre of East Africa the ship of the desert had to concede to the humble mule. Corpses and skeletons marked the route but they did not last long as the forces of mother nature soon removed every trace of them.

The intrusion of vast numbers of machines and mammals of the two and four-footed kind caught Africa by surprise. They needed vast amounts of food, fodder and water for sustenance. The water supply from the wells of Mombasa was barely adequate for the locals, let alone for the steaming and sweating hoards of newcomers. It was, therefore, imperative to find water to fulfil the need for at least 10,000 gallons per day and desalination machinery was installed in Mombasa. In addition, a dam was built at Changamwe. The only water supply beyond this was at four places. Maji Chumvi's brackish water, however, was unsuitable and at Voi the supply ran out before the end of the dry season. The only viable solution to this problem was the introduction of water trains, for work had to proceed come what may.

If things sometimes appeared chaotic it was always organised chaos. One gang using hoes turned the sod and rendered the surface smooth. All the soil from cuttings was used to fill holes and hollows and to build embankments. The soil and slurry was shovelled into metal *karais* which the other gang of coolies carried on their heads in a sort of continuous human conveyor belt.

The trusty turban was very handy. It not only acted as a cushion to protect the scalp from the steel and sun but the long loose end at the back was invaluable to wipe away the streams of sweat that rolled down the face. This six-yard piece of muslin or cotton was perhaps the most versatile single item in the tropics. It was often used as a cover to ward off mosquitoes and other creepy-crawlies at night or it doubled up as a ground sheet. It provided a ready filter when the drinking water was muddy or green with algae. It often came in use as a rope and on many occasions a turban was cut up and used as bandages.

As soon as the rail bed was smooth and level, a second team of coolies placed the sleepers at regular intervals and dropped the rails in their places. They then delivered the necessary keys, fish-plates, nuts and bolts. Next it was the turn of the men who fixed the rails to the sleepers and linked the rails. Finally, the packers moved in to finish the job by filling the space around the sleepers with soil and ballast. Then the train was ready to roll.

The sound of the steaming, smoking, clanking engine of the water train was the cue for everyone to down tools and take five. The coolies squatted, sat *chawnkri* (cross-legged) fashion on the bare earth or used a nearby stone to rest their behind. The *bwana*, of course, had the luxury of a rickety folding chair and a parasol. If the coolies, wearing a *kurta*, a vest, a cotton *lungi* and an enormous turban looked over-dressed and somewhat comical, the white surveyor with his khaki jacket, trousers and pith helmet seemed even more so. Once the thirst was quenched with cupped hands or tin cans and the salty crust washed off the face, it was time to get back to work again.

The line at last reached Tsavo at mile 130. The terrible semi-desert, Taru, had been conquered and they were now at an oasis. This was the traditional place of rest and replenishment. The water was sweet and the supply unending. The men were happy as they plunged in the cool river water to wash away weeks of dirt and grime and put on clean crisp white clothes and fresh *pugrees* (turbans). They looked forward to a smoke, a game of cards, spending the cool evenings telling stories and of course, *sheiro shairi* (poetry recitation) by the weak light of a flickering hurricane lamp. There were smiles on their faces and a song in their hearts.

However, not one of them knew the meaning of *Tsavo*, which was the Kikamba word for 'slaughter'. The green vegetation and the cool winds were just a mirage that had lulled them into a false sense of security. In fact, the place was surrounded by an aura of ill luck. Here, men had disappeared without trace and porters had abandoned caravans seemingly without reason. Deep in the jungle lurked a cunning and a powerful enemy, a *shaitan* (satan) who was about to turn their heaven into hell and their dreams into nightmares. This purgatory was to last for months and many of them would never see their sweethearts and children again, but instead, end up in a shallow, hastily dug grave with a cover of red soil and a few rough stones to mark the final resting place for their bodies, or what was left of them.

It did not take long for the adversary to strike as one of their buddies disappeared from a tent during the dead of the night, leaving behind no trace except a blood-stained *dhoti* which was found at the river's edge. They did not have to look far before they discovered his half eaten body a little distance away, and knew at once that it was *sher ka kaam* (work of a lion). They set about fortifying the *boma* with thorns and anything else they could find, but they had hardly time to mourn their loss when another of their colleagues was dragged away from his tent and met the same fate. The camp was now in a state of panic but the engineer, named Preston, managed to restore some order as he encouraged the men to work even harder so as to speed them on their move away from what he called a 'hell hole'.

Meanwhile at Voi, at mile 100, a white road engineer, O'Hara, was snatched from his tent while his wife and two children were asleep beside him. At Kima (mincemeat in Urdu) a ferocious man eater had tried to tear off the corrugated iron sheets from the roof of the station building, prompting the terrified *babu* to send the following message: *"Lion fighting with station. Send urgent succour."*[23] On 6 June 1900, a superintendent of the Railway Police who was on his way to Nairobi was persuaded to dispose of the beast. His private carriage was shunted into a siding and there, Inspector Ryall, along with two white companions, Huebner and Parenti, waited for the adversary. They all sat on guard in the

---

[23] Ref: p 45 – Foran, W Robert – A Cuckoo in Kenya. Hutchinson. London 1936

51

inspection carriage during the early hours of the night. The two friends went to sleep while Ryall kept watch. Huebner occupied the high berth while Parenti slept on the floor. Apparently, Ryall came to the conclusion that the lion was unlikely to appear, and he too lay down on the lower berth of the carriage and fell asleep.

The lion, in fact, had been watching its prey. Silently, he crept on to the little platform and shoved open the sliding door into the carriage, which shut behind it, for the carriage had a list due to the poor state of the siding. The lion had to plant his feet on Parenti as he seized Ryall. The commotion woke Huebner who was so panic-stricken that he climbed over the lion and escaped through the second sliding door communicating with the servants' quarters. The lion broke through one of the windows carrying Ryall in his jaws and leaving Parenti shivering on the floor. The 'Kima killer' had hunted the hunter.

Lt. Col. Patterson

At this stage, Lt. Col. Patterson, an Indian Army Officer, with a long experience in railway construction, arrived on the scene with a

53

mandate to design and construct a permanent bridge on River Tsavo. At first, he was sceptical of what he was told by Preston and he suspected the Indians of killing their own fellow workers. He believed *"The unfortunate men had been the victims of foul play at the hands of some of their comrades... I thought it quite likely that some scoundrels from the gangs had murdered them for the sake of their money"*[24]. It was not long before he realized his error when a third coolie, *jamadar* Ungan Singh, was snatched from his tent in the dead of the night. On the next day, his half eaten body was buried, but curiously, not his head, which was brought back for identification by the Medical Officer. Patterson came to the conclusion that there was not one but two animals involved in the killing and he 'vowed there and then to rid the neighbourhood of the brutes'.[25] This was the start of a vigil, to stalk the stalkers, and his experiences were destined to excite the imagination of many generations to come.

Shifting Camp

[24] Ref: p21 – Patterson J.H. – *The Man-Eaters of Tsavo.* St. Martin's Press, New York, NY 1986. Originally published in London by Macmillan, 1907

[25] Ref: p322 – Miller, Charles – The Lunatic Express

At the very outset Patterson was faced with the logistical difficulty of policing a camp that was not only situated on both banks of the river, but in which the tents were in pockets scattered over an area of eight miles in diameter. The lions were free to attack any conglomeration of tents they desired. In addition, they often wandered away and targeted the nearby Wakamba villages. The attacks were sporadic and as soon as a semblance of peace returned to the camps they would be back with a vengeance. This was very frustrating to say the least and Patterson tried various tactics such as changing the position of his nightly vigil and using live goats as bait, but to no avail. As time passed, the lions became very bold and unafraid of noise, even gunfire, and they almost seemed to prefer the vicinity of the camp for their nightly meal. In one instance, they seized a man at the railway station and dragged him all the way to the camp to enjoy their kill at leisure.

At the end of March 1898, the labour force was suddenly reduced to 500 men instead of 2,000 as the railhead gangs moved on out of the area. The remaining labourers were scared witless and panicked as they realized that the odds against them were even greater. They threatened a mass walkout to Mombasa, causing a temporary suspension of all work on the bridge, but eventually agreed to stay when the *bomas* were further reinforced. Meanwhile Patterson, supported by a companion called Dr. Brock and *jamadars* with guns, continued his quest for the quarry which became bolder by the day. They started attacking the hospital tents and vandalizing everything in sight, necessitating change to three different locations. They attacked the new hospital too, carried away the *bhisti* (water carrier) and almost completely devoured this victim leaving behind only a skull and a few fingers. Patterson wrote, *"On one of these was a silver ring, and this, with the teeth (a relic much prized by certain casts), was then sent to the man's widow in India"*[26].

The dual in the dark continued, but without success, and Patterson's frustration was compounded as work on the bridge and its vicinity slowed down to a snail's pace. This resulted in Patterson becoming over-sensitive and petty and venting his anger on the labourers. He started scolding them in public each day at noon: *"It was my custom to have evil-doers brought up for judgement"*[27]. He over-reacted to workers who had lied about their expertise as stone

[26] Ref: p34 – Patterson J.H. – *The Man-Eaters of Tsavo*

[27] Ref: p329 – Miller, Charles – The Lunatic Express

masons in order to claim higher wages, or those who were guffing off at work. He set light to the bed of a patient named Karim Bux who he rightly suspected of being a malingerer. The relations between Patterson and his workers continued to deteriorate and he responded by disciplining, degrading and imposing fines on them. It all came to a head when a plot was hatched by the men to murder Patterson during his noon visit to the quarry. He was warned of this conspiracy in advance by one of his masons and again by his headman, Heera Singh. Patterson visited the quarry undaunted and confronted the men *"carrying crowbars and flourishing their heavy hammers…"*. Luckily, there was no violence and Patterson emerged unscathed: *"It was with feelings of great relief that one hour later I made my way back, safe and sound, to Tsavo"*. Another murder plot was hatched against Patterson soon afterwards which was revealed to him by his timekeeper. The ring leaders were arrested and taken to Mombasa where *"All the scoundrels were found guilty and sentenced to various terms of imprisonment in chain-gangs"*[28].

The lions continued their work unabated. A coolie was eaten but Patterson, under stress, reacted in a bizarre fashion by refusing the last rites to be carried out. *"The few scattered fragments that remained of the body I would not allow to be buried at once, hoping that the lions would return to the spot the following night"*[29]. Patterson now found the situation getting out of control as all the white riff-raff and wealthy 'sportsmen' descended on Tsavo and started to shoot anything that moved including pregnant lionesses and cubs, giving slaughter a new meaning. This carnage disturbed Patterson profoundly. Patterson next resorted to build a large steel trap but the man-eaters were too clever to fall for this ploy.

The coolies had had enough. They announced: *"They would not remain at Tsavo any longer for anything or anybody; they had come from India on an agreement to work for the Government, not to supply food for either lions or 'devils'"*[30]. They forcibly stopped the train to Mombasa late one afternoon by lying on the track and clambered all over it. The train with its unscheduled passengers steamed off eastwards leaving the exasperated Colonel to rant and rave and pull his hair out. His work had come to a halt, he was alone

---

[28] Ref: p332 – Miller, Charles – The Lunatic Express

[29] Ref: p335 – Miller, Charles – The Lunatic Express

[30] Ref: p337 – Miller, Charles – The Lunatic Express

with a few dozen coolies and the enemy was still at large devouring victims as they pleased.

At last, all good things must come to an end – for the lions that is! The dawn of 9 December 1898 was eventful. Patterson was just leaving the *boma* when he was informed that a lion had been feasting on a donkey. Patterson had an instant rush of adrenaline and grabbing his rifle he went after the beast. The lion was spotted, but just then, the snapping of a twig under foot warned the quarry who bounded off into the jungle. Patterson summoned his workers to act as beaters to flush out the animal while he hid behind a large anthill. This was 'a huge maneless lion' ready for a dual. Patterson raised his rifle. *"The moment I moved to do this, he caught sight of me, and seemed much astonished at my sudden appearance, for he struck his forefeet into the ground, threw himself back on his haunches and growled savagely"[31]*. The gun misfired. Both the adversaries appeared confused for a split second but Patterson recovered first and fired again, only to wound the lion which disappeared into the bush.

Patterson was disappointed but not disheartened and he prepared for round two. He noticed that the dead donkey had hardly been touched and his instinct told him that the lion would be back. He had built a wooden scaffold about twelve-foot high and he tied the donkey to it. At dusk, Patterson climbed into the rickety perch. It was several hours of still silence before the lion showed up, but instead of attacking the hunter or partaking in the feast provided, it began to stalk at a safe distance and this dance of death lasted all of two hours. At last, he came within a few feet of the scaffold and Patterson could just make out his shape. He held his breath and, peering into the dark, squeezed the trigger. *"The sound of the shot was at once followed by a most terrific roar, and then I could hear him leaping about in all directions. I was no longer able to see him, however, as his first bound had taken him into the thick bush; but to make doubly sure, I kept blazing away in the direction in which I heard him plunging about. At length came a series of groans, gradually subsiding into deep sighs, and finally ceasing altogether, and I felt convinced that one of the 'devils' who had so long harried us would trouble us no more"[32]*. The next morning, the lion was

---

[31] Ref: p339 – Miller, Charles – The Lunatic Express
[32] Ref: p340 – Miller, Charles – The Lunatic Express

found lying beside the donkey. It measured nine-foot eight-inches and eight men were needed to carry it.

The battle that lasted eight months was won but the war was not yet over. There was another enemy still lurking in the woods. He was also bold and fearless and he made several attacks during one of which he was wounded by a bullet from Patterson's gun but the lion continued its activities undaunted. One moonlit night, Patterson was in a tree with his Swahili gun-bearer, Mahina, when the lion made its appearance and began to prowl. The conditions for once were in Patterson's favour as a full moon in a cloudless sky lit up the area of hostilities. Patterson shot the beast four times before the lion disappeared into the surrounding bush. The next morning they found it wounded but alive in a thicket. Patterson fired and shot the animal but it still charged. Patterson fired again and the lion kept coming. Patterson had to take refuge in the nearest tree, but luckily for Patterson, the lion could not follow as its hind leg was badly shattered. Patterson fired again and this time it brought the animal down. Patterson was elated and immediately jumped to the ground only to find that the lion was still alive and two more shots were needed to silence the ferocious feline forever.

Patterson became an instant hero and all the animosity between him and the workers vanished. A foreman of the masons named Roshan, a Punjabi from the district of Jehlum, composed an epic poem in praise of 'Patterson Sahib' and his exploits. Patterson was very flattered and wrote: *"Instead of wishing to murder me, as they once did, they could not now do enough for me, and as a token of their gratitude they presented me with a beautiful silver bowl, as well as with a long poem written in Hindustani describing all our trials and my ultimate victory"*[33]. The inscription was signed by the Overseer and Clerk of Works, Baboo Purhotam Hurjee Purmar.

The bridge over river Tsavo was completed and on 7 February 1899 it was opened to traffic. It stood the test of time until it was blown up by Germans during the East African campaign of the First World War. The two lions are now on display in Chicago's Field Museum – although it is uncertain as to whether they represent the courage of man or beast. Their pelts show the ravages of nature and the gun. In their capacity as the 'king of the jungle' their fight was perhaps symbolic of one last stand against the intrusion by foreigners, with their new fangled contraption, who came with the

---

[33] Ref: p104 – Patterson, J.H. – *The Man-Eaters of Tsavo*

sole aim of exploiting the country with no regard to the harmony in which man and beast had co-existed for thousands of years.

After Tsavo, the progress was much more satisfactory. The curious rhino would sometimes turn up at the railhead and delay the proceedings by scattering the construction gangs, and on one occasion challenged the oncoming engine and nearly derailed the train. Lions continued their harassment, especially at Simba station, and frequently held up the trains.

There was an occasional deluge which would wash away the new embankments or turn them into a quagmire. In one downpour a herd of zebra got caught in the *ugali* of soft black earth and had to be rescued with lassos made out of the workers' turbans. In another instance a flock of guinea fowl undermined the embankment with equally disastrous results. The problems were also compounded by a plague of army worms and locust which turned into a slippery soup under the engine wheels, preventing all traction.

Once the tracks reached Kiboko (Hippopotamus) at mile 217 the conditions improved even more as the place was cool and pleasant. The large mimosa trees with their flat tops provided much needed shade, but the abundance of water proved a double-edged sword, for it made the mosquito raise its ugly head. Before long the railhead gang were afflicted with malaria.

Behind the railhead things were beginning to happen. During 1898 the railway carried 28,799 troops and porters, 1,241 transport animals and 2,468 tons of goods and at long last began to generate some revenue. During the year it accounted for 70 first-class, 200 second-class and 30,000 third-class passengers.

By May 1899, the tracks were nearing the highlands. The Kapiti and Athi plains were easy prairie country for the track layers. The lush, long, tender grass attracted all kinds of game and every newcomer to the area had marvelled at the abundance and diversity of the fauna.

The antelope were in such large numbers that they made the gentle slopes look like a golden-brown carpet and the slow movement of the herds gave the illusion that the whole hillside was on the move. Interspersed among a profusion of *phunda malia* (zebra) and conglomeration of grey, bearded, sad looking wildebeeste was the graceful long-legged giraffe nibbling at the choicest tender shoots from the top of the trees. Then there were shortsighted rhinos muscling their way like army tanks, and an occasional family of lovable, funny looking warthog running nervously in a single file with their tails pointing skywards at right angles to their fat bodies.

The animals instinctively gathered to the south of the railway following a government decree allowing shooting of game only on the northern flank. There they grazed nonchalantly and with such indifference that most did not even raise their heads at the sound of the E.Class Garrat hurtling through the landscape.

The approach of the railway was viewed with considerable trepidation. The railway authorities feared that the arrival in Kikuyuland of thousands of construction coolies with accompanying prostitutes and catamites would cause discipline problems for 'they raid and steal whenever opportunity offers and it is almost impossible to bring a charge home to a particular man'.

White traders, transport contractors and buccaneers were equally hedonistic, and getting into conflict with Kikuyus, three were killed. John Boys, the most shadowy of all east Africa's pre-settlement pioneers, was illegally taxing the natives and cheating them out of ivory. *"He thought"* writes Chenevix Trench, *"they called him 'King of the Wa Kikuyu'"*. Actually they called him 'Eater of beans'[34], a tribute presumably to his flatulence. By 1902, the administration was given legal powers to keep all undesirables out of native areas.

On 30 May 1899, the railhead at last reached mile 327. The Masai called the area *Nakusontelon*, 'the beginning of all beauty'. This area, too, was teeming with game and according to Preston it 'did not boast a single tree'. A small river called *Uaso Nairobi* (cold water) ran through Nakusontelon and its banks were lush with tall papyrus. Thick elephant grass lined the valley and the flat area all around was ideal as a terminus, so Whitehouse decided to develop it as the principal railway centre. Little did he realise that this was the beginning of a metropolis which a hundred years later would be home to many million inhabitants. Patterson, who was by now a Divisional Engineer, was charged with the responsibility of transforming the grassland into the nerve centre of the railway.

The arrival of the railway was celebrated with a champagne lunch. Thirty sat down, including five ladies, to enjoy a sumptuous spread of salmon, lobster, beef, beefsteak pie, partridges, hams,

---

[34] Ref: Trench, Charles Chenevix – *Men Who Ruled Kenya.* The Radcliffe Press, London 1993

tongues and fowls. The dessert included fruit salads, blancmanges, jellies, tarts, custards and other luxuries.

In July 1899, fourteen months from the arrival of the railhead at Nairobi, the railway headquarters were moved from Mombasa to Nairobi. A month later the line was opened to the public and regular services were scheduled.

The railway had its own administration, law courts, police, fire department and health facilities. It owned the land through which it passed and the adjacent land in Nairobi was its property. The only telegraph line in the country belonged to the railway. Such a degree of autonomy made the railway a government within a government.

The transfer of the Municipal Council headquarters from Machakos in 1899 was not a popular decision. John Ainsworth, the Provincial Commissioner, was sent to Nairobi, to bring order and rule of law as the place was becoming more and more like a Wild West town in America. Ainsworth was very meticulous and a stickler for proper paperwork and this did not endear him to many of his colleagues. He replaced rough justice with proper courts in accordance with the Indian penal code and questioned many other practices. This caused so much animosity between him and the Chief Engineer, Whitehouse, that when Ainsworth built his house, a tin shack, he faced it towards the forest, away from a beautiful view over the plains, just to avoid the sight of his adversary's house. The conflict was resolved by a sort of gentleman's agreement and the two administrations learnt to co-exist.

By 1903, there were several thousand Indians in Nairobi, who were beginning to play a very important role in the development of Kenya, beyond the vital role played by the coolies in the development of the railway. They were also beginning to move into the hinterland and open dukas (from *dukan* in Hindi, meaning a shop) where no other person wanted to go. Up to 1905, European capital and enterprise were almost absent and 80 per cent of capital was Indian.

Nairobi in the early days was just a ramshackle collection of paraphernalia on a landscape that was pleasant but not spectacular. It consisted of row upon row of hastily built corrugated iron bungalows on stilts a couple of feet above the ground in order to keep flood waters and vermin at bay. Weather-beaten tents still dotted the landscape. The main thoroughfare, Victoria Street, could not by any stretch of imagination be regarded as a compliment to the great Queen. At its western end towards the swamp was a collection of Indian shops. They, according to Sir Charles Eliot *'built their houses so close together that they neutralised the natural advantages of air and light, and allowed the most disgusting filth to accumulate'.* [35]At the swankier end was the European, WOOD'S HOTEL, in a building rented from Jeevanjee. The town now boasted a post office, a soda factory and the proverbial centre of European activity – a club. Before the opening of Indian Bazaar, the Protectorate Government, was a sort of shopkeeper, for it had to keep stores of trade goods at each centre, since they formed the sole medium of exchange with the natives. Beads, Americani and Bombay cloth, wire rings, looking glasses, umbrellas and bells all had a recognized value at each centre. Indian stores spelled the demise of these government stores and Indian currency came into use on the 9 May 1898 with all payments made in rupees and pice.

In 1899, 'a case or two' of plague was discovered in the Indian Bazaar and Patterson, without consultation, 'gave the natives and Indians who inhabited it an hour's notice to clear out, and on my responsibility promptly burned the whole place to the ground'[36]. For this outrage, he wrote, *"I was mildly called over the coals".*

In 1902, the plague revisited the Indian Bazaar and there were 63 cases with nineteen deaths. This time, a Goan doctor, Rosendo Ribero, Nairobi's first medical practitioner, diagnosed bubonic plague in two Somali patients[37]. The Medical Officer of Health, with no experience with tropical diseases, panicked and ordered the Bazaar to be burned down. Dr Ribero's surgery met the same fate as the rest. Dr Ribero was compensated with a gift of a plot near the station where he built a bungalow-cum-surgery. Later, for his report on the plague, he received a gift of sixteen acres of land behind Victoria Street[38]. The Indians were housed on the racecourse until a third Indian Bazaar arose, phoenix-like, from the ashes. There were proposals to relocate the Bazaar from this 'temporary site' but the estimated cost of £83,000 was so horrendous that it remains there to the present day – albeit as the Asian Bazaar.

[35] Ref: p366 – Miller, Charles – The Lunatic Express

[36] Ref: p296 – Patterson J.H. – *The Man-Eaters of Tsavo*

[37] Ref: Younghusband – *Glimpses of East Africa.* 1910

[38] Ref: p44 – Trzebinski, Errol – *The Kenya Pioneers.* Heinemann, London 1985

From Nairobi onwards, the progress was a piece of cake – '*An absolute picnic*'[39] as Preston described it. As the train emerges from the thick green Kikuyu forest on to the Kikuyu escarpment, the eyes can only stare in disbelief as they come upon a truly magnificent vista – the unfolding panorama of the Great Rift Valley. Suddenly, it is as if the horizon has gone and the eyes can see forever. Sitting on the vast plain of the Rift Valley is Mount Longonot, with its extinct crater, and a little distance away the extinct peak of the equally impressive Mount Suswa. Tucked to one side of the base of Longonot is Lake Naivasha, a hauntingly beautiful sheet of still water, twelve miles by eleven miles. The mirror like surface of the water, however, belies its treacherous nature, for a sudden squall can awaken the monster within and turn it into a death trap for the unsuspecting mariner. Surrounding the water are sentinels of massive ancient acacia trees with turmeric bark and wide flat canopies standing in meadows of lush green grass. Their fibrous twigs and agreeable taste nearly proved their undoing, for the Indians started using these as *datans* (toothbrushes). Timely legislation put an end to this vandalism and hopefully saved them for posterity.

This picnic was soon ended as the 2,000-foot drop of the eastern wall of the Rift Valley confronted the builders. The problems of descent into the valley were not insurmountable but necessitated the building of expensive and time-consuming viaducts. The Railway Committee was in a great hurry and it wanted to continue laying the track along the valley floor without any hold-ups. Whitehouse and Preston took up the challenge and they came up with an ingenious arrangement which allowed the railway to proceed unimpeded.

The descent comprised of four successive inclines. The first 400-feet sloped at an angle of sixteen degrees but the next two slopes covering 700-feet had an angle of 45 degrees. The slopes were formidable as the railway is only expected to negotiate inclines of no more than two-and-a-half degrees. For the first slope the rolling stock was to be moved by gravity. A steel cable was passed around a break drum at the head of the slope and the cable ends were attached to the wagons running on parallel lines of tracks. The loaded trucks descending the incline would pull the empty bogies up. For the next two slopes the rolling stock had to be carried on

---

[39] Ref: p376 – Miller, Charles – The Lunatic Express

specially built flat platforms with the front wheels ten-feet below the rear wheels. The power was provided by a steam-operated winch. The last 400-feet of the fourth incline of a mere nine-and-a-half degrees was negotiated by gravity once again.

**Rope Inclines in the Rift Valley
during Construction in March, 1900.**

The construction itself was quite hazardous. The coolies could hardly get a foothold on a terrain more suited to mountain goats. The rains and low clouds made life even more miserable by turning the inclines into ski slopes. The loads often got away from the slipping and sliding labourers and went crashing down to the bottom. It was a miracle that the whole operation did not cause a single fatality. Preston had to station a coolie at each end of a sleeper to hold it in place until the rails could be clipped to it and the whole assembly secured to the ground. Once completed, the arrangement worked like clockwork.

This *modus operandi* lasted for eighteen months, and during this time, the railway went ahead by 170 miles. The arrangement was dismantled on 14 November 1901, but not before the railway celebrated the occasion by running a special excursion round trip from Nairobi to Naivasha. Passengers on the up-train descended into the valley by cable and on the return trip ascended the escarpment on the down -train using the new line.

Track laying across the floor of the Rift Valley was plain sailing and Preston was able to spare time to go sailing on Lake Naivasha, Lake Elmenteita and Lake Nakuru where a sort of yacht club was already in existence. The railhead rumbled past a natural rock formation known as the Sleeping Masai and into Nakuru at mile 447. This station, in the shadow of Menangai Hill, was destined to become the district centre. To the south of this hick town lay one of Africa's most beautiful sights – Lake Nakuru. The blue waters of the lake were surrounded by a halo of pink. This was flamingo country and the presence of thousands of these long-legged birds with rosy-white plumage turned the whole area pink. This in turn was surrounded by a silver fringe of a chalk-like chemical called *magadi* soda and around it all was the dark green of the tropical forest.

As one approached the edge of the lake the birds would slowly but deliberately move into the deeper waters as if luring the visitor into the soft *dal dal* (mud) where an unsuspecting person could easily sink up to the waist in a split second. Suddenly, for no apparent reason, the flock would take off, turning the azure of the sunny sky into a swathe of vibrant pink – a truly spectacular sight. The Lakeland area of Nakuru and Elmenteita also attracted vast herds of zebra down the Rift Valley from Baringo but this migration was gradually checked by the encroachment of man and his wire fences.

The workers had hardly said adieu to the flamingos when they came against the western wall of the valley. The railway would climb 2,600 feet in a mere 42 miles. This involved massive, back-breaking cuttings and earthworks and the building of 27 viaducts over the ravines and gorges that scarred the mountain sides. The viaducts varied in length from 156 feet to 881 feet and with long, spindly legs, stood like giant preying mantis over chasms ten storeys deep. The engineers of the American Bridge Company, contracted to build these structures, became very popular with the Europeans, for they introduced a variety of novel tinned foods into East Africa and their hospitality was much sought after. Some of the larger of the steel bridges were built like a crescent and could accommodate the entire train. The view from the window of a train rushing full tilt through a low cloud high above a deep valley with a river snaking in its lap remains a truly awesome sight even for the most seasoned of rail traveller.

By early 1901, the railhead was perched atop the Mau summit at 8,700 feet above sea level, 490 miles from Mombasa and just a shade south of the equator. From then onwards, it was downhill all the way to Muhoroni, a descent of nearly 4,450 feet in 58 miles.

An unexpected hazard came, not from animals, but from humans. So far, the macho Masai and the clever Kikuyu had put up surprisingly little resistance, but the Nandi proved to be a different kettle of fish. They had always been hostile to foreign incursions and had attacked Uganda-bound caravans and the railways' advance survey parties in the past. The Nandi found the enormous supplies of steel to their liking as they could forge these into spears and other weapons. Nandi men were similar to the Masai in physique and customs but they did not shy away from confrontation. Their raids forced the authorities to fortify all railway stations with barbed wire fences. The trains were prohibited from travelling through Nandi country during the night and armed *askaries* had to ride the trains during the day.

According to the whites, a further cause of Nandi hostility was the behaviour of brown workers. They were accused of not only laying the tracks but also every Nandi girl and boy they could lure into their tents. Sir Frederick Jackson, writing about two camps on the western slopes of Mau called them a 'scandal' and says, *"I passed them on foot and that was enough; I never had the courage to walk through one. It was quite sufficient to view them from the line ... Apart from the squalor, they were crowded with prostitutes, small boys and accessories to bestial devices so commonly practised by Orientals. Complaints by Nandi and Lumbwa natives were frequent ... on account of so many of their young women being inveigled away from their homes and harboured in those sinks of iniquity".* Jackson continues, *"Considering the horrible vices and corruption practised before the eyes of local natives, the effect was not as serious as it might have been, but that was due more to the good sense of the natives and their disgust ... well illustrated by a question once put to the District Commissioner at Ndi by a Mteita: 'Bwana, are these people men?'"*[40]

By the summer of 1901, the line had descended the western slopes of the Mau and arrived at Muhoroni which became the supply

[40] Ref: p387 – Miller, Charles – *The Lunatic Express*

base for the railhead. Only 35 miles of marshy flat lands of Kavirondo lay between the men and their destination. Preston called the men together and urged them to work like the Trojans in order to traverse the malarious semi-swamp as quickly as possible. The men responded with enthusiasm and they replied, *"We will, Inshalla, be there by the New Year"[41]*.

The Allah was not listening. Kibos Village, merely six miles from the lake, was reached at record speed, but then disaster struck. The men were hit by a double whammy of malaria and dysentery and half the work force, including Preston, became ill. The rains came down with such fury that the entire lowlands became a morass. The new embankments were either washed out or became soft like *Ugali* and were barely able to support the trains that wobbled along so dangerously that a disaster was waiting to happen.

To add to all these troubles, the Nandi started raiding the stores and they stole so much wire and materials that the telegraph lines began to lag behind the plate layers. This was a very frustrating setback as messages could only be relayed by engine drivers. The telegraph engineer, Turner, was at his wits end and one night, he set out by train from the railhead to Muhoroni to investigate the delay. He was accompanied by Nesbitt, the bridge engineer, who had completed his assignment and was preparing to leave for England. It was a miserable night and the visibility was poor due to the lashing rain. Someone in Muhoroni had blundered and despatched an unscheduled train to the railhead. The two locomotives approached each other like two blind dragons and collided at full speed. Preston, on hearing this news, got out of his sick bed and at once took the inspection trolley to the site of the accident. He was not prepared for what he saw. Poor Turner was so badly smashed up as to be barely recognisable, and Nesbitt had only sufficient breath left to remark that he had built his last bridge. The two men, so cruelly denied the satisfaction of a job well done, were buried beside the line on the platform at Kibigori station – a stone's throw from the final destination.

This arduous task came to fruition at mile 572 when the railway reached the lake on Friday, 20 December 1901, just in time for Christmas celebrations. The next day at 4 o'clock in the afternoon, an official ceremony marked the occasion. A photograph of that moment shows that in comparison with the inauguration at

---

[41] Ref: p338 – Miller, Charles – The Lunatic Express

Mombasa, which appeared to be a well-orchestrated formal occasion, driving home the last key was a very ordinary affair. The rail track seems to extend almost to the water's edge. Five sturdy, overdressed Englishmen wearing plus-fours and jackets graced the occasion. Four sported pith helmets and one a wide-brimmed trilby. A black mastiff represented the animal kingdom. Someone forgot to invite the natives and the coolies. Florence Preston, the wife of the Chief Engineer, in a long, elegant white dress and hat, seems to steal the show as she gingerly taps the last key into position and *voila!*

Florence Preston
Driving home the last key

The entire enterprise was an example of grit and co-operation between the people of three continents and three colours. The brainchild of the British needed Indian and African brawn to achieve this dream. This was a unique telescopic railway, built not to unify a country or to provide transport in an already developed country, but an undertaking to provide a passage through one country to get to another, a long distance away from the sea. The railhead literally preceded everything else and dragged all the paraphernalia of a modern age behind it. The project involved about 31,983 Indians, many hundred Africans and a handful of Europeans. It was a triumph over drought, disease, the elements, the animals, the natives and the idiosyncrasies of the labour force.

The final cost of £5.5 million, instead of the projected £1.9 million, was enormous but pales when compared to the horrendous cost in human terms. Of the 2,495 coolies who died, 28 were eaten up by lions. A majority of them succumbed to a multitude of tropical diseases. An untold number suffered physical injuries and mental anguish. Many Africans gave their lives in a similar fashion but no one even cared to record their names and numbers. Only a few Europeans died, but they too, gave all they had in planning and surveying, and suffered the same hardships as the men in their service. At the end of the day, however, the railway remains a triumph of human endeavour and courage and a permanent monument to all the *babus, boys* and *bwanas* who contributed to its success.

Chapter 3

Duel of Turbans and Topees

"When the missionaries came to Africa they had the bible and we had the land. They said "Let us pray." We closed our eyes. When we opened them we had the bible and they had the land."

Bishop Desmond Tutu

Race relations in East Africa were acrimonious from the very beginning of the twentieth century. The cut and thrust between the Indians and Europeans continued unabated, with one or two periods of relative calm. At the beginning of World War II the Europeans had virtually all they wanted. The European grip was eventually loosened by the events of the second half of the century. The Indians were politically naïve and trusting. They were, in fact, on a losing wicket from the start as they could only ask and hope to receive. The Europeans were rich, united, and had influence and support in high places. The Governors, in East Africa, with one exception, tended to support their fellow Europeans and the Imperial Government was largely pro-European when it most mattered.

Although there was a suggestion from well-meaning people in India and Britain that East Africa should become an Indian colony, this was an idle dream and some Indians in high political positions fell into this trap. The Indians' older civilisation, equal intelligence, entrepreneurship and resilience became a source of jealousy and fear for the Europeans. The by-product of this constant bickering was the emergence of support for the African who was pushed forward by one side to thwart the other, and the eventual rise of the native to claim the land which was his in the first place, and neither the white man nor the brown man had any right to usurp it.

At the dawn of the century, Sir Charles Eliot was appointed the Consul-General at Zanzibar and Commissioner for the East African Protectorate, resident in Mombasa. He was a brilliant Oxford man with mastery of at least six languages including Sanskrit. Elspeth Huxley called him 'the progenitor of white settlement in East

Africa.'[42] Initially he was in favour of Indian and European settlement in the Kenya Highlands, but by 1902 he wanted the area exclusively for the Europeans. He advocated the restriction of Indian settlement to the lowlands and he wrote to the Secretary of State *"believing as I do that East African Highlands are for most part a white man's country and hoping that they will be taken up by white colonists in the near future, I doubt the expediency of settling large bodies of Indians in them."* [43]He believed that the Highlands were 'distasteful to the Hindu' and the claims of the Europeans were 'paramount'.[44] He supported his views by disclosing reports by railway officials, Whitehouse and Rogers, and the Superintendent of Police Farquhar. Land was offered to the Europeans at Rs 2 per acre freehold up to 1,000 acres for farmers and later 5,000-acre blocks were offered to them free of charge. By the end of 1903, 130 Europeans had taken advantage. Eliot also prevented land sales to Indians covering an area from Machakos to Fort Ternan, thus heralding the official beginning of 'White Highlands'. In 1904, there was an intervention from the Foreign Office and this led to Eliot resigning his office.

Eliot's views were opposed by some of his subordinates. In 1903 Frederick Jackson warned the Foreign Office that most European settlers were *'a lot of scallywags'*[45] under the influence of their leader, Lord Hugh Delamare. The opposition, however, was never strong enough to change the course of events in the Protectorate. In 1906, the constitution was changed and the title of Commissioner was changed to Governor and Commander-in-Chief. As well the seat of Government was moved from Mombasa to Nairobi. Sir James Hays Sadler became the first Governor of Kenya. Executive and Legislative Councils were established. The Legislative Council had three unofficial and six official members – all European. At the same time the Colonial Secretary, Lord Elgin, gave assurances confirming the reservation of the Highlands for the

---

[42] Ref: p 75 – Huxley, Elspeth – *White Man's Country.* London 2nd Edition 1956, Vol I

Pg 74 – Gregory, Robert G – *India and East Africa. A History of Race Relations within the British Empire 1890-1939.* Clarendon Press, London 1971

[43] Ref: p 72 Gregory, Robert G – India and East Africa

[44] Ref: p 72 Gregory, Robert G – India and East Africa

[45] Ref: Jackson, F to Sir Clement Hill, pvt, 25 May & 4 August 1903, in F.O.2/270

Europeans. By 1908 these assurances were confirmed by the Colonial Secretary and this became known as 'the Elgin Pledge'.

Meanwhile, the whites formed a Colonists' Association in Nairobi and in 1905 they presented a petition pointing out that 'the East Africa Protectorate is governed as if it were a province of India...' They were opposed to the application of Indian laws, Indian currency and Indian methods of government and they demanded restriction of Indian immigration and reservation of the Highlands. A Land Committee with Lord Delamare as its Chairman reported in 1905. It favoured the segregation of the races in the towns, reserving the Highlands for the Europeans and confining the Lowlands for Indian agriculture. This policy was supported by Elgin's Liberal Government in Britain and by Governor, Hayes-Sadler. So successful was this policy in excluding Indians from the Highlands, that in 1934, the Carter Land Commission reported that the only Indian settlement in the Highlands was a small block of farms east of Mohoroni.

Earlier, the plight of 6,000 railway coolies who had applied to stay in East Africa at the end of their contracts gave the Europeans added ammunition. They were destitute and trying to make a living any way they could. Some roamed about as petty traders and others set up shops in the interior, giving rise to haphazard, unsanitary Indian bazaars. The problems that arose made them a target of European criticism. Sir Donald Stewart in August 1903 supported the European position that the Highlands were a 'comparatively small area' while 'enormous tracts of land' suitable for Indians were available elsewhere and that because 'owing to the unsanitary habits of Asiatics and Africans, they are not fit persons to take up land as neighbours of Europeans'[46]. The extremist, Colonel Grogan, asked for the exclusion of Indians in the same way as in South Africa.

This racist policy resulted in a surge of European population, which more than tripled in five years from 501 in 1901 to 1,813 in 1906 and increased more than tenfold in fourteen years. The first census of 1911 showed that there were 11,886 Indians, 3,167 Europeans, 9,100 Arabs and 3 million Africans in Kenya.[47]

Both Jackson and John Ainsworth opposed the Colonists' Association by pointing out that its leaders had South African connections and that they were anti-Native and anti-Indian.

---

[46] Ref: Stewart, Donald to Alfred Lyttleton, 14 August 1905

[47] Ref: p 77 Gregory,Robert G – India and East Africa

Ainsworth highlighted that the Indians were an important factor in Kenya as they owned 60 to 70 per cent of the trading and other capital. Holly emphasised the fact that Indians were paying 25 per cent of municipal rates in Nairobi whereas the European settler only contributed 6½ per cent. He also addressed the accusation that Indians always transmit their savings to India and pointed out that this 'accusation may with some weight be laid against Europeans'[48].

The Indians were perturbed from the very beginning and to oppose this racism they formed the Indian Association of Mombasa in 1900 under the leadership of L.M. Savle, a Maratha who ran a small business, as manufacturers' representative in Mombasa. He was supported by Seth Allidina Visram, a Khoja, and by the two brothers, A. M. Jeevanjee and T. M. Jeevanjee, who were Bohras. The Aga Khan was approached to use his influence to obtain farmland in the Highlands but he discouraged his petitioners. He stated *"I do not think the country between say, Machakos and the Mau Escarpment is suited to Indians, and I think it would be a pity if Indians tried for land there, since it is not a country where Indians can show what they can do"[49]*. The Indians ignored his advice and continued their agitation.

In 1906, Visram became the founder President of the Indian Association of Nairobi. In April of that year came the first real opposition to the racial policies when a mass meeting was convened at Mombasa. The point that particularly troubled the Indians was that non-British Europeans would have preference in public matters over British Indians in a British Protectorate. The Indians subscribed Rs 20,000 towards the presentation of their grievances to the local, Imperial and Indian Governments. A.M. Jeevanjee led a deputation to the Colonial Office with the objective 'not to obtain equal rights with the Colonials in British Colonies in Africa, but only to secure a fair treatment of the Indian subjects of the King-Emperor'[50].

---

[48] Ref: p101 – Mangat, J.S. – *History of the Asians in East Africa.* C.1886 to 1945. Oxford 1969

[49] Ref: p 82-83 – Gregory,Robert G – India and East Africa

[50] Ref: p 307 – Ross, William McGregor

Seth Allidina Visram – 'King of Uganda'.

In 1907, a British East Africa Indian Association was formed, with headquarters in Mombasa, to represent the Indians in all parts of the country. In the autumn of that year, Indian grievances and views were presented to Winston Churchill, who in 1908 published his book, **My African Journey**. In Churchill the Indians found an ally. He assured the Indian delegation that although he hoped to confine the Highlands mainly to white population, the Government would keep its promises to Indians.[51] He wrote *"Is it possible for any Government, with a scrap of respect for honest dealing between man and man, to embark on a policy of deliberately squeezing out the native of India from regions in which he has established himself under every security of public faith".*[52]

In 1908, the Indians demanded equal rights and representation on the Legislative Council. Governor, Hayes-Sadler, who had good relations with Indians and spoke Gujarati,[53] told the Indians that they had 'a legitimate claim to representation.'[54] In a dispatch to the Colonial Office he wrote, *"European non-official feeling in the Uplands will doubtless be opposed to the Indians being represented, but I do not consider that any such feeling should outweigh the legitimate claims of that community"*[55]. The Europeans were irritated by the Governor's friendliness towards Indians and in 1908, a disorderly European mob led by Lord Delamare, marched to Government House and shouted for the Governor's resignation. Hayes-Sadler responded by suspending Delamare from the Legislative Council. The settlers nicknamed the Governor 'Flannel Foot'.

In 1910, A.M. Jeevanjee was appointed to the Legislative Council, but only as an unofficial Indian member. As there was hostility from the Europeans and his was a voice in the wilderness, Jeevanjee decided to present the Indian case to Government in London. Some of his claims were exaggerated and promptly refuted by the Legislative Council, and at the expiry of his term in 1911, no further appointment was made until 1919.

Meanwhile, in London, the All Indian Muslim League took up the cudgel on behalf of the East African Indians and made representations to the Imperial Government. The grievances advanced by the League included the reservation of the Highlands for Europeans, Government sponsorship of European immigration, discriminatory education policies, denial of trial by jury, refusal to appoint Indians as Justices of Peace and denial of certain plots of

---

[51] Ref:p 83 – Gregory, Robert G. – *India and East Africa*

[52] Ref: p49 – Churchill, Winston – *My African Journey.* Hodder & Stoughton, London 1908

[53] Ref: p104 – Mangat, J.S. – Quoting: East African Standard, 6 January 1906

[54] Ref: p104 – Mangat, J.S. – Quoting: East African Protectorate. Minutes of the Executive Council, 13 April 1908

[55] Ref: p104 – Mangat, J. S. – A History of the Asians in East Africa

land in Nairobi. Sir Percy Girouard, the new Governor of Kenya, issued a rebuttal, dismissing Jeevanjee as an illiterate and pointed out that the East African Colony had to be 'controlled by our own kith and kin'. He predicted that with 'the announcement of grant of agricultural lands to them (the Indians) in the Highlands, mob law would be in vogue within 24 hours'.[56] Frederick Jackson, who had previously supported the Indian cause, changed his tune and called the Indians 'hucksters and usurers' who were using unscrupulous business methods and accused them of being carriers of disease.

The Indian arguments fell on deaf ears and the Colonial Secretary, Lewis Harcourt, brought forth all the old chestnuts, claiming that the Highlands were a comparatively small area unsuited to the Indian agriculturalist and that segregation was needed to maintain proper sanitary standards because most Indians were of low caste and unsanitary. He did not, however, appreciate that most Indians in the country were not ex-coolies.

Indians continued to demand a representative in the Legislative Council but Girouard turned this down, claiming that there was 'no prominent Indian of sufficient educational qualifications'.[57] The Indians reacted by withholding payment of the poll tax which was introduced in 1912.

In 1914, the East African Indian National Congress was formed in Mombasa with T.M. Jeevanjee as its President. Further pressure was brought to bear on the Government but the new Governor, Sir Henery Belfield, came out with the same lame excuses. However, the Government of India supported the Indians and pointed out that there was 'no justification for assigning in the Crown Colonies or Protectorates to British Indians who are not indentured labourers, a status in any way inferior to that of any other class of His Majesty's subjects resident in the Colony'.[58] But no one was listening. Local European settlers, missionaries and officials spoke in unison and the Imperial Government, too, jumped into bed with them.

The events in German East Africa more or less paralleled those in Kenya. Earlier benign attitudes towards the Indians began to take

---

[56] Ref: p106 – Mangat, J.S. – (India Office Emigration – May 1911, Pros 1-2,file48, part A, memo by Sir Percy Girouard)

[57] Ref: p108 – Mangat, J. S. – (C.O. 533/102, Girouard to Crewe, 19 Feb 1912; and E.A.P. Minutes of the Executive Council, 17 Feb. 1912

[58] Ref: p110 – Mangat, J.S. – (India Office Emigration – August 1914, Pros.22,file34, Part A, Crewe to Harcourt, 29 July 1914)

on a malignant hue. Indians were accused of being crafty and unsanitary, of gun running and of keeping accounts in their own language. Except for Parsees and Goans, all Indians were to be tried by a 'native judge' – a second class official without legal training. Curbs on Indian immigration were also demanded.

The official policy in Uganda more or less followed along the same route. The same innuendos and accusations were made. As the Indians had no ginneries, rules were brought in for direct purchase of cotton by the ginners, thus excluding the Indian middleman. Visram retaliated by building a ginnery in Kampala. On the whole, however, the general attitude of the Ugandan Government towards the Indians was softer, as illustrated by the 1920 report of the Uganda Development Commission which provided that: *"The country owes much to the Indian trader and we consider that a broad policy of toleration should be adopted towards him. He has shown energy and enterprise, and has assisted in the opening up of the more remote districts".*[59]

The Europeans continued to highlight Indian vices and ignore their virtues. A cascade of measures to weaken the Indians and to make the Europeans paramount were brought in after the war. In 1915, the Crown Lands Ordinance sought to legalise reservation of the Highlands for the Europeans. Segregation was introduced and in 1919 Europeans were granted elective representation that ensured their predominance in legislative and municipal councils. In 1920 the status of Kenya was changed to a Crown Colony and in 1921 the rupee currency was abolished. The Governor, Sir Edward Northey, declared in 1919 that 'British European preponderance in the Government is essential' and pointed out to the Indian Association that 'the principle has been accepted at home that this country was primarily for European development…'[60]

The Indians protested against these measures over and over again but they were ill-organised and their efforts were unsuccessful. In 1915, Manilal A. Desai[61], a lawyer's clerk, arrived

---

[59] Ref: p114 – Mangat, J.S. – (Quoted in Gvt. Of India dispatch of 21 October 1920 in *Correspondence regarding the Position of Indians in East Africa.* Cmd.1311(1921)p9

[60] Ref: p117 – Mangat, J. S. – A History of Asians in East Africa. C. 1886 to 1945

[61] Ref: p39 – Gregory, Robert G. – *Quest for Equality. Asian Politics in East Africa 1900-1967* Oriental Longman, New Delhi 1993

from India and after a brief spell in business and law, he turned to politics and journalism. He re-organised the Indian Association of Nairobi and by touring the Protectorate he founded Indian organisations in almost all the communities. Desai had a 'hypnotic capacity to draw talent to any cause he espoused' and he soon 'lifted the lethargic community from political inertia'.[62] He founded and edited the EAST AFRICAN CHRONICLE which became the mouthpiece of the Indians. It folded in 1923 and its role was taken over by the MOMBASA WEEKLY DEMOCRAT which was founded and edited by Sitaram Achariar. Next, Desai re-organised the East African Indian National Congress (EAINC) and was supported by excellent men like Suleiman Virji, an Ismaili businessman who became the President and B.S. Varma, a Hindu lawyer who was appointed the Secretary.

The rejuvenated EAINC demanded equal rights for Indians in Kenya and elsewhere in the Empire. A deputation was sent to London which presented a position paper to Lord Milner, the Secretary of State for Colonies. Milner offered the Indians two elected seats on the Legislative Council but nil else. The vehement Indian protest found an ally in the Government of India. The Milner 'solution' was rejected, except by the Europeans.

At this juncture in 1921, the Imperial Government convened a Joint Parliament Committee and Governor Northey called a round table conference in Kenya to resolve the impasse. The Europeans were adamant and the only concession offered was the abandonment of commercial segregation. The Joint Parliamentary Committee, however, strongly supported the Indians. The Europeans countered by seeking support from the European settlers in South Africa. The Europeans claimed that they were acting as trustees for the Africans and the sole aim of the Indians was domination. Governor Northey sided with the Europeans and claimed that he had received strong protests from the Arabs and Africans who were against the granting of common roll and equal status to Indians as proposed by the Joint Parliamentary Committee. This was found not to be the case when it was discovered that the meeting of Arabs and Africans had been promoted by a leading settler, Frank Watkins, and that Watkins himself had drafted the resolutions.[63]

---

[62] Ref: pp70-1 – Pandit, Shanti – *Brief History of the Development of Indian Settlement in East Africa.* Nairobi, 1961

[63] Ref: pp20-1 – Kyle – *Gandhi, Harry Thuku*

The Indians sought help in India and elsewhere. The Nationalists in India regarded the Kenya controversy as a test case for the Imperial Conference resolution passed in 1921 that India was an equal member of the Empire. An Indian delegation of A.M. Jeevanjee and Varma was sent to London to explain the Indian viewpoint, following the departure of the hostile Governor Northey for consultation with the Colonial Office. Mr Harry Thuku, leader of the Young Kikuyu Association, sent a telegram to the Colonial Office emphasising that Indian presence in Kenya was not prejudicial to native advancement as alleged by the Europeans, and he declared *"Next to missionaries, Indians are our best friends..."[64]*. He also stated that natives had authorised Jeevanjee, Varma and Colonel Wedgewood (who, along with Gandhi's old South African friend Henery S.L. Polak was in London to support the Indian delegation) to represent their cause.

The Indians had been helping the natives all along. Desai helped to publicise various African grievances over land, labour and wages policies. He printed articles and pamphlets in Swahili for Thuku, who distributed these to his followers. The African leaders were allowed to use the offices of the Indian Association of Nairobi for their political activities and were probably given financial assistance. Thuku was arrested and an African riot followed in March 1922 in which at least eighteen Africans were killed. Indians were accused of complicity, and were in a no-win situation. If they sympathised with the natives, they were regarded as politically dangerous, and if they kept aloof they were accused of doing nothing for the people of the country.

In February 1921, Churchill succeeded Milner as the Secretary of State for the Colonies. During his first year his policy was pro-Indian, conforming to his ideas expounded in 1908. Churchill had said *"The British Empire could have only one ideal on this matter, namely, there should be no barrier of race, colour or creed preventing any man by merit from reaching any station if he was fitted therefore"[65]*.

In spite of Churchill's public statements, it was rumoured that he was leaning towards General Jan Christian Smut's view that Kenya and South Africa should be treated differently. Churchill set

---

[64] Ref: p124 – Mangat, J.S. – *A History of Asians in East Africa.* Oxford University Press, 1969

[65] Ref: p200 – Gregory, Robert G. – India and East Africa

up a review of the Kenya situation by his Under-Secretary, E.F.L.Wood and Secretary of State for India, Sir Edwin Montagu's Under-Secretary, Lord Lytton, and he summoned the Governors of Kenya and Uganda to London. He also invited a delegation of Kenya Indians for consultation.

On 15 August 1921 the Montagu-Churchill proposals on Indian Policy in Kenya were published. The basis for the policy would be 'equal rights for civilised men'. A new constitution was to be announced at the end of 1922 or early 1923. In the interim, Indians were offered, and in January 1922 accepted, four representatives to the Legislative Council. Churchill was hesitant as there was a real threat of a mutiny on the part of the Kenya Europeans who were very active, well-organised and feared that Kenya was about to become 'a dependency of India with its supreme control transferred from London to Delhi'. They formed a Reform Party and proclaimed 'a policy of stern opposition to the present claims of Indians'.[66]

By contrast, the Indians of East Africa were lulled into complacency. They called off the non-co-operation movement and were at pains to emphasise their support for the African community. One of the resolutions stated *"There is no conflict of interest between the Natives of this country and the British Indians. The Indians have never expressed their desire or ambition to rule the Natives or gain supremacy over them, and further the British Indians fully-endorse and support the policy of the rights and privileges asked by them being extended alike to all subjects of the British Government including the indigenous Natives of the Colony".[67]*

In spite of general Indian satisfaction, Churchill was intimidated enough by Europeans that he quickly abandoned the proposals. On 27 January 1922, Churchill dropped this bombshell at the East African Dinner in London. The issue was wide open once again. He pledged his Government to 'reserve the Highlands of East Africa exclusively for European settlers' and referred to it as 'a matter which is definitely settled'. As for Kenya's future he said, *"We do not contemplate any settlement or system which will prevent British East Africa or Kenya becoming a characteristically and*

---

[66] Ref: pp98-9 – Huxley, Elspeth – *White Man's Country.* London, 2nd Edition 1956, Vol II

[67] Ref: Desai, M.A. to Prime Minister *et al.,* telegram, 21 July 1921

distinctly British Colony looking forward in full fruition of time to complete, responsible self-government".[68]

This radical departure from the early proposals was welcomed by the Europeans but bitterly resented by the Indians and their supporters and aroused a storm of protest. Jeevanjee wrote to Churchill of Indian 'utmost surprise and alarm'.[69] Polak wired to Sapru in India that 'Churchill betrayed Kenya Indians'[70].

As a result, a rift developed between Montagu and Churchill and led to Montagu's resignation. Criticism from all quarters seem to have persuaded Churchill to think again. Governor Northey was replaced by Sir Robert Coryndon as Churchill wanted a governor who did not hold pronounced anti-Indian views. Renewed discussions between Parliamentary under-secretaries of the Colonial and India Offices, Wood and Lytton's successor, Winterton, and consultation with Indian and European delegations from Kenya resulted in new proposals known as the Wood-Winterton Report in September 1922. Indian demand for a common elected roll was accepted. The Kenya Government and the Europeans rejected the report and then later threatened a *coup d'etat*. In October 1922, Lloyd George's coalition collapsed and with it Churchill not only lost his post but also his seat in Parliament. Churchill had, like Milner, failed to solve the Kenya problem.

Churchill was succeeded by Victor Cavendish, the Duke of Devonshire. The change was welcomed by the proponents of the Indian cause. Polak wrote to Andrews. *"We stand a very much better chance under the new Government than under the old. Ormsby-Gore is even friendlier than Wood and the Duke of Devonshire has the reputation of being an honest man, which is hardly a virtue that one would attribute to Churchill".*[71] The Duke of Devonshire, however, had very little knowledge of East Africa and he relied heavily on the advice of his two principal assistants, Sir James Masterton-Smith and William Ormsby-Gore.

The relations between the Europeans and Indians reached their lowest ebb in February and March of 1923 and elections were

---

[68] Ref: p213 – Gregory, Robert G. – India and East Africa

[69] Ref: Jeevanjee, Polak & Tadwalker to SSC, 9 February 1922

[70] Ref: Polak to Sapru, telegram 30 January 1922, in G of I, Dept.of R&A, Emig.A, October 1922, nos 1-55

[71] Ref: Polak to Andrews, 8 November &1922, quoted by Ewbank in note, 22 December 1922 in G of I, Dept. of EH &L, Overseas A, June 1923, nos 26-73

postponed. The Europeans were plotting a rebellion and the Governor was openly pro-European. Three British cruisers were moored at Zanzibar just in case things went haywire. The Indian Commissioner in Kenya was forced to resign when his duplicity was discovered by the Mombasa Indians. A Reverend Shaw of Nyeri wrote to the Standard comparing Mohammed to Belial and this caused a worldwide protest from the Muslims. In response to European criticisms Achariar published a disparaging editorial on the morals of Kenya white women in the DEMOCRAT, resulting in his arrest. He was found guilty and remanded for deportation, prompting a hartal 'observed from Mombasa to the lake'. Eventually the Europeans, led by Delamare, the Governor Coryndon and an Indian delegation, left Kenya for consultations in London. The Indians were led by Jeevanjee, who was accompanied by Desai, Varma and Virji, the President of the Nairobi Indian Association. Coryndon, on the eve of departure, declared to a group of Europeans, *"You may remember that I am South African born"*[72].

The negotiations in London were held between April and July 1923. Representations were made by a delegation of Kenya Indians, Indians, Kenya Europeans and others. Opinions were expressed supporting the Indian position by the Theosophical Society, British Auxiliary of the National Conference in Delhi and the Labour Party's Advisory Committee on International Questions. Lady Emily Lutyens gave her untiring support and Mr Jinarajadasa brought moving eloquence and moral fervour to the Indian arguments. The British newspapers, THE MANCHESTER GUARDIAN, THE OBSERVER, THE NATION, THE DAILY NEWS and THE DAILY HERALD supported the Indian arguments. Humanitarians like Polak and Andrews played a very active role, and as a result suffered abuse from the Europeans. Governor Coryndon described Andrews as a 'poisonous renegade'[73].

Everyone seemed to agree, however, that 'native interests' should be paramount. Andrews, with the aid of Mahatma Gandhi and Polak, was instrumental in convincing Indians at home and abroad that Africa belonged to the Africans. Polak, in a letter to

---

[72] Ref: Hill, Mervyn F. – *Dual Policy in Kenya.* Nairobi 1944
Huxley, Elspeth – *White Man's Country.* London 1956, Vol.II
[73] Ref: Gregory, Robert G – *India and East Africa*
Oldham and Davidson, 25 May 1923, in *Oldham Papers.* Edinburgh House, London

THE TIMES, explained that Indians favoured a policy of administering Kenya *'primarily as a native trust'.*[74] Polak, according to the Indian delegates was 'practically in charge of our deputation's activity and never grudged time, energy or money'. There was a general belief that Smuts had given support to the European position by threatening to withdraw South Africa from the Commonwealth.

The White Paper, **Indians in Kenya: Memorandum,** was published on 25 July 1923 and this came to be known as the Devonshire Declaration. The natives' interests in Kenya became paramount. Indians were granted five seats on the Legislative Council to be elected on communal rather than common roll. The Highlands reservation was to continue. All segregation between Europeans and Asiatic in towns would be abandoned. Restrictions on immigration were to be imposed 'in the economic interest of the natives'. The Indians were thus denied their two most important demands – access to the Highlands and a common roll. It also frustrated European aspirations to achieve self-government.

This document was a devastating blow as all Indian hopes were dashed. Desai called the decision 'both shocking and alarming – completely betraying Indians' cause showing queer sense of British justice'. Polak remarked *"The whole result is tragic. We may properly congratulate ourselves on having won a clear declaration of policy for the native Africans but in practice, I fear the old evils will remain… The stage is being set for a world wide racial struggle between white and coloured peoples".*[75] The London DAILY HERALD asserted, *"The Government of the Empire has declared to the world that its Indian citizens are an inferior race…"* In India there was a tremendous outcry. Lal Bahadur Shastri, a leading member of the Congress Party, who had previously been unable to accept Gandhi's conviction of the importance of attaining *Swaraj*, (independence) changed his opinion. Shastri wrote a number of articles and emphasized 'Kenya lost, everything lost'. A mass meeting in Bombay, chaired by Mrs. A. Besant, Irish-born theosophist who had come to love, live and work for India, passed six resolutions, the sixth being 'that only when India attained dominion status abroad and *Swaraj* at home would she be able to protect her nationals'. The Indian Viceroy, Ewbank, also expressed his disappointment in the settlement.

---

[74] Ref: p10 – *The Times.* 17 April 1923
[75] Ref: p250 – Gregory, Robert G. – Indian and East Africa

On 23 November 1923, Coryndon published the Immigration Bill and this precipitated another crisis. However, the Imperial Government intervened and Devonshire directed the Governor to postpone the Bill. Early in the following year, Coryndon informed the Indians that he had 'earmarked provisionally' two lowland areas for Indian occupation and invited the Indian Government to inspect these. This scheme did not materialize because 95 per cent of the land offered was unfit for human habitation because of the lack of water and pestilence. Leys called the offer 'a brazen-faced humbug'. The offer would have also jeopardized the principle of non-segregation.

It was not until 19 January 1924 that the E A I N C formally considered the White Paper. The reaction was predictable and the E A I N C retaliated by passing a resolution against the payment of poll tax by Kenya Indians, excepting the Government servants. Mrs. Sarojini Naidu, who was one of the three Indian delegates, was honoured with the presidency and she delivered a fiery but unfortunate address declaring, *"East Africa is, therefore, the legitimate Colony of the surplus of that great Indian nation".*[76] It was S.G. Vaze who had the difficult task to persuade the militant Indians that it was to their benefit to merge their interest with those of the Africans instead. In late January 1924, the Labour Party of Ramsay MacDonald replaced Baldwin's Conservatives and this spelt the end of the Devonshire era.

In March 1924, Desai and Virji were imprisoned after a huge demonstration in Mombasa where national songs were sung and support for the non-payment of poll tax was urged. The boycott turned out to be a miserable failure due to the disunity among Indians. The Indians then decided to accept 'under protest, one of the seats in the Executive and five seats on the Legislative Council on a nominal basis'. [77]The Indians also began to realize that appeals to the Indian Government were fruitless as long as it remained subordinate to the Imperial Government in London.

In July 1924, Leopold Stemett Amery, who was Secretary of State for the Colonies, set up the East African Commission – usually referred to as the Ormsby-Gore Commission – as an instrument for furthering Amery's ideas. The Commission recommended the

---

[76] Ref: p264 – Gregory, Robert G. – *India and East Africa.* (Quoted in *Indian Quarterly Register,* 1924, I,312)

[77] Ref: p277 Gregory, Robert G. – *India and East Africa*

84

building of roads and railways for future development. It advocated that the cultivation of Arabica coffee be reserved exclusively for Europeans. It urged that the African's right to land be given a legal status and recommended that 'some form of income tax should be adopted'. The question of a federation was thought to be 'premature'.

In December 1924, the Indians abandoned the policy of non-co-operation and compromise arrangements were made for a three-year trial period. This decision was a result of the Immigration Bill being withdrawn and an offer from the Kenya Government to nominate Indian representatives on the Legislative Council and Local Government Commissions, and an offer for more Indian representation on the Municipal Councils. This compromise lasted a fleeting moment because the Europeans began to push for Dual Policy and closer union of East African Territories. The auction of plots in Mombasa by the Kenya Government exclusively to Europeans only proved to be the last straw.

In February 1925, Coryndon died during an appendectomy operation and Sir Edward Grigg became the Governor. He was also appointed High Commissioner of Transport for Kenya, Uganda and Tanganyika. The post was created to pave the way for Grigg's advancement to Governor General of East Africa.

Governor Grigg was a good friend of Kenya Europeans and he was committed to their advancement. Besides encouraging a closer union of East African countries, he began to promote the concept of Dual Policy which was, in fact, the brainchild of Coryndon. But, in addition to just economic advancement, he began to include political evolution. He described Dual Policy as 'complementary development of native, and non-native communities' – a new version of Cecil Rhodes' dictum 'equal rights for all civilized men'. The doctrine professed equality but aspired to European superiority. The Indians did not figure in this equation as they were soon to discover. They were excluded from a public auction of thirty-nine residential plots in Mombasa and their poll tax was increased from 30 to 50 shillings.

In 1926, Desai fell ill and died under suspicious circumstances. Newer leaders were already waiting in the wings and several young Indians, notably Sitaram Achariar, Dr A.C.L. de Souza, Mohammed Hussain, Malik and Isher Dass started the revival of political activity which had slipped into the doldrums after the failure of the boycott. Dr de Souza founded and edited two publications – FAIRPLAY and

85

GOAN VOICE and he entered the legislature. He also became the President of Desai Memorial Library and the Goan Overseas Association.[78] Isher Dass, a Marxist, arrived from London in 1927 and served as Jeevanjee's Secretary. He was described as 'young, bold, outspoken, rash and stubborn'. As General Secretary of the Congress and Legislative Councillor, he became the leader of the non-co-operation movement and the most militant defender of both Indian and African interests.

The Indians became fragmented on the subject of co-operation with the Government and when they all resigned from the Legislative Council, Malik alone chose to stay on. In December 1927, Achariar asked for Grigg's recall. A year later in December 1928, he described the Governor as 'the Arch Anti-Indian of Kenya' and he charged Grigg with breach of faith and treachery towards the Indian community.[79]

Meanwhile, the Indians were helping the natives and Achariar and his assistant editor, Thakur, printed MWIGWITHANIA, the Kikuyu Central Association's journal, and guided Johnstone (later Jomo) Kenyatta, its General Secretary, 'through editorial and printing intricacies'.[80]

In 1927, under the influence of radical leaders like Isher Dass and U.K. Oza, demands for common role were resumed and non-cooperation was reactivated. This resulted in an almost total boycott of the Legislative Council elections in March 1927. Malik was the only one to break ranks and he was elected unopposed by 360 voters who had registered on the communal roll. The situation became very tense when Grigg accepted the recommendations of the Feltham Commission promoting a European unofficial majority. Furthermore, his support for communal roll and his questioning of the Indian fitness to be associated with Dual Policy added fuel to the fire.

In July 1927, Amery published a Command Paper which altered the existing policy in three ways: 1) Dual Policy was

---

[78] Ref: p71 – Pundit, Shanti – *Asians in East Africa and Cental Africa.* Nairobi, 1963

[79] Ref: Quoted in *Intelligence Report* for the Year ending 31 December 1928, Northern Frontier Dist. p13, *ibid*
p268 Pundit, Shanti

[80] Ref: Thakur was the son of S.L. Thakur who had helped found East African Indian National Congress

86

substituted for native paramountcy; 2) it accorded the Europeans a share in trusteeship; and 3) it implied that the East African territories were proceeding rapidly towards self-government. The paper also included terms of reference for a Royal Commission designed to prepare the way for an East African federation. This Commission under the Conservative Chairman, Sir Edward Hilton Young, reported in January 1929. This was a majority report, the Chairman having dissented. The report was not favourable to the Europeans as the Commission was in favour of 'a common roll for Europeans and Indians with a franchise based on a high education and property test'.

The Europeans and Governor Grigg were very disappointed and Grigg issued a press statement backing the minority report. The Europeans opposed the common role as they feared that the admission of Indian votes on the same terms as the Europeans might lead in the end, through superiority of numbers, to the control of their interests and institutions passing into the hands of another race.

Amery then tried to circumvent the recommendations of the Hilton Young majority by sending his Permanent-Under-Secretary of State, Sir Samuel Wilson, on a special mission to East Africa. While Wilson was in East Africa, Amery was blatantly championing the cause of the European settlers and self-government. On 2 June 1929 Baldwin's Conservative Government lost the election and Amery lost his Colonial Office. The Labour Government under Ramsay MacDonald was sworn in and Sidney Webb (Lord Passfield) became the Secretary of State for the Colonies. A month later, Wilson produced his report. This report was very pro-European and it pleased the Europeans and the Governor, but it drew howls of protest from the British Humanitarians. After intense pressure from William Temple, Archbishop of York and prompting by Wedgewood Benn at the India Office, Passfield took steps to dissociate the Government from the views expressed in the report. Kenya Africans and Indians too were very critical. The Kikuyu Central Association claimed, 'His enquiry was only one-sided and natives were totally excluded'.[81] Malik, the only Indian elected member in the Legislative Council stated, *"Surely the Indian community was not a party to the alleged agreement, nor were the natives"*.[82]

---

[81] Ref: *East African Standard.* Nairobi, 2 November 1929
[82] Ref: p40 – East African Standard (15 Feb. 1930)

The Kenya Indians had so far presented a joint front but chinks were beginning to appear in their solidarity. The 'Mombasa Group' spearheaded by J. B. Pandya, A. B. Patel and G. A. Kaderbhoy were pro-co-operation with the Government but the radical 'Nairobi Group' led by Isher Dass, Oza, Varma and Shamasud Deen favoured non-co-operation. Furthermore, a rift developed between Dass and Deen as they both sought the post of Secretary of Congress in 1931. The moderate Mombasa group therefore assumed control of the organisation and they were quickly recognised by the Government. The two groups soon resolved their differences and in May 1931, all the members supported non-co-operation and this policy continued for two more years. In 1933, co-operation was resumed following the Joint Committees' conclusions against European demands for self-government and against the Indian demands for immediate adoption of common roll. The moderates had won the struggle.

Waiting in the wings were, however, the inter-racial separatist tendencies among the Indians. Although the Legislative Council elections of 1933 had the cooperation of all the communities and resulted in the election of Pandya, Deen, DeSouza, Mangat and Dass, the Municipal Council elections in Nairobi managed to expose the Achilles' heel of the Indians. The Muslims demanded reservation of the seats for themselves and the elections of 1936 saw one seat reserved for Goans and one for Muslims. These tendencies were in fact a reflection of the growing differences between Hindus and Muslims in the mother country, and this rift eventually culminated in the granting of separate religious representation to the Muslims in 1951.

On 20 June 1930, eleven months after the publication of the Wilson Report, Passfield issued two White Papers, one entitled 'Statement of the Conclusions of His Majesty's Government on the United Kingdom as regards closer Union in East Africa' and the other, 'Memorandum on Native Policy in East Africa'. In the Paper on closer union, Passfield proposed the appointment of a High Commissioner who would administer native policy as well as essential services like customs, defence, posts and telegraph in Kenya, Uganda and Tanganyika. He also recommended a second nominated representative for African interests and supported common roll based on education and advancement in civilisation. In the second Paper he accepted that 'the interests of the African natives must be paramount, and that if, and when, those interests and the interests of the immigrant races should conflict, the former should prevail'[83]. No mention was made of lowlands.

These two White Papers were highly favourable to the Indian community. The Indians in Kenya supported African Native Paramountcy and trusteeship but opposed closer association of East African territories. The natives were also pleased and Kenyatta, on behalf of the Kikuyu Central Association, sent a letter to the EAST AFRICAN STANDARD in praise of the two Papers.[84] The Kenya Europeans were incensed and called them 'Black Papers'. Governor Grigg was most critical privately and in public. The Conservatives in England denounced these proposals. Passfield, who had not expected such a great protest, announced only five months after the publication of the two White Papers that a Joint Committee would be set up to review both papers – yet another review!

Meanwhile, events in India were moving fast. At the instigation of Congress, 26 January 1930 was celebrated all over India as Independence Day and in April, Gandhi made his famous march to the sea in protest of salt tax. The Government responded by imprisoning Gandhi and adopting stern repressive measures. The en masse resistance led by the Indians and skirmishes with the police and military led to 100 Indians killed, 500 injured and 60,000 thrown in prison. The East African Indians protested, called a *hartal* throughout East Africa on 22 May 1930 following Gandhi's arrest, and congratulated Nehru and others for their sacrifices.[85]

The Joint Committee, set up by the Labour Government, had a curious composition. It not only had a Conservative majority but also a Conservative Chairman. The Committee met 53 times and heard 51 witnesses. Only one day was devoted to hearing Indian opinion, when two Indians from Kenya, A.B. Patel and V. V. Phadke, and two from Uganda, P. V. Mehta and George Ismael, were interviewed. Four days were devoted to evidence from Africans and 49 days were reserved for the European viewpoint.

A.B. Patel declared in his submissions that the Indians 'whole-heartedly support the paramountcy of the native interests'[86] supported African demands for the removal of restriction from

---

[83] Ref: Gregory, Robert G. – *India and East Africa*

[84] Ref: *East African Standard.* Nairobi, 10 January 1931

[85] Ref: Gregory, Robert G. – *India and East Africa*
(Majumdar *et al.,* p987)

[86] Ref: Joint Select Committee. Appendices, no.23

growing certain crops and owning livestock and he called for the abolition of *Kipandi* (identification cards) for Africans. Patel also discussed the inadequate Indian political representation, the Highlands Policy, residential segregation in towns, insufficient funds for Indian educational and medical needs and lack of proportional representation on Government Boards and Committees.

The Europeans had a totally different point of view. Lord Francis Scott, a Kenya settler, claimed that *"Indians would swamp us"* and he added *"We cannot admit that the Indians have the same right to control as the people of our own race. It is a fundamental belief we have that this country is British and not Indian".* [87]J. A. Cable, founder of the TIMES OF MOMBASA, asserted *"Indians ought not to be allowed to make a peaceful conquest of the Government of Kenya through the vote".* [88]

The Joint Committee reported on 4 November 1931. The report was very pro-European and contrary to the interests of the Labour Government, Africans and Indians. It decided against the Indians on most of the major issues such as the common roll, increase in representation in Kenya's Legislative Council, the Highland issue, municipal segregation and discrimination in the public services. Thus the Committee destroyed any plans or hope for reforms.

Meanwhile, in August 1931, the Labour Government collapsed and Passfield lost his job. A new Government was formed by a Labour and Conservative national coalition. The Joint Committee's decision came at a time when the limelight was shifting away from East Africa. Important events elsewhere were beginning to hold the attention of the world and the problems of East Africa were not attracting the intense interest of the twenties. The world was facing economic crisis, India was embroiled in the struggle for independence and conflicts had broken out in various parts of Africa. In India, there was a general acceptance of the idea 'Africa for Africans' and the Kenya Indians were becoming reconciled to European supremacy and the futility of efforts in achieving common electoral roll, proportional representation and access to the Highlands. The Kenya Europeans were in turn becoming less paranoid of the 'Indian menace' and less bent on driving the Indians 'home'.

---

[87] Ref: *Ibid.,* pp661, 700, 712

[88] Ref: *Ibid.,* Appendices, H.C.156, no 19, p126

The Joint Committee's decision was favourably received in England. The Kenya Indians were disappointed as they had made no gains but the Kenya Europeans were pleased overall. The new British Government wasted no time in implementing the report and this diverted attention from the report itself. Sir Philip Cunliffe-Lister, a Conservative who succeeded Passfield, was a man of action and by December he asked the three Governors of East Africa for their views. In July 1932, Cunliffe-Lister directed the Governors to implement the Joint Committee's recommendations. He also appointed three Royal Commissions. The one-man Commission of Lord Moyne was directed to investigate the economic health of the colony. The second Commission, composed of three members, with Sir Morris Carter as Chairman, was to report on land in Kenya. The third Commission was to look into the administration of criminal law in the three territories.

The principal recommendation of Moyne was the imposition of a non-native income tax. Whilst the report drew praise in England, in Kenya, it drew criticism from both Europeans and Indians. The Europeans threatened 'general obstruction and non-cooperation'. They proposed an alternative tax and Major Grogan led a deputation to London.

On June 1933, Cunliffe-Lister directed Governor Byrne to abandon non-native income tax and give a 'full trial' to the alternative tax. This decision was claimed by the Europeans as 'the greatest constitutional victory in the history of the Colony'.[89] This subsequently proved to be a dismal failure. A non-native progressive poll tax was then adopted, but this too proved unsatisfactory, and after a study by Sir Alan Pim, a financial expert, non-native income tax went into effect on 1 January 1937.

The Carter Commission was very thorough in its investigation but gave the Indians a cold shoulder. He interviewed at least 100 Europeans and 487 Africans but only six Indians. The Indians opposed the system of African reserves as it did not meet the growing needs of the Africans for more land and restricted the free movement of tribes. They also opposed the reservation of Highlands exclusively for Europeans. Dass recommended that 'no more land should be alienated to non-natives, irrespective of race – Indian or

---

[89] Ref: p13 – Words of the Nairobi correspondent, *The Times,* London, 15 June 1933, p13

European'.[90] He predicted future trouble between the sons of the soil (Africans) and Europeans.

The Commission's recommendations, released in May 1934, defined the Highlands as consisting of 16,500 square miles and favoured the reservation of this land exclusively for the Europeans. The Commission, to provide a feeling of security for both Africans and Europeans, recommended two Orders-in-Council: one to declare the African's exclusive right to the native reserves and to extinguish any African claims to land in other areas; the other to recognise the Europeans' special claim to the Highlands. The Orders were not issued until 21 February 1939. The British Indians were excluded but any European regardless of nationality had the right to settle in the Highlands.

The publication of Orders-in-Council coincided with Gandhi's contest with Subhas Chandra Bose for Congress leadership, new threats to Indians in South Africa and when Indian legislature was involved in a debate, whether India should withdraw from the League of Nations. But they did not go unnoticed and there was a lot of support for Kenya Indians. The Congress declared the Order-in-Council as 'an insult to India'. The Indians in Kenya, led by A.B. Patel, joined the Africans to form Kenya Highlands League to fight this injustice. A *hartal* and a *jalus* (street procession) took place on 1 March. An assembly of 10,000 Indians, Africans and Arabs in Mombasa passed resolutions of protest. The campaign had hardly started when an even greater campaign, World War II in September 1939, put an end to it.

---

[90] Ref: Kenya Land Commission: Evidence and Memoranda,2887.

Chapter 4

Riding The Rails

**Faster than fairies, faster than witches,
Bridges and houses, hedges and ditches;
And charging along the troops in battle,
All through the meadows the horse and cattle.**

Robert Louis Stevenson

The pleasures of travel by *Gari ya Mosi* (Swahili for smoking gharry), Kenya's version of Stephenson's rocket, are surely unmatched by any other railway journey in the world. The diadromous dragon begins its travels from the tiny picturesque island of Mombasa, with the historic salt waters of the Indian Ocean almost lapping against its wheels, the same waters that had brought the *dhows* of ancient mariners from India and Arabia and the galleons of Ibn Batutta and Vasco da Gama. In more recent times, these waves had wafted the sturdier steel hulls of the Victorian merchant ships and men of war. This marathon trip, in old times, took days before the passengers reached the sweet, cool and unlimited waters of Ukerewe (Arab name for Lake Victoria Nyanza). The journey took even longer if a *bwana* took a fancy to one of nature's beautiful creatures and decided that he needed to exercise his gun and collect a trophy or two. Occasionally the train ran out of steam, a not too uncommon happening, and the passengers had to cool their heels until the right head of steam was generated. Sometimes the driver decided that the spirits and stomachs of the crew and the travellers needed replenishment and stopped at a wayside stall, like the one run by an eccentric Englishman, a convert to Islam, who laid out a spread of cakes, cookies and coffee alongside the track a few miles out of Nairobi[91].

En route, the train has to meander uphill through the Rabai Hills with their giant baobabs and onwards across the semi-desert of Taru. It then proceeds along the cleavage, of Africa's two great

---

[91] Ref: p510 – Miller, Charles – *The Lunatic Express.* The Macmillan Company, New York, NY, 1971

mountains, rising from the continental chest like enormous breasts with nipples of ice and snow. The train then hurries along the savannah, with its myriad of animals and the thick green Kikuyu forest before abseiling down the escarpment into the Rift Valley, a geographical feature of breathtaking proportions. Here, this steel centipede is dwarfed by mountains with cavernous extinct volcanic craters and the smoking hills of Eburu. Further along, the navel of the valley is filled with the shining blue waters of the lakes at Elmenteita and Nakuru. Then come the Mau Hills with their deep ravines and valleys before reaching the Kano plains, in the shadow of the Nandi Hills, and finally Victoria Nyanza, at the very heart of Africa, at a height of 3,762 feet above sea level.

Those lucky enough to ride the rails over the bridge at Jinja are rewarded by the awe-inspiring sight of the lake water spilling over the 'stones' of Rippon Falls to form the source of the Nile, the greatest river in Africa. The scene is at its most magnificent in the evenings when the sun, balancing precariously at the rim of the lake, turns the waters into a shimmering expanse of green and yellow, like molten gold. This magic moment is short, but its memory lingers on for a lifetime.

It is surprising to know that the source of the Nile was well known to and recorded by ancient Hindus, as *Amara*[92], in their religious tome, the *Puranas*. They christened the river *'Cali'*, or 'Great Krishna'. Francis Wilford wrote an article in 1792 based on excerpts from ancient Hindu writings. In a second article thirteen years later, Wilford retracted many of the statements claiming that he had been deceived as to their authenticity. Speke was not aware of the second article and unintentionally perpetuated Wilford's false impression and thus over-emphasized India's contacts with East Africa. This elixir-laden river has flowed northwards since time immemorial to provide life-blood to the humble *falahin* and the mighty Pharaohs of Egypt and cradled the first expounder of the Jewish faith. The same waters have quenched the thirst of Alexander the Great and his armies and cooled the garden playground of Cleopatra and her Roman lovers Mark Anthony and Octavius Caesar. So dependent was Egypt on the Nile that when the river waters fell below normal during a worldwide drought 4,200 years ago, the underbelly of the oldest and greatest civilisation was

---

[92] Ref: p25 – Speke, J.H. – *Journal of the Discovery of the Source of the Nile.* J.M. Dent & Sons Ltd., London & Toronto, E.P. Dutton & Company, New York

exposed and it took only a few years before it and its magnificent monuments began to turn into dust.

The very first 'passengers' to ride the rails were the coolies, who were transported from the base camp to the railhead and back every day. The real upheaval came whenever the camp was struck for a move to the new railhead further up the line. The coolies would clamber lock, stock, chair and *charpai,* all over the bogies wherever there was an inch of space to spare. The engine was no exception. On one occasion when this 'Punjab Mail' was ready to depart, the engine's whistle refused to co-operate. The frustrated driver climbed onto the roof of his cab to investigate and was not amused when he found that one of the coolies had placed his cushion on the whistle and was sitting on it.

By the time my generation came on stream, the days of the VIPs riding in front of the engine perched above a cowcatcher had sadly come to an end. The need to stick to schedules due to increasing congestion on the line had put paid to stops to bag a lion and other such whimsical behaviour – almost, but not absolutely.

.

Prince of Wales sitting on the front of the Royal Train in Kenya, 1928.

During the 30s and 40s, travel for travel's sake was almost unknown and taking holidays for recreation was not yet in vogue. Businessmen travelled only if they had to, for the cost and time did not justify the gains. People saved their cash to go to India on 'long leave' to visit their families, and more often than not, to get married or to marry off their children. As connections with India became more tenuous and locally born talent became available, however, interest in India began to wane.

The first known Hindu marriage in East Africa took place in Mombasa when a lay Arya Samaj pundit named Shiv Chand Bowry married Krishan Nair to Krishna. Although there were many Sood families in Kenya, the first Sood wedding did not take place until 3 July 1928, when Ram Karan Mayor married Maya Wati in Nairobi. Both the bride and groom were born in India. *"The ceremony was performed"*, writes the groom, *"with great pomp and show, the band played by Arya Vir Dal".*[93]

The railway men were fortunate in that local travel for them and their families was highly subsidised. They were hampered, however, by the lack of hotel accommodation for Indians. The rudimentary accommodation in some temples and doss houses was hardly conducive to fun and relaxation. Relations and friends were generally hospitable but usually unable to put up guests in their spartan accommodation which often comprised of one, or at the most two rented rooms brimful with their own large families.

The European hotels all practised colour bar and were in any case beyond the means of the *babus*. The handful of Indians who were wealthy enough would not have used such places, even if they were open to all, for they were uncomfortable with the European lifestyle and bland Western cuisine, which often contained beef and pork products. As far as one knows, such social exclusion in the first few decades was not of much concern to Indians anyway.

Our family seemed to be an exception, as we were always on the move. My father, *Dhupaji*, as everyone called him, was a Senior Clerk in the railway and he was allowed one free pass and three *PTOs* (Privileged Travel Orders) every year for the whole family. So every fourth months, when we had school holidays, we would get our *bistra-boria* (luggage) ready and take the uptrain from Nakuru to Grandpa's farm at Miwani or Kibos. When my older brothers travelled alone, the train would stop at the signal beside the farm at Miwani and wait for my brothers to run down to the farm to see if Grandfather was there. If he was not, they would climb back into the train and continue onto his farm at Kibos. At other times, we went elsewhere and stayed at various trackside stations between Nairobi and Kisumu. The places with good climate invariably had good and

---

[93] Ref: p32 – Mayor Ram Karan – Memoirs of Ram Karan Mayor. London, 1984

spacious bungalows as they were initially built for European staff who had long since moved out to more lucrative pastures. More often than not, these stations were manned by a member of the Sood fraternity, who was either a friend of my father or had served under my Grandfather's tutelage in Kisumu.

Here we had a chance to experience the fresh air, the cool water and the sights, sound and smells of the Highlands area that was the cause of so much acrimony between the Indians and the Europeans. The rest of the time, we messed around the railway facilities. We pretended to send Morse code messages on the telegraph equipment and were thrilled by the exchange of 'line clear tablets' with the drivers of the incoming trains. A treat came one day when my uncle, D.D. Mayor, the Station Master, asked me to do it for real – an experience for a young lad to die for. He held me aloft as the steaming clanking Garret thundered by and the driver bent down and garlanded my outstretched left arm with the hoop of his tablet while he scooped the new tablet from my right hand held high above my head. This was an experience of a lifetime, surpassing by far the excitement I felt when I was allowed to wave the green flag and watch the train pull out of the station platform.

My earliest recollection of riding the rails was that of the evening up train pulling out of Mombasa and puff-puffing across the Makupa Creek. The beautiful view from the Salisbury Bridge seemed to draw every passenger to the windows of their compartments. To propitiate their gods the Gujarati passengers were armed with coconuts which were tossed into the blue waters below. These were certainly God-send for the Swahili boatmen in their dug-out boats who scooped them up as soon as they hit the water and without doubt sold them to the passengers on the next train to Nairobi. That night I remember insisting that I wanted to sleep on the upper berth, so my father tucked me away behind my elder brother out of harm's way. During the night, I somehow managed to roll over my sibling and the safety net. The sickening thud in the dead of the night was my head bouncing off the floor.

In the heady days of the pioneers and for decades after, the trains would slow down at mile 59 at McKinnon Road to pay homage, not to the high and mighty, but to a humble railway *pagazi* (Swahili for labourer) known to his fellow workers as Seyyid Baghali. He was killed along with two other workers when an out-of-control inspector's trolley overturned and he was buried in the vicinity of the tracks. Seyyid Fateh Shah had joined the railway under a *nom-de-plume* when his father fell on hard times. The young Punjabi was known for his prowess rather than his piety. *"He was so fast"*, writes Akbar Shah, *"that he could easily catch a peacock or a vulture before they were able to fly away. Once he caught a running cat that had devoured his cockerel... he could easily run fast carrying three maunds over [over, not on] his head".*[94] A myth grew that Baghali was a *pir* (holyman) as he was a distant descendant of the Seyyids who had gone from Saudi Arabia to Iran to teach Islam. When Genghis Khan invaded Persia, the Seyyids were forced to seek refuge in India.

A simple, hurriedly-dug grave became a focal point for not only Muslims but Hindus and especially Sikhs. Here they would stop, tie a thread on the surrounding grill, pray in silence and ask for a boon. As the legend grew, so did the donations, and alas, the size of the tomb.

The gathering darkness, a heavy dinner and the swaying of the coaches all conspired to spread somnolence and sent most of the travellers deep into slumberland. Only those who stayed up all night playing cards or merrymaking were rewarded by the surreal sight of the moonlight reflecting from the distant snows of Kilimanjaro. The rest were not only denied this splendiferous sight but slept through some of the areas of most dramatic encounters between the hoards of foreign *homo sapiens* and *felis leo* – the real masters of those lands.

The first rays of the rising sun were timorously transforming the night into dawn as the Mombasa-Nairobi mail train steamed into Simba, an unpretentious run of the mill wayside station. This post was aptly named as it had a history. Here the man-eaters had let the construction work progress without hindrance, only to take over once the railhead had moved on. They became regular visitors in the evenings, strutted along the platform and the tracks and often held up traffic by preventing the *babu* from lighting the signal lamp.

In March 1902, the SM telegraphed the traffic manager in Nairobi. *"Lions on platform. Please instruct driver and guard of down-mixed to proceed carefully without signal in Yard. Guard also please advise passengers not to alight from train and be cautious when desiring come office"*. Again, in August 1902: *"Two lions on platform. Train approaching and pointsman up water-tank. Lions*

---

[94] Ref: p169 – Salvadori, Cynthia – We Came in Dhows. Paperchase Kenya Ltd., Vol 1

won't let down. I very nervously frightened and secured in office. Cannot dare give 'line clear' signal oncoming train. Please arrange matter over personal satisfaction and dispose of two lions who great bane my existence". In April the following year the exasperated Station Master reported: *"Please inform station master Makindu instruct driver up-mixed approach station with caution or beware serious troubles and life dangers. Four lions with consorts, aggressively on platform and completely in charge my official functions. Regret impossible perform duties necessary. Please therefore arrange grave matter under report as said lions and consorts making fearful roars and acting savagely. Am in terror of own life"*[95].

Not much had changed by 1920 when Chunilal Amin, the son of a titled Patel, arrived from India and got his first job as a station master at Simba. He was uneducated, as his wealthy father had withdrawn him from school after the teacher had hit him. The huffy father had also ordered a cannon to demolish the school only to relent at the last minute. Upon his father's death, Chuni soon lost his inherited wealth and had no choice but to escape to Africa. *"My father"*, writes his son Vinubhai, *"first got a job as a station-master at Simba station, but he only stayed there for one or two years. The station was a building of c. i. sheets, and it didn't have a toilet inside. He had an assistant, an Indian but I don't know his name. One evening the assistant went out to urinate squatting, as is our Indian custom. While he was squatting, a lion pounced and took him away. My father resigned the next day"*[96].

Simba station had another claim to fame. Here the passengers on the up train, many of whom were still trying to rub the sleep out of their eyes, first caught sight of the most picturesque of humans in Africa – the Elmoran. Here, the ochre-haired ebony warriors came to see *Gari ya Mosi* and stood nonchalantly or even arrogantly on one leg with a decorated heavy shield in one hand and an eight-foot spear in the other. They ploughed nothing, grew nothing and reaped nothing, for their entire diet was milk mixed with blood tapped from the necks of their cattle. The ample slit in the blanket, tied toga-fashion over the right shoulder, revealed a lithe and muscular body and an endowment no other two-legged creature could match, the

---

[95] Ref: p64-65 – Foran W.R. – *A Cuckoo in Kenya*

[96] Ref: p178 – Salvadori, Cynthia. Interview with Vinubhai C. Amin. *We came in Dhows.* Paperchase Kenya Ltd., Vol I

craning of curious necks and side glances of salivating *memsahibs* in first class amply attesting to this.

Not all the SMs were in terror of the lions. Major Foran wrote: *"the Indian babu at Tsavo earns my undying admiration for requesting a rifle and only a single cartridge to defend himself and family from a marauding lion. His confidence in marksmanship was surely misplaced?"* The message, sent in 1901 from the SM at Tsavo to the Traffic Manager in Nairobi, read: *"Just a lion twice or thrice to break office and fencing doors, leaving office door on bell ringing half hour. Myself and family, consisting two wives and three children, narrowly escaping danger of life. Now seeking safety in office. Kindly despatch rifle and one cartridge to aid on first incoming train so can deal with intruder"*.

Another *babu* at Tsavo was threatened by a marauder of a different kind. During the hostilities with Germany, he was prepared to single-handedly repulse an attack on his patch. He telegraphed the Headquarters: *"One hundred Germans advancing on station, please send one rifle and one hundred rounds of ammunition"*[97].

Another brave railway man in the annals of Kenyan history was popularly known as *Simba Mbili*. Abdul Hamid Khan stood six-and-a-half foot tall with wrists the size of an ordinary man's calf. He arrived in IBEA around 1890 and worked for the railway as a Senior Permanent Way Inspector, or 'SPWI', in railway jargon. Khan combined his official duties with hunting. He was often called upon to kill lions – sadly considered vermin in those pioneer days – that were attracted to stations where the shade and dripping water from the overhead water tanks provided a salubrious environment.

One day while riding his inspection trolley with his entourage of African pushers in the vicinity of Tsavo River, he came across a pride of lions crossing the tracks ahead. Ikram Hassam of Mombasa, who knew him well, takes up the story: *"They stopped and went on a nearby ridge, and from there they saw a whole pride pulling down a giraffe. Abdul Hamid had his .303 rifle with him and twelve bullets. He picked off the lions one by one, killing ten of them. The eleventh bullet killed two lions, for it went right through one, and got the one behind in the neck. Someone watching from the top of the hill shouted 'simba mbili, simba mbili!' Abdul thought he had killed all the lions, and was drinking from his water bottle, when one lioness that had only been stunned got up and charged at him. She*

---

[97] Ref: Reitz, Deneys – *Trekking On.* Travel Book Club, London 1933

was so close that he shoved the barrel of the rifle right into her mouth and fired, killing her at the very last minute with his very last bullet".

"...One day when he was going for guinea fowl he started up a buffalo. The buffalo charged at him and gored him repeatedly. He stayed nine months in hospital and never hunted again until I started hunting in the 1940s.

"He took me under his wing because he knew my father very well...The Government had given him a plot at Mtito Andei where he put up the small SIMBA MBILI HOTEL. *I, and my family would stay with him there. He had two wives but no children, and he died in Nairobi in the 1950s".*[98]

Afzal, yet another Khan from Punjab, whose father was a station master, went one better. He acquired the name of *Simba Tatu*. In 1946, a pride of three lions ambled across the causeway one early morning and startled the inhabitants in the Makupa area of Mombasa. Afzal Khan shot all three, using only two bullets – one bullet somehow killing two of the big cats. Manmohan Singh, my classmate at Allidina Visram school in Mombasa, takes up the story: *"When the news reached the railway Landis, I along with other boys ran to the scene still wearing only my cachera (*traditional Sikh shorts*). There on the ground were the three beasts. Women in the neighbourhood started plucking their whiskers and hair to make amulets and bracelets, and people collected the churbi (*fat*) in jars and any other pot they could find, as lion fat is regarded as the ultimate healer of all joint and muscle problems. The pelts went to the brave hunter".*[99]

Lal Singh, the station master at Naivasha, had an encounter of another kind. One day he was returning from a visit to Kijabi, where he had taken his brother, Kehar Singh, a farmer from Kibos, for a bicycle ride. The darkness was closing in as they approached the area of *Mswaki* trees, within a stone's throw from the railway station, when they spotted a pride of lions beside the footpath. They were faced with Hobson's choice for behind them lay twenty miles of jungle. Fearing that the sound of the machines would startle the animals, they decided to abandon their bikes and walk. They held

---

[98] Ref: p180 Salvadori, Cynthia. – We Came in Dhows. Paperchase Kenya Ltd., Vol 1

[99] Ref: Personal communication

their breath as they gingerly walked past the lions. They lived to tell the tale for the lions did not even bother to raise their heads.

The lions were not the only bane of the *babu*'s life. The *Mzungus* were another source of his woes. They were often rude and demanding and a law unto themselves. When bullying did not achieve the desired result, they sometimes resorted to violence. The beating of subservients, it is said, came easy to such products of a public school system where caning even for petty offences was an integral part of their culture.

Thus, Norma Lorimer spent the night at Londiani station toying with the *'baboo'* who had the temerity of demanding payment for excess luggage. When this was not forthcoming he had the cheek to threaten her 'with all the terrors of the law, the general manager, and everyone else'. Every time he made a list of her luggage she tore it up. She wrote: *"As the general manager is a friend of mine, I was able to laugh up my sleeve"*. And: *"This entertainment went on, without the slightest variation, until I heard the train whistle, when I paid what I meant to pay, and not a penny more"*[100].

On another occasion, 'because of some technical omission', a passenger called Humphry was made to pay for his entire luggage when boarding a train from Kisumu. *"This made the charge against it 60 shillings instead of six",* complained the traveller, *"and I had to contribute 54 shillings to the dumb-headedness of that turbaned, cross-legged son of Mahomet who ruled Kisumu's baggage room"*[101].

The imperious white settler, Lord Delamare, was not only arrogant but very xenophobic and used to having his own way. Once when travelling upcountry from Mombasa, he found that the overnight train had been shunted into a siding, to allow a senior official to go hunting the next morning – a not uncommon practice in those days. The Indian engine driver too had joined the party. Delamare, who was in a hurry to get home, became so enraged that he ordered one of the African firemen, who had never driven before, to get on to the footplate and drive the train to Nairobi – where mercifully it arrived safely!

---

[100] Ref: p81 – Lorimer, Norma – *By the Waters of Africa.* Robert Scott, London 1917

[101] Ref: p181 – Salvadori, Cynthia – *We came in Dhows.* Paperchase Kenya Ltd., Vol I

The station master at Elmenteita had to learn fast that there was only one way and that was the Lord's way! When a new SM refused to accept one of Delamare's cheques and a shipment from his estate at Soysambu until the freight had been paid in advance, His Lordship became unhappy. An urgent message received in Nairobi read: *"The Lord has kicked me. Please advise"*[102]. The station master was transferred to another station.

On another occasion, two Indian policemen were sent to Soysambu, following a case of stock theft. Delamare, who was allergic to all police, was away and so the policemen decided to spend the night in an unoccupied tent on his estate. The Baron returned late that night and finding the Indians in the tent, he got the Masai servants to make bloodthirsty noises. As the startled men rushed out of the tent Delamare laid them out with a native wooden club. A summons was subsequently issued against Delamare and served to him at the Nakuru railway station where he was in conference with the Governor in his state coach. The European officer who delivered the subpoena was fired on the spot for disturbing His Excellency, as it was early in the morning and he was recovering from a settler's dinner the night before[103].

The Africans fared even worse. Their lack of education and poverty had pushed them to the bottom of the totem pole. They were unable to assert themselves and there was hardly anyone who was prepared to speak up for their rights. The European attitude arose, it is said, out of a fear that unless there was a strict hierarchy, their prestige would be eroded and lead to increasing African insolence. They were comfortable with the class system in Europe and its propagation in Africa came naturally. The punishment meted out depended on the whim of the *bwana*. Fred Roy admitted, *"My men cannot stand the kiboko, I gave a man 50 the other day and he howled from first to last"*[104].

---

[102] Ref: p304 – Huxley, Elspeth – *White Man's Country.* Chatto & Windus, London 1956

[103] Ref: p303 – Huxley, Elspeth – *White Man's Country.* Chatto & Windus, London 1956

[104] Ref: p125 – Trezbinski, Errol – *The Kenya Pioneers.* Heinemann, London (Fred Roy's letters 1907)

It was not uncommon for the farmers to take pot shots at their labourers. Paice [105] devised a particularly bizarre means to 'teaching them a lesson'. The Masai and Kikuyu tradition of enlarging their earlobes by inserting bigger and bigger things into the pierced ear until it forms large loops made them a target. He wrote, *"...once I came across a herd boy who had... gone to sleep... when I met him, he was wandering about looking for cattle he should have been herding... by way of punishment as I was mounted... I took the crupper of the pony and fastened it through the ear and on the D of the saddle. Then I shoved my heels in my pony and set off at a canter... the nigger had to canter too..."* On another occasion, we tied a lot of trespassers together by the ears and made them carry timber from the forest. In one instance a Boer farmer at Nanyuki chased one of his stock men in his car and when the man fell, drove over him, fully aware that despite the terror it would cause, he would not maim the man because the car chassis would clear his body by several inches!

In 1907, Col. Grogan, one of the pillars of European society, and his two friends, publicly flogged his three rickshaw boys for their insolence towards his sister, Dorothy Hunter and her friend, Miss MacDonald. This took place in front of the courthouse despite the protestations of the magistrate, Mr E.R. Logan. Each offender was given 25 strokes while a crowd of more than 50 Europeans watched the spectacle.[106]

In 1911, a settler, who was a relation of Lord Delamare, shot dead one of the three Africans who had rustled his sheep. The jury of Europeans acquitted the settler, who claimed to have done so in self-defence of his property. Following an outcry in the press against this miscarriage of justice, the man was deported by the Secretary of State for 'inciting to racial enmity'. He was smuggled back into Kenya, dressed as a Somali, during the war and the Government allowed him to stay.[107]

In 1943 or 1944, I witnessed a European police officer interrogating two African houseboys after a burglary in the railway

---

[105] Ref: p125 – Trezbinski, Errol – *The Kenya Pioneers* – Heinemann, London (Arnold Paice's Letters 1910)

[106] Ref: Trezbinski, Errol – *The Kenya Pioneers* – Heinemann, London Bowker – *The Grogan and Bowker Flogging Case* (unpublished)

[107] Ref: p286 – Huxley, Elspeth – *White Man's Country.* Chatto & Windus, London 1956

quarters in Nakuru. The policeman beat the suspects repeatedly and mercilessly until blood started to drip from their mouths and noses. He then marched them away from the surrounding crowd but the beating did not stop.

The Indian policemen resorted to such tactics too. A police officer known to us as 'Giddi' was notorious for his cruelty and unorthodox methods of obtaining evidence and admission of guilt.

The railway *babus* too resorted to violence against the houseboys but it was usually confined to pulling and pinching of the ear or threatening them with a hockey stick – a weapon in most Punjabi houses in those days. Many *landiwallas* took to employing *totos* (young lads) as they were easy to manage and discipline!

Violence against the Europeans was rare but not unknown – until the days of Mau Mau that is. Popatlal Jethwa recalls a rare incident when a European station master became the victim of an Indian's wrath. *'Father didn't take any nonsense from anyone. Like all our family members, he was a bit short-tempered... One time he went to the railway station, I think to see a friend. The station master, a European, tried to stop him from going on to the platform – so my father beat him up. It was all over town, that an Indian had thrashed a European, and even today you'll find that the old people remember the episode* [108].

Relations between the settlers and the SM were sometimes quite amicable as long as the little fellow knew his place. Tom Delamare, 4th Baron and Tara Chand Sood, who spoke good English and used his charm to keep the *bwana* happy, developed a sort of symbiotic relationship. In return for prompt service the landowner kept him supplied with produce from Soysambu and sent him so much milk that his wife, Vidya Vati, resorted to making butter and cheese and sending it to her friends and relations in Nakuru.

Such backhanders were not uncommon. The *babu* was a lynchpin at these wayside stations and the farmers and *dukawallas* made sure that he was on their side. Nasinje, in Uganda, was the epitome of this practice. The *dalals* (agents) paid a fixed amount for each bale of cotton loaded into the wagon and it was of mutual benefit for the *babu* to make sure that a supply of bogies was waiting in the siding at harvest time. Two or three years here and the SM was set for life!

---

[108] Ref: p50 – Salvadori, Cynthia – *We Came in Dhows.* – Paperchase Kenya Ltd., Vol II

The station masters were very 'house proud' of their outposts. They kept the tiny buildings clean and well swept and the name boards and signs were washed regularly. *"Nearly all the station-masters are Indians"* wrote Bache[109], *"and many of them are keen gardeners, and anxious to win the prize for the best-kept station garden. One little wayside station (plants and seeds supplied by the ladies in the district) had a most elaborate garden – flowerbeds in tiers round the two lampposts, kept in place by strips of corrugated iron; roses and creepers in half-barrels, masses of flowers in borders, gum and pepper-trees, rows of cannas; and planted out to Babu's delight, in two rows small beds divided by a path, the loyal sentiment, 'GOD SAVE THE KING'.* Roosevelt too, on his hunting safari in 1909, found *'The stations at which the train stopped were neat and attractive".*[110]

At one of the stations, a Gujarati station master surrounded his house with an enormous fence of *Limri* (bayleaf or European laurel). Word eventually got out as to what it was and many Indian passengers on the passing trains felt free to raid it in spite of the protestations of the owner's wife. Eventually the vandalised hedge became so scraggy that the frustrated woman chopped it off altogether.

Travellers were required to buy their tickets at the point of departure and these were collected at the destination. However, many passengers from the Highlands did not bother and beat the system by disembarking at the NORFOLK HOTEL on the outskirts of Nairobi. Many others 'forgot', 'overlooked', or were 'in a hurry to catch the train'. In any case, they could always buy one at the other end – one man is supposed to have reached England on a second class ticket from Nakuru to Elmenteita, a distance of eighteen miles.

On one occasion Delamare, on his way to Nairobi, got on the train at Elmenteita with his bull-terrier bitch and a litter of four puppies. He did not buy any tickets. After the train had left, the vigilant station master, too scared to confront the Baron, telegraphed Nairobi, warning, *"The Lord is on the train with one bitch and four sons of bitches. No tickets. Please collect".*[111]

---

[109] Ref: Bache, Eve – *The Youngest Lion.* Hutchison, London 1934

[110] Ref: p14 – Roosevelt, Theodore – *African Game Trails.* John Murray, London 1910

[111] Ref: p479 – Millers, Charles – The Lunatic Express.

Some Indian rascals also tried to travel without paying but they were usually subjected to much closer scrutiny. Ralla Ram, a questionable character from Kisumu, managed to beat the system by collusion. When the assistant station master at Nakuru discovered the misdemeanour of his penniless friend, 'a Sood brother', he could not bring himself to hand him over to the authorities. Instead the venerable gentleman was advised to lie low until the coach was shunted into the siding from where he was smuggled out through the back door.

Another Indian, a schoolteacher, tried to beat the system by jumping off the moving train before it reached the station. The price of this folly was however very high. Being a novice, he jumped opposite to the direction of the train and broke his shoulder.

When a suitable train was not available, it was not uncommon for senior railway men to hitch a lift with the guard. My grandfather did that quite often, even after his retirement. I too have travelled in the break van of a goods train on several occasions. On one memorable occasion in 1948, I went to Jinja with my father and half a dozen railwaymen to see Uganda Hockey XI play Indian XI, prior to their departure to the Olympics. On the return journey to Kampala, the train had to wait for several minutes at a level crossing outside Jinja to pick up my father who was delayed at a Sundowner hosted by his friend, the industrialist Inder Singh Gill. In 1951, I was travelling from Lugazi to Kampala after a visit to the sugar mill of Nanji Kalidas Mehta when the engine ran out of steam. The guard and I had to walk back along the track to attach detonators to the rails to warn other trains. After another short conference with the driver, it was time to have a cuppa hot sugary tea. By then the engine had recovered, the devices were removed, and off we went.

It was not uncommon for the engines to sometimes run out of steam. Edward Rodwell[112], a columnist with the *EAST AFRICAN STANDARD,* recounts the story of a train driven by a Goan driver, Emedio Lobo, that ran out of steam near Makindu. After a couple of attempts at the gradient ahead the red-faced driver had to ask the passengers to alight. Another attempt again ended in failure. At this juncture, he noticed that the fuel tender was also empty.

Lobo had no choice but to ask the passengers to cut wood if they had any intention of reaching Mombasa. What Lobo did not know was that among the passengers was Sir Fredrick Jackson, the

[112] Ref: p107 – Rodwell, Edward – *Coast Causerie.* Heinemann, Nairobi

Deputy Governor of Uganda, several Provincial Commissioners and other officials. Sir Fredrick asked for a *panga* and the others followed. Soon the tender was full and there was full head of steam. Lobo gave the loco the throttle and asked the ladies and gentlemen to push for all their worth. The game old engine overcame the incline and the passengers climbed aboard.

In 1943, a Sikh SPWI agreed to take a group of young boys in the overnight goods train to Nairobi. He was taken aback by the size of the party as we climbed into his private coach only minutes before departure. As soon as the meal was over the crusty 'uncle' instructed us to sleep and switched off the light. Soon afterwards, one of the lads developed a stomach ache. His moans and groans and appeals to 'Uncle' to do something were met by Mr Singh urging him to 'take deep breaths and go to sleep'. The general commotion got all the others excited and fully awake. Mr Singh, who was friendly at first, became more and more agitated and began to curse and swear. His colourful language only helped to keep the boys amused, and of course, awake. His misery lasted the entire way to the destination. With the first shafts of daylight he unceremoniously bundled us out into the railway yard where the coach had been shunted overnight. It is not difficult to imagine his relief as he saw the innocent critters walk away as he no doubt muttered to himself – never again.

A short trip in 1940 from Miwani to Kisumu proved to be less than the usual exhilarating experience and caused an excitement of a different kind. I was accompanying my grandfather and was sitting on a stack of railway sleepers in an open bogie. A large, smouldering ember managed to nestle beside me and I only became aware of it when it began to burn my skin. By then, it had made a largish hole in my white shorts. The embarrassment of walking around Kisumu with charred "knickers," as they were then called, was short lived as the permanent scar became a trophy and something to boast about. Many other travellers were not so lucky and they became the victims of much more harrowing experiences.

Shadi Ram Phakey, a railway shunter, was on his way from Kisumu with his bride of a few hours when an African thief scrambled into his compartment and grabbed a purse full of the bride's jewellery. The victim gave a chase but the thief jumped out of the moving train. Just then, the door slammed shut on the young man's thumb, which got amputated. Phakey overcame his handicap and not only resumed his job but continued to keep goal for the

Mombasa Railway Hockey First XI, and fortunately, his sporting career was unaffected.

On one occasion, a petrol tanker and the guard's van broke off from the goods train. The two units rolled backwards down the steep incline, overturned and burst into flames. Mr Bajaj, the guard, tried to run away from the engulfing inferno. He managed to save his life but his body and face were so badly burnt that he was forced to retire. The loss of career in the prime of life and the psychological repercussions of disfigurement and isolation was perhaps a fate worse than death.

Another railwayman, Ravjibhai Patel, our neighbour in Nakuru, became the victim of a bizarre accident. He had spent a lifetime riding the rails, first as a guard and after promotion as a train ticket examiner 'T.T'. He was travelling to Kampala on holiday, when the two corridor coaches of the train became uncoupled. Mr Patel, who was just then crossing the connecting bridge when the two sides sprung apart fell on the rails below and was run over. Thakurbhai, his son was my childhood buddy and had taught me the rudiments of cricket. When this accident happened we had long left Nakuru and lost contact. Thakur eventually moved to the United Kingdom. In the early sixties, I was one day reading the newspaper when I saw Thakur's photograph on the front page. His luck had turned, for he had won an enormous sum of money on the pools. I wanted to call him to congratulate him but decided to leave him alone and let him enjoy his good fortune in peace.

When Dhani Ram, a young fireman, died of burns aboard a locomotive a lot of eyebrows were raised. The driver, Hukum Chand Sood, claimed that the assistant had fallen into the fire while chucking logs into the hearth. By the time he realised what had happened and pulled the victim out, it was too late. In spite of the fact that the Indian community knew the two men did not see eye to eye, his explanation was accepted – the alternative was too horrendous to contemplate!

A pioneer engine driver, Pherozeshaw Nowrojee, also breathed his last on a train to Mombasa. He was brought to Kenya by Darabshaw Motabhoy, a veteran driver from Indian Railways who was among the first batch of drivers recruited by Uganda Railways in 1896. Although Motabhoy had no engine to drive for this was before a single rail had been laid, there was promise in the air.

By the time Nowrojee joined the elite group of men like Motabhoy, D'Souza and N. Pinto in 1900 the railway was well on its way. Nowrojee was a hardworking man with the looks of a demi-god and the confidence of a musketeer. On one occasion while awaiting a train, he was pacing along the edge of the platform when he met a Government official who said, *"Get out of my way"*. The Indian stood his ground and replied, *"Get out yourself"*[113].

On another occasion when he disagreed with Governor Belfield as to the extent of his injuries received during a train crash in 1916, he chose to resign instead of compromising. He was back in the cab three years later and was the driver of choice for the V.I.P. trains. In 1906, with Pinto, he was asked to drive the Duke of Connaught's train from Mombasa to Nairobi. He died as he had lived. On the railway, proud of the fact that he had made a significant impact in the development of Uganda Railway from its fledgling days.

---

[113] Ref: p183 – Salvadori, Cynthia – *We Came in Dhows.* Paperchase Kenya Ltd., Vol I

Pheroze Nowrojee. Engine Driver – First Class. In Drivers uniform. Circa 1900.

The mention of the *GREAT TRAIN ROBBERY* of 1950 still causes a stir among the Asians of Kenya. *"Although a very law-abiding community,"* wrote the Commissioner of Police O'Rourke in 1949, *"it nevertheless produces crime which is usually of a most complicated nature"*[114]. But such gangster crimes were out of character. The only previous case was that of a highway robbery in Mengo (Kampala) in the early thirties. A Punjabi named Pyara Lall Seth and some *Kaburus* stopped a car carrying a large amount of

---

[114] Ref: p161 – Foran W.Robert – *The Kenya Police 1887-1960.* Robert Hale Ltd, London

cash for the cotton ginnery workers' wages. One of the bandits lay beside the road feigning sickness and when the unsuspecting Indian driver stopped the car he was attacked with chilli powder. In the ensuing chase, according to the legend, the robbers' car lost a tyre and still got to the top of the Mengo Hill, where the men were arrested. They all received stiff sentences.[115]

However, in the more recent version of such banditry, the unsuspecting victim was an African guard and the perpetrators were all Punjabi Indians from Nairobi. According to R.N. Dhiri, a senior station master at Nairobi, security if any, was very lax and large amounts of cash were often left unattended in a room at the Nairobi railway station.

The bandits, Kartar Singh Garewal, Balbir Joshi, Bacho Singh and Jiti Sharma were all the sons of railway employees and as they themselves worked for Kenya Uganda Railways they were in possession of some inside knowledge. Sharma was a school friend and neighbour of mine in the early 1940s in Nakuru.

The guard of the train from Nairobi had seen the *Muhindis* (Swahili for 'Indians') and their motorcar at more than one level crossing along the track to Nakuru but thought nothing of it. Near Morendat Station, three masked men boarded the train, and after holding the guard at pistol point, jumped off with two boxes containing £25,000 in currency notes. The accent of the robbers gave the game away. Within 24 hours, the police had arrested all four dabbling dacoits in Nakuru and recovered their vehicles, their disguises and the loot they had buried at the railway cricket ground.

The news of the robbery caused quite a commotion in Kenya, especially among the Indians, many of whom knew the participants and their families. Joshi became a crown witness but all the criminals received long sentences. As the amount stolen was five lakhs of Kenya shillings, the foursome became part of Kenya folklore as the *Panj Lakhias*.

At one time, the up and down trains were kept busy ferrying husbands and wives to be, to India and Europe. Indian marriages were virtually all arranged and the brides invariably accompanied their husbands to Africa. Some couples were well on their way to Kenya before the young man took his first good look at the bride. By contrast, the European men usually got engaged in Europe and returned to set up house before inviting their fiancées. The new

---

[115] Dhupa, Lila Vati. Personal Communication

arrival would be taken straight from the ship to the church or D.C.'s office, the bride stopping at some stranger's house to hurriedly change into a wedding gown. The young man, to impress his partner, not uncommonly upgraded his train ticket to a higher class only to regret it later.

But there were no such financial constraints for Karen, also known as Tania, Dinesen. She married her Swedish Baron, Bror Von Blixen-Finecke, at the D.C.'s office a day after her arrival in Mombasa and rode the rails to Nairobi in a style that most brides could not even dream about. The Governor, Sir Harry Belfield, sent her his private dining car and the American millionaire Northrup McMillan, his cook, to accompany them. But life in Kenya for many newcomers was hard, even cruel, and often full of surprises. The Baroness was no exception.

She started a large coffee acreage at the foot of Ngong Hills near Nairobi and was soon accepted as part of the European blue-blooded elite of Kenyan society. But she was never fully comfortable with the carryings on among the rich and often powerful. She found the British bourgeois, dreary, ill-bred and philistine. The farm was failing, not for lack of hard, back-breaking work on her part, but because of unsuitable soil. Her husband too let her down. Unknown to her, she had married a philanderer, more interested in hunting and chasing women than getting his wellingtons wet. Bror Blixen fell for a married woman named Cockie, so named by her father after cock-a-leekie soup, while he was still married to Karen. The two communicated by concealing their love messages in the barrel of the Baron's rifle which was given to Karen's farm manager who acted as a go-between. The marriage ended in a divorce in 1922.

Karen too had fallen deeply in love with a handsome white hunter named Dennis Finch Hatton. Dennis and Bror Blixen were friends and the two of them escorted the Prince of Wales on his safari in 1928 to shoot a lion in Tanganyika. The playboy prince would play his accordion late into the night, thus rendering everyone unfit for early rising, sharp-eyed tracking and a steady aim the next morning. He was also interested more in pursuing the young women, single or married, than the game. At Dodoma, he disappeared into the night with the wife of a very junior official and turned up several hours late at a formal dinner party. The shindig was to end abruptly due to the sudden illness of King George V, by which time the Royal visitor had bagged his lion.

Karen's love affair ended in disaster when Dennis was killed in a plane crash. The dejected and depressed Baroness was eventually forced to throw in the towel. She abandoned the land of her dreams, took the down train to the sea and returned to Denmark, but not before she had left an indelible mark on Kenya. The area where her farm once stood has become the Nairobi suburb of Karen. Her book, OUT OF AFRICA, the essence of her letters to her aunt in Denmark, published under her pen name Isak Dinesen, has captured the imagination of the world and endeared her to the people of a once far-flung outpost of the British Empire – the people she loved.

A young Hindu maiden, named Yash, the daughter of a railway *babu*, travelled reluctantly in the opposite direction to Karen's first rail trip to meet her beau in India. She was a Kenya girl and that is where she wanted to live, but circumstances had conspired against her. She was, it was said, a radiant happy-go-lucky beauty who had fallen in love with a young Station Master. He reciprocated her feelings and she wanted to get married as soon as he returned from his long leave to India, but when he returned he had a bride in tow.

The parents had no choice but to take their jilted daughter to India and marry her off. The husband turned out to be a namby-pamby and his domineering mother constantly complained about the modest dowry. Besides, a year had gone by and there was no sign of a new prince. The unremitting pressure eventually got to Yash and in a fit of temper she let the old battle-axe know that there would be no patter of tiny feet as her own prince was nothing but a pansy.

A few months went by and Yash became pregnant. She was very happy but she decided to keep it a secret until the festival of Divali. Meanwhile she sent a letter of happy tidings to her parents in Kenya. On the morning of Divali she was in the kitchen preparing sweetmeats and things and waiting for the auspicious hour when she would share her happiness with the family.

The gods and mother-in-law, however, had a different agenda – and the secret would never leave her womb. As the fat hit the fire, she burnt like a torch. *"A kitchen accident",* the matriarch proclaimed. The others joined in the chorus to blame her 'bad karma'. Like many hundreds of brides in the motherland, *'The lady was for burning'*- TWICE.

The platform at Nakuru station, for the up trains to Kisumu and Kampala which departed in the evenings, had the atmosphere of a *mela* (Punjabi for fete). Crowds of people would turn up 'to meet the train' on the off chance that someone they knew was travelling.

They were usually not disappointed. Others would arrive carrying tiffin carriers for friends who were on the train. It was very common for people to send a telegram, *"Passing through on… Meet with food"*. To limit the numbers, the railway introduced a charge of ten cents in the early 1940s but it did not have the desired effect. The railway station was the pub, club and hub of activity in the town – and no one was going to stop that.

While the effusive Indians were busy meeting, greeting, eating and backslapping, the European scene was much more subdued. As soon as the train came to a halt, they would make a beeline for the nearby NAKURU HOTEL. The men in their suits and women in long dresses looked so very elegant. Whereas it was a common sight to see Indian children of all ages horsing around the platform wearing ill-fitting shirts, 'knickers' and often no shoes, European children were noticeable by their absence. They would only appear at the beginning or the end of a school term on their way to or from the residential schools in Nakuru and Nairobi. They were always expensively dressed in blue or red blazers, grey shorts or skirts and matching knee-length stockings. There they would sit on a trunk, often looking bored, sad and lonely. These English *bachas* (children) did not escape the notice of and criticism from the Indian parents who regarded the *dorias* (whites) as uncaring and alleged that they were only too happy to bundle their children off to boarding schools. The hugging and kissing by Europeans in public they contended was 'all show'!

One visit to the platform at Nakuru will remain indelibly etched in my memory. I was standing next to a shy African woman who was trying to ignore the advances of two burly males. As the train began to move, they suddenly grabbed hold of her, bundled her into an open bogie and jumped in behind her. The blatant kidnapping was over in a trice. No one seemed to care. A mere woman – black at that!

Time on such visits grew wings and soon the train was ready to depart. A sudden jolt from a fresh, steaming, clanking Garret and the leisurely return of the *bwanas* and their *memsahibs*, many with a slightly unsteady gait due no doubt to some hurried tippling, was the signal for the others to reassemble their tiffin carriers and leave the carriages. The African hawkers ran from window to window of third-class carriages crying out *"Chai, Chai, Kutumbua"* in the hope of a last minute sale. A few stragglers always needed to be flushed out by the 'T.T' who came rushing around from cabin to cabin shouting *"Time to go – clear the train"*. Then there were always one or two show-offs who even ignored the green flag and the engine's whistle and waited for the train to move before jumping off.

Travel in the down train from Kisumu was always great fun as the section to Nakuru was covered during daylight hours. My mother made sure that there was never a dull moment by pointing out interesting features along the line and quizzing us on various crops as they whizzed past. She was a master of mixing entertainment with education. Before long we had memorized the order, the names and the height of each station and the flora and fauna along the whole network. My favourite scene was the field of white chrysanthemums, stretching as far as the eye could see. These aromatic pyrethrum flowers were the source of an insecticide universally sold as *Flit* and every household in Kenya had a can-full and a pump to spray the house every evening. This reminds me of a story I once read of an Englishman who was invited to an old lady's house in India. On arrival, he was amused to see the matron standing in the hall and holding up her long skirt while her manservant pumped *Flit* up her petticoat – guaranteed to drive away the mosquitoes and other things!

More often than not, my parents knew the station masters along the line as many of them were either recruited by my grandfather or passed through his tutelage in Kisumu. Many were my father's contemporaries and as he was in the Traffic Superintendent's office, they wanted his support to get the good postings. There was always a smile and a quick friendly *Namaste* during these whistle-stops. Often a tray of tea and homemade sweetmeats was awaiting the arrival of the train and a *toto* would appear balancing the tray precariously on his head. The hot thick milky brew fortified with lashings of sugar and *masala* was like manna from heaven. Time was always short and often we had to resort to slurping it from the saucer much to the annoyance of my father. No sooner we handed back the tray the SM would unfurl his green flag and off we went leaving behind a cloud of steam and dust.

At mile 547 at Muhoroni and mile 484 at Molo, the train would stop for about twenty minutes for the Europeans to have tea at the dak bungalow. At Lumbwa at mile 515, the stop for lunch was almost an hour. The steward at Lumbwa always made sure that there was surplus food, recollects my brother Dev Dhupa, who lived with his uncle and station master Tara Chand, and as soon as the train departed the Indian staff would gather together and have a feast. I too can remember my holidays at Molo where we stayed with my uncle, station master Dharam Dev Mayor. Molo was one of the two sites where there was a 'bacon factory'. The idea was to enjoy the cool crisp air of the high country. But the protests and the squealing of the young porkers being led to meet their maker shattered the mornings. Curiosity, however, got the better of some members of our family and the SM was goaded into arranging a visit to the abattoir. The visitors, all vegetarians, were not prepared for the blood and gore and the dangling carcases. The trip lasted all of a few minutes but the vertigo it caused lingers to this day.

Years later in 1949 I was travelling from Mombasa to Kisumu with a contingent of school friends when the train made its customary fifteen-minute stop at Uplands, where the other factory was situated. This gave us an opportunity to visit the factory outlet just off the platform. Two of my Sikh friends, who like the rest had no idea of what the various cuts were, decided to buy 'meat'. At lunchtime, they opened their packets with great panache, smacking of lips and obvious glee. While one chomped through his purchase with great relish, the other to everyone's amusement began to choke on the very first slice. One had managed to buy cooked ham and the other raw bacon.

Corridor trains were introduced in 1927 and with that came the advent of the restaurant car. Initially the new coaches were quite unpopular because the compartments were smaller and there was less lavatory accommodation. The *ensuite* facility was replaced by toilets at the two ends of the long coach which were marked 'European' and 'Non-European'.

The old prostatic gentlemen rued the walk down the corridor and the loss of the bottle opener fixed near the sink, attesting to the fact that a lot of elbow bending went on during the journey. They also missed the good food and the ambience of the old dak bungalows. My grandfather, Fakir Chand Mayor, disliked the new coaches for a unique reason and he continued to travel in the older 'horse boxes' as they were affectionately called. He was in the habit of having a bath in the *en suite* lavatory. A pail of hot water was delivered to him at one station and at the next station, the SM had an African servant standing by to collect the empty pail and to mop up and polish the loo. Nevertheless, the extension of the line, in part through unhealthy country, made the adoption of corridor trains essential to a satisfactory timetable. After some modifications, these coaches became the order of the day.

For children the corridor coaches were a Godsend. Each coach was furnished with a water filter and a stack of conical paper cups and on a folding seat at one end sat a well-turned-out African steward wearing a long white *kanzu* and a fez. He was at our beck-and-call and was kept busy supplying us with endless soft drinks. The new coaches also gave the kids the run of the whole train much to the annoyance of the adults, especially the Europeans, who found that the children did not respect their exclusive coaches or the signs of apartheid.

The corridors provided a racecourse that ended in the most exciting part of the train – third-class coaches. Their allure was their contrast and because they were somewhat of a forbidden territory. Here, too, we could gorge ourselves on delicious African foods like *Mogho, guachi, Karanga, kutumbua and miai* which most Indian adults would not touch with a barge pole.

The compartments on Kenya and Uganda Railways were usually allocated in such a way as to separate the sexes, the races, and where possible, even religious groups. But not uncommonly, the accommodation had to be shared with complete strangers. These chance encounters could occasionally be trying but were never uninteresting. Sometimes they resulted in the formation of life-long friendships.

On one occasion, I was travelling alone from Miwani to Nairobi. As the train stop was only for a minute or so, my luggage was hurriedly piled into the corridor for me to sort it out later. I was carrying the customary tin trunk and a bed roll, an oversized *kikapu* of fruit and vegetables and a bundle of fresh sugar cane neatly cut into equal lengths and tied together with twine. If this was not enough, my grandma had lumbered me with a large earthenware *matungi* (Swahili for 'vessel') for one of the 'aunties' in Nairobi – everyone was called an aunty or uncle in those days. On entering the compartment, I found that my companion was a Gujarati boy about my age and that he was carrying even more luggage than I was – mostly in cardboard boxes. He had spread his belongings on the second berth that was legitimately mine, and what was more, he was reluctant to vacate it. His resentment did not last long and by the time we arrived at the next stop at Kibigori, we were chatting like old friends. Soon Ramu, whose olfactory senses were tickled by the scents arising from the fruit, was rummaging through the *kikapu* and offering me bars of Cadbury's chocolate in return. The purpose of his trip to Kisumu was, I discovered, to collect provisions for his father's kiosk on Lumbwa Station. We had a long bartering session, and at Lumbwa, we parted as friends with a promise to meet and exchange goodies after each of my quarterly visits to my grandfather's farm in Miwani.

The *matungi* in my charge presented a tricky problem. Once in Nairobi, I would have no choice but to hire a taxi at an exorbitant cost of two shillings, but without grandma's unwieldy water pot, I could manage in a bus for just ten cents. There was only one thing to do – dump it. With deep remorse! I informed aunty that her terracotta had become a victim of a sudden jolt due to the incompetence of the engine driver. My aunt was not impressed. She called me 'irresponsible' and much more besides, for not molly coddling her prize possession and cursed the modern engineers for the *kamikazi* way they drove the engines. I have stuck to this story – until now that is.

The beginning of the second half of the twentieth century ushered in what could only be described as a radical change in the attitude of the railway authorities, a reflection perhaps of what was happening elsewhere in eastern Africa. The dak bungalows on the Nakuru-Kisumu line and the restaurant cars on the rest of the network were thrown open to non-Europeans. In practice, it meant the admission of Asians, as the socio-economic conditions of the Africans were still tenuous. The changes in these bastions of social elitism had taken place at snail's pace. The ambience and the fayre had changed but still lagged behind times. The old standard Nazareth menu of 'watery soup, tinned salmon, meatballs, fruit and custard' had given way to newer versions but the quality was still lacking. In 1933, Elspeth Huxley described the establishment as 'grubby, unadorned dak bungalows lit by safari lanterns; the food was pretty dreadful and the drinks tepid'.

In 1950, I made my first foray into the uncharted waters of a European catering establishment – the dak bungalow at Muhoroni. This was in the company of a bunch of high-spirited hockey players, on our way to Mombasa after winning the Inter-school competition in Kisumu. Our captain, Hardev, a gregarious Sikh, assured us that there was no need for apprehension. He was on his way even before the train came to a complete halt and the rest of us followed like sheep. The Goan steward was rather flummoxed at the sight of so many young Indians in this one-time white citadel. In hushed tones, he tried to usher us to the side tables but Hardev would have none of it and plonked himself at the main table.

The place was dark and dingy, even with the mid-morning sun high up in the sky. The tables were covered with crisp white linen and fresh napkins to match. They were laid out with polished silverware and clean, shiny crockery. Jars of marmalade and fully loaded racks of toast stood in the middle. Pots of fresh *Kenya Creameries* butter had long replaced Mrs Sandbach Baker's homemade *siagi ya Queenie* which had in turn, been light years better than the tinned Bombay 'axle grease' of the pioneer era. The tea was still lukewarm.

The Europeans sharing our tables were friendly, chatty and interested in our sports activities. They were amused at the speed with which we gobbled up the cold, woody toast and all the fruitcake. The harried steward had to rush around and come up with fresh hot toast and cake – a bonus for those who had to wait. We could almost hear the steward's sigh of relief as the engine blew its whistle, warning: *"Time gentlemen, please"*.

A trip by train sometimes created strange bedfellows. Occasionally, there was a mix up of surnames and a European was allocated a berth in the same compartment as an Indian. This left the SM red-faced and open to criticism and abuse from his superior and the train was held up until a satisfactory reshuffle was achieved.

The Indians were often quite intolerant of their other countrymen. They had come from a background of a caste system, class-consciousness and religious bigotry and these traits had followed them to Africa. An interesting encounter is described by Kuldip Rai Moman[116] when he was a 20-year-old Hindu postal worker on his way from Mombasa to Kisumu.

"The train halted at Nairobi railway station...

"At the platform while I was having an aimless ramble, a gentleman who was around 45, got into conversation with me. It transpired he was a teacher and was moving on transfer to Kisumu, where I was employed in the Posts and Telegraphs Department as a postal clerk and telegraphist – learner. Masterji was pleased to learn that our destination was the same. I was travelling third-class while my new acquaintance was entitled for a second-class ticket for travel on duty. It was a custom in those days that if one had a second-class ticket and there was no second-class compartment

---

[116] Ref: Moman, Kuldip Rai – *Sood World.* London 1995

available in the train, the railway authorities would allow the passenger to travel in a cabin meant for use by the railway guard or the train ticket examiner. This made the second-class ticket holder think he was a cut above the third-class passengers and was a man of prestige. There were two wooden seats, one opposite the other, two-and-a-half-foot in length, near the windows.

"*Masterji invited me to have midday bhojan, of puri and allu ki sabji with him in his second-class. The train was at Naivasha or Gilgil. I am not certain which station and the mwalimu accompanied me to my compartment to have a further chat. While he was there, the passenger next to me, an Ismaili youth, addressed me by my last name Moman and asked me to share his lunch. He specifically mentioned fish. This was a bombshell for my rifiki, the master. All of a sudden, with machi* (fish) *and Moman, I became a Mussulman! At the next station, without much ado, he got down and left for his seat – without any mention of the delicious lunch I was awaiting. I felt he was not keen on his invitation. However, I had decided, I must have the midday meal with him. Nakuru came and then the train stopped at Njoro, Molo and Turi, but there was no sign of my host. When Elburgan came, I alighted and went to his cabin. He greeted me half-heartedly and I made myself comfortable opposite to him.*

"*What about the puris, I asked. Oh yes, he placed a page from a newspaper on my seat, dropped the puris from a height of 30 inches, followed by allu sabzi from a distance as well. I asked for the mango pickle which he had in a tiny bottle. He obliged. I was intent on a bit of further fun and asked him for the burfi which I knew he had in a potli or a paper packet. He again obliged. I was amused and enjoyed the special lunch throughout.*

"*I shall not be able to retrace my footsteps into the safari and shall not pass through those colourful railway stations between Nairobi and Kisumu, some forlorn, distant, desolate and wild, beyond the horizon. There was a time when a good number of these were manned by our Sood pioneers. I can visualise them waving the red and green flags.*

Kuldip Moman.

"Finally although I had no thirst, I requested for drinking water. I opened my hands joining them together to form an 'oak' as it is called in Punjabi. Again, he poured the nectar from a distance. The train went gurgling through Londiani, Lumbwa, Kedowa, Fortenan and Koru.

And ever again, in the wink of an eye,
Painted stations whistle by.
And here is a mill and there is a river:
Each a glimpse and gone forever!

Robert Louis Stevenson

"We reached Kisumu and what I saw – Ramji Dass Phakey, my uncle! He had received a communication from someone in Nairobi, asking him to put up masterji and help him as necessary. I greeted my uncle with Namaste and he addressed me with my first name 'Kuldip'. Masterji was once again flabbergasted – from Moman and machi to Namaste and Kuldip!"

In 1945, the year of victory, celebrations were held throughout Kenya. In Nakuru, a large sign, 'GRVI', tattooed in the side of Mount Menangai at King George's coronation was re-etched with chalk and an enthusiastic multicultural crowd gathered at the aerodrome near the lake to enjoy the festivities and all the hoopla. The highlight of the evening was the drop of miniature candle bearing parachutes from a plane. The sight of hundreds of lanterns floating about in the sky was a sight to behold. My brother managed to catch one and that remained our prize possession for years to come.

The Kenyans had another cause *celebre* that year. It was the 50th anniversary of the arrival of the late Sir George Whitehouse in Mombasa to build the Uganda Railway. Flags were flown on all stations and office buildings and a large crowd had gathered at Nairobi station to greet the mail train from Mombasa. Among the celebratees were four long-time employees, R.O. Preston, Gulam Mohammed, A. Stubbs and A.M. Khan, who had all joined the railway in its infancy.

Gulam, in 1899, was the driver of a *machanga* (construction) train that brought his mother to Nairobi. This hookah-smoking lady

124

was the first Indian woman to arrive in the future capital and lived there to a ripe old age of 112 years.

A.M. Khan by contrast was a coolie, hired to push the Makindu-based PWI's trolley and carry his baggage. He was allowed to enter the house, but only by the back door. On one occasion, he was huddling in the front verandah during a rainstorm when he was spotted by the *bwana* and was ordered to leave at once. The hardworking Khan eventually became a P.W.I. himself and when Makindu was re-graded as an Indian post, he was allocated the same bungalow from which he had been unceremoniously expelled.

The railways had ruled the roost for nearly five decades of the twentieth century. The motor transport during that era was unreliable and the roads were no more than corrugated dirt tracks crossed by numerous runnels and rivulets. Every trip by road had the potential of turning into an adventure. The possibility of spending the night stranded in a sea of gooey mud or due to a broken axle was a daunting prospect. Because of safety in numbers people tended to travel in groups, and that, too, during daylight hours.

My first ever motor trip into the wilderness was in Uganda where my host, Mr Loroia, in Kampala, had arranged a visit to Murchison Falls. This truly magnificent wonder of eastern Africa was named by Speke, after Sir Roderick Murchison, the President of the Royal Society in London. Our outward course was uneventful but the return journey nearly turned into a nightmare. We were motoring along in the cool of the evening and softening daylight past a herd of elephants when the tyre developed a puncture. The first hurried attempt at changing the tyre was a dismal failure. The car did not budge but the jack sank into the soft mud. The only solution was to dig a hole and fill it with roadside grit to form a firm base. The darkness was beginning to engulf the area in its inky mantle as the job was completed. The sound of the boot lid or something else alarmed our hitherto docile onlookers. The agitated jumbo suddenly raised his trunk and trumpeting and flapping his ears made a beeline for the car. All we could do was to sit still and hold our breath while the wild juggernaut sniffed and pranced around our Hudson. Perhaps it was our prayer to Lord Ganesh – the elephant-headed god – that saved the day for the beast turned around and ambled away to the waiting herd.

The first decent all-weather road in Kenya was built during the Second World War when the 'white *pagazis*', the Italian P.O.W.s, were put to work. Travelling between Nakuru and Nairobi by train, one could see hundreds of Italians working on this highway, a menial job hitherto reserved for the Africans. The quality of their work was of such high standard that the road continues to be one of the best after so many decades.

The railway, following the war, was under considerable strain. The rolling stock was old and decrepit and prompt replacement was not in sight. Competition from airways was looming and road transport was threatening to overtake the slow and rattling *gharri*. The authorities were confident that the third-class passengers would continue to use the railway but the second-class and first-class punters were unpredictable and quite likely to seek alternate means. Unless their comfort and service were improved, the future could be bleak. The times they were a-changing and the whole country was in a flux. The days of innocence would soon be over and the next couple of decades would usher in changes of unprecedented proportions.

The African masses were rapidly growing conscious of their social status and political rights – or lack of them. The natives were congregating nearer the larger towns and developing expensive tastes in liquor and goods. The first five decades had seen the host nation relegated to last place and there was little chance that the incomers were going to let it have a fair piece of the action by legitimate means. The young and the restless could not wait for slow and laborious political and social change and the alternative of direct action was becoming increasingly attractive. Poverty, insecurity and greed were a sure-fire mixture to lead many into gangster crimes.

Pickpockets and jewellery and handbag snatchers became increasingly common. They were no doubt, encouraged by uncouth Asian goldsmiths of Nagara and River Road who provided a ready market for the ill-gotten gold. These trinketers melted the jewellery overnight, re-fashioned it into brand-new pieces and resold them to Asian women for whom gold was the ultimate status symbol. The muggers became so bold that even the police officers were attacked downtown in broad daylight.

When women gave up the wearing of expensive adornments in public the Africans took to pole-fishing and burglary. The criminals were unsophisticated and their crude ways would have made the '*Kilimani Bat*' turn in his grave.[117]*

---

117 Kilimani Bat was a smooth African operator who in 1926 gained entry into many Nairobi homes and stole only money. He carried a pistol and a

My father's house in a railway landi was broken into one afternoon. The hapless men got in by chopping down the wooden doors and a steel trunk but stole only the less valuable flimsy pieces leaving behind heavy gold items in cardboard boxes, thinking perhaps that they were made of brass.

This, however, was just the beginning of a period of lawlessness which would escalate into ever more grotesque and bloody killings until life for foreigners, especially Asians, would become untenable. Kenya came to be known as *Killya* and Nairobi's notoriety earned it the name of *Nairobbery*. The Asians left their beloved country in droves for pastures fresh and woods anew but their soul remained behind.

The aggrieved Asians were hardly a paragon of virtue. Their *modus operandi* was much more subtle. Many had long swindled the natives by under-weighing his produce, substituting goods of lower quality or giving short measures. An occasional attempt at big crime was not unknown. In 1926, a cleverly forged cheque in the amount of 50,000 shillings was cashed at a bank in Mombasa and the man immediately left for India. He was caught, extradited to Kenya, where he along with his partner who had contrived the actual forgery, was sentenced to long-term imprisonment with hard labour. About half the proceeds were recovered. In 1933, an attempt by a clever gang of Sikhs in Nairobi to pass off spurious but well-made coins ended in their arrest and conviction. They were sentenced by the Supreme Court to five years' hard labour.

The criminals gradually became much more sophisticated and their activities involved megabucks as they increasingly delved into commercial crime. Asians, Africans and Europeans all joined in this orgy of ill-gotten gains. Container loads of foreign goods were imported and sold without paying taxes. Money laundering and export of money became a very lucrative business for the big fish. The practice became so common that it was no longer perceived by ordinary people as a crime. Smuggling of coffee, cotton and other produce, especially during the troubles in Uganda, netted the 'businessmen' vast fortunes. Sadly, Government Ministers and officials of foreign embassies were also a party to this binge. It was claimed that these people made more money in a few years after independence that they had in a 'lifetime' before.

---

flashlight and wore nothing but a layer of oil. He was never caught.

By the time the World War ended, breezes of a different kind were blowing in from the Indian subcontinent. The sails and spinnakers were now filled with a powerful message – Independence.

The British had decided to quit India but they were not quite ready to loosen their grip around eastern Africa. Slogans of freedom began to fill the air. But rhetoric is just that – it stirs the senses but does not sustain. The country owed its very existence to the much-maligned *Mzungus* who, by their hard work, foresight, discipline and efficiency had built a nation and civilised and modernised its people over a period of just a few decades. Unlike other colonial powers, they had invested more than they had taken out. The day was not far when they would cease to be the fall guy.

The events in Africa were moving fast and the moment of truth was fast approaching. The freedom fighters were ready to lay down their lives. But, who would replace the British? The power would inevitably fall in the lap of whisk-waving, tub-thumping, political *tuchuns*. Were they up to the task of looking after the *Kinder*, *Kirch* and *Kuche*? – UHURU.

Chapter 5

Bwana Governor

The reasons why young men from India landed up in Mombasa were many and varied. Each person has a story to tell and each story is more fascinating than the other. Unlike most other Indians, Fakir Chand Mayor, my maternal grandfather, was not driven to crossing the *Kala Pani* (deep ocean) to the land of *Kala Log* (black people) by the pain in a hungry stomach, but by a passion for adventure, the challenge of a new world and perhaps a desire to get away from the humdrum life of an Indian village. He was recruited by the railway as a *babu*[118] and on arrival he found his niche in Port Florence where he became known as the Governor.

Babuji[119] Fakir Chand was born on 11 November 1878 in the village of Hiran, about fourteen miles from the city of Ludhiana in the province of Punjab. His father, Sultani Mall, was the adopted son of Banna Mall who had no progeny of his own. Sultani Mall became the 'village squire' after he inherited 300 *bigas* of land from his father. He lived in the hope that one day, his favourite son, Fakir Chand, would take over the reins of office.

Hiran was a peaceful, sleepy village of 300 – 400 souls. A narrow dirt road ran across the hamlet and on either side of it were single storied *hutties* (shops) of burnt brick with roofs of local thatch. To one side of the village was an open *maidan* (open ground) where grain was delivered from the surrounding fields and villages. A little distance away was the *toba* (pond) where some of the locals gathered, washed their clothes and watered their animals. The village proper was set back from the shops which acted as the first line of defence. The vigilant shopkeepers kept a weather eye open and noted all the comings and goings of daily life. Strangers were treated with caution and suspicion.

For Sultani Mall, life could not be better. His four sons were healthy and strong. His farmland was fertile and it boasted of three wells. One of these was fitted with a Persian wheel which moaned and groaned from morning till night. The villagers drew their water

---

[118] An Indian Clerk. A Hindu gentleman. A form of address corresponding to Mr

[119] or *Bauji.* A way to address a respected elder, a father or a grandfather

from the shallow wells or collected it from the canal that ran from the wells to the fields. A constant stream of women came to the wells to replenish their supply of drinking water and to exchange gossip. The old hands trouped in with two or three *matkas* (water vessel) on their heads, filled them up and disappeared. The comely maidens sauntered along in twos and threes, laughing and giggling with one *matka* on the head and another resting delicately on the hip – with a tight *choli* (blouse) and a *gagri* (skirt) tied low on the waist. They came to linger, to notice and to be noticed. This was an opportunity to flirt, a chance for romance or even a village scandal. Richer Hindu women did not go to the well or mix with the riff-raff. Instead, their supplies were delivered by a *bhisti* (water carrier) who spent all day carrying two large brass vessels attached to a long pole which was slung across the shoulders.

The villagers toiled in the fields all day, much as they did all over Punjab. The Muslims, who were usually the *mazdurs* (labourers), were easy to spot for they wore a white kerchief around their heads and a loin-cloth. The Hindus wore a large white turban, a short *kurta* (shirt) and a *dhoti* around their hips. At noon, the more well off Hindus would go home for midday meal and a siesta whereas the labourers had their food delivered to them in the fields and took rest wherever they could.

But none of this for Sultani Mall whose farm hands and minions did all the digging, hoeing and other backbreaking jobs. The squire was awoken at 5 o'clock every morning and after morning ablution and a short prayer he was ready for a substantial breakfast of eggs, *paratha,* a *pinni* (sweetmeat) and hot milk. He would then slip into a fresh white cotton *kurta* and a white silk *lungi.* His large turban of seven yards of white muslin was tied in a style that reflected his position in the society. The morning was spent at the shop wheeling and dealing in cotton, grain and other commodities and discussing day-to-day matters. During the summer months, a jug of cool *sherbat* was always at hand and the smoke from a large ornate *hukka* filled the air all year round. This was shared only with friends and someone of equal status. In the evenings, the village *panchayat* (council), of which Sultani Mall was a member, met to discuss village matters, exchange news and generally shoot the breeze. The ever-present *hukka* was shared by all the participants – each person making sure that the nozzle was kept dry by drawing the smoke through a closed fist covering the end piece.

As darkness fell, it was time to adjourn and go home for the main meal of the day. The men sat on reed mats with their individual *thalies* (brass trays) in front of them. Each man was served with a *phulka* as it came off the hot plate strictly according to the pecking order. The meal usually consisted of *dhal* (lentils), *sabzi* (vegetables), *dahi* (yogurt) and pickles. Goat meat was generally cooked by men and eaten only by men. Large quantities of it were fed to boys in the general belief in Punjab and elsewhere that the sons would grow up to be tall and strong.

Gandhi, who was born on 2[n] October 1869 in Gujarat, also succumbed to this belief and was persuaded to eat goats' flesh to improve his physique and courage. He forced himself to swallow the meat supplied by his friend, Sheikh Mehtab, and became sick immediately. That night he kept dreaming of a live goat bleating in his stomach. Gandhi considered that 'meat eating was a duty' and performed it for a year at a secret rendezvous with Sheikh. Then, his dishonesty repelled him and he gave up meat consumption until he could resume it openly after his parents' death[120].

The villagers consumed *titer* (pheasant) and *batera* (quail) with relish and occasionally fish when available from the nearby river. Beef and pork were shunned by all as they were a taboo for Hindus and Muslims respectively. When mustard was in season, *saag* (pureed leaves) and *maki di roti* made of yellow maize flour were a great favourite with the rich and poor alike. In Punjab rice was a rarity. Boiled rice soaked in hot milk and kedgeree was cooked only if someone in the household was sick.

Education in Hiran was available up to primary school level. Only the bright children from well-to-do families went to secondary school in Ludhiana. The rest had to look for jobs. Fakir Chand had no such constraints. He would get on his horse and trot off to Dayanand Arya Vedic High School. The horse was tied outside the school with a supply of hay and water.

Most of the traffic along the dirt road consisted of two-wheeled, two-ox carts overflowing with wheat, hay or sugar cane, creaking and jolting on their way to the market. The sight of a *tonga* was uncommon. The villagers hardly, if ever, left the village and a visit to the city was a rare event. The pedestrians, mostly males, were almost all barefoot. Some of them carried their shoes in a

---

[120] Ref: p11-12 – Fisher Louis – *Gandhi, His Life and Message for the World.* Mentor: Pub by the Penguin Group, Penguin Books, USA Inc., New York, USA

satchel until they reached the outskirts, where they would wash their feet, put on their sassy spats and saunter into the city.

It was the year of 1897 when Fakir Chand received a letter from his friend in Nairobi. Mathra Dass who hailed from the nearby village of Sanewal had met Fakir Chand at school in Ludhiana and the two of them had taken an instant liking to each other. Here they came under the influence of Maharishi Dayanand Saraswati, the founder of Arya Samaj, an institution based on the Vedas. It propagates universal doctrines of humanity but it is neither a religion nor a sect. The letter extolled the virtues of British East Africa and encouraged Fakir Chand to join him in the opportunity of a lifetime. It contained the following verse:

Ram nam ki loot hai,
Looti jai so loot;
Phir piche pachtae ga,
Jab pran jayenge choot[121]

Fakir Chand was smitten. The call of his friend and the opportunity for adventure in the African wilderness proved greater than his intended journey through the human body. His decision to forsake Agra Medical School caused a lot of consternation but the family rallied round and decided to support his venture. They perhaps took solace in the fact that his three-year contract would soon be over and he would get over his wanderlust.

The farewell was very emotional and the tears could have filled the Ganges. Prayers were said early that morning, dry chillies were waved over his head to ward off evil spirits, and a donation of cash and sweetmeats was made to the village Brahmin. He said a sad goodbye to his young wife, Mathra Devi, and soon he was on his way to the train station in Ludhiana. Any apprehension that he felt was soon dispelled by the thoughts of better prospects in Africa and as the train chugged into Calcutta Station[122] he began to bubble with excitement. After a cursory examination and some paperwork it was anchors ahoy and Africa here we come.

---

[121] In the name of our Lord, the land abounds in milk and honey, You will regret forever, if you squander the chance to make money

[122] Under normal circumstances, the ship would have sailed from Karachi, but the port was closed temporarily due to an outbreak of plague. The authorities were thus forced to use the Port of Calcutta.

As soon as the ship's holds were full and the hatches battened down, it was time to board. This was a free-for-all mad dash to clamber on to the tarpaulin-covered boards and establish a pitch. Battered metal trunks, bed rolls of cotton filled *rajai* (duvet), a pillow rolled in a *dhurrie*, rations and the rest of the caboodle were quickly arranged to demarcate one's territory. This was the 'third-class cabin' where one had to cook, relax, sleep and dream of life in the new world and the beckoning wilderness. Disputes over space were not uncommon and occasionally ended up in fisticuffs. Those whose bedding was sparse, which was in most cases, had no choice but to grin and bear the hardness of the boards of their four posters and the resultant stiffness of the muscles and aching of the bones.

The mornings started with the appearance of the *Khalasis* (deck hands) and the banging and clanging of steel buckets as they hosed away the debris and scrubbed the decks with stiff long-handled brooms. The days at sea were long and often monotonous and spent by pacing the decks or gazing at the blue-black waters of the endless ocean. The open decks and stiff breezes were Godsend as they carried away the air thick with stench from unwashed human bodies and smoke from a large number of *jikos* used for cooking meals. Cooking was a welcome pastime but even this was disrupted if the seas were rough. The meals became progressively austere as days passed and the supplies of fruit and vegetables were exhausted. At best they consisted of various watery *dhals* and *chapattis*.

The afternoons were the time of *araam* (siesta) and the cooler evenings were given to card playing or *shatranj* (chess). Some of the passengers got together in small knots for a singsong or a spontaneous *mushaira* (poetry recitation). These get-togethers sometimes ended with the forging of friendships or future business associations which lasted a lifetime.

Occasionally, the monotony was broken by the sighting of flying fish swooping over the surface of the water or the appearance of dolphins and other creatures of the deep. Sometimes, a dhow or two or a whole flotilla would appear from nowhere and everyone rushed over to wave and greet them. Beautiful as these ancient craft of rough sawn timber and handmade sails looked against the vast canvas of the ocean, the recruits were glad that unlike the earlier emigrants, they did not have to sail in these leaking, creaking vessels. A trip by dhow was hazardous and could take months for it was at the mercy of the unpredictable power of the winds and in the charge of a *Nakhoda* who depended on experience, the shadow of the sun in a box sextant and a compass if he was lucky.

On breezeless, overcast days all the passengers could do was to watch the helpless craft bob up and down like a rubber duck on a still pond. The *Nakhoda* sat on the deck counting his prayers with his ivory bead rosary and shouting instructions to men who were kept busy scraping mussels from the hull or mending the sails. He kept a tight control on the supply of fresh water which was stored in wooden tanks above decks, for he had to make port before his stores ran out or face thirst, hunger and a watery grave. The mayday signals were not of much use as they were generally ignored by passing ships.

The conditions in third-class were luxurious in comparison to those in a dhow. Here, only men could go above decks to stretch their legs. Women had no such privilege and they were allowed on the top deck only to use the toilet facilities which consisted of a slimy two-foot square wooden platform with a low railing around it and a large hole to squat over. The contraption was slung lower than the deck so that only the occupant's head and shoulders were visible. A small bucket at the end of a rope provided the supply of seawater. During long voyages, women would often lose the use of their legs and had to be carried ashore.

The *Nakhodas* were drawn mostly from the Muslim *Badalas,* Hindu *Bhatias* of Cutch Mandavi and ancient mariners from other parts of India who had plied these waters for many millennia. It is said that *Kana Maalim*[123], meaning 'Master of the Tiller', a *Badala* from Gujarat, was in Malindi when Vasco da Gama arrived on the East African coast in 1498 and that it was he who acted as a pilot and took the Portuguese adventurer to India.

Mombasa appeared on the horizon one morning and a buzz went up throughout the ship. Everyone moved over to the rails to take a good look at the distant shore. Young Fakir Chand's heart began to race as the moment of truth and the land of his aspirations came into sharper focus. Soon the ship was steaming through the

---

[123] Ref: p4 – Salvadori, Cynthia – *We came in Dhows.* Paperchase Kenya Ltd., Vol I
Kana Maalim Ibn Majid – *The Sun is in Our Blood.* From an interview with Yakub Abbas Kana, Mombasa

mouth of the creek with the historic island of Mombasa on the starboard and the mainland area of Likoni portside. Suddenly, the sound of the engines stopped and the ship glided to a ceased, the rattling of cable announced the lowering of the anchor.

Port Kilindini (Swahili for deep water) was nothing more than an ugly scar in the side of a lush landscape. The once pristine sands were desecrated with patches of diesel and the beach was pockmarked with industrial bric-a-brac. Massive girders were stacked to one side of a straight-railed jetty which protruded quite rudely out to the water's edge and beyond. At the fringe of the vegetation stood truncated stumps of once graceful coconut palms vandalised in the name of progress. Milling about the sand were a few Indians and Swahilis and two or three *bwanas* in their white uniforms and pith toupees. The human cargo was soon transferred to small unsteady dug-out boats and other craft and taken ashore. From here everyone had to walk to makeshift accommodation until it was time to move inland.

Most coolies had only a short time to find their land legs and get used to the blinding sun and hot sweltering nights. The loose end of the turban was handy to wipe away the rivulets of sweat that ran down the face and spine. The island was covered with the gold and green of coconut palms which swayed gracefully and waved about their feathery fronds like elegant ladies trying to keep cool. Strong, majestic and immovable baobabs dotted the island as if guarding against intruders. Elsewhere, mangroves with their prep roots formed thickets at the water's edge.

On the eastern flank of the island lay the old historic harbour that had witnessed the comings and goings of dhows from coastal ports of Gedi, Malindi, Zanzibar and from distant shores of Arabia and India. In more recent times the galleons from Europe had made their presence felt. All had come with the common purposes – trade, re-supply, exploitation and even military control. The galleons have departed but dhows remain to this day. They lie around, as they have done since time immemorial, bobbing and creaking with each wave and surrounded by small boats which cling to them like barnacles to a whale. Each cluster is enveloped by its own peculiar aura which comes from the stench of cargo holds, incense burners and cooking pots on three stone fireplaces on the top deck.

Keeping a watchful eye on the entrance to the old harbour, the visitors saw the towering, thick mottled grey battlements of Fort

Jesus[124]. This was built by the Portuguese with labour from India, almost a hundred years after the visit of Vasco da Gama. His arrival heralded a new era of commercial enterprise. His objectives of trade and military control proved so successful that within a short period the Portuguese started to dominate the western Indian Ocean. But theirs was a regime of cruelty, plunder, exploitation and subjugation and so despised were they that all trace of their culture and contribution have disappeared from the coast except for the fort and a few words in Swahili[125].

Every visitor to the old harbour had to step onto a few slime covered steps which led to a small wharf, the unpretentious gateway to Africa. Immediately outside was the old fish market with its stinking fly-covered *fruit de mer,* and beyond this lay the old Arab town of Mombasa – a haphazard conglomeration of motley buildings. Only Vasco da Gama or perhaps *Nadia Ku* with some imagination could be called a street.

The houses and shops on either side of this narrow dark gully belonged to wealthy Arabs and Indian businessmen from Cutch and Gujarat. These were either single story structures built of *boriti* (mangrove poles) and mud with roofs of *makuti* (coconut thatch), or two or three-storey buildings with walls of coral rag hewn out of the earth with axes. The newer buildings had roofs of *mabati.* These corrugated iron sheets heated up in the sun, turning the rooms into furnaces. The buildings had quite uninteresting plain facades, pierced by shuttered windows to keep the heat out. The door was the most imposing feature of the Gujarati houses. This was designed to reflect the owner's prosperity and to ward off evil spirits. These were elaborately carved and often incorporated the images of *Ganesh*, the lovable elephant-headed god of the Hindus, as a dominant feature. The Muslims decorated their doors with verses from the Quran and flower motifs. Each door had a sturdy chain and a ham-sized padlock to keep the things and thieves at bay.

Near the fish market was the AFRICA, Mombasa's oldest hotel, run by a Goan named d'Souza. This and the other two hostelries, the CECIL and the GRAND, did not cater to the

---

[124] Fort Jesus was built by the Portuguese with Indian labour from 1593 to 1595

[125] The Portuguese were probably responsible for introducing maize, potatoes and cassava into East Africa

Indians[126], which was a blessing in disguise as they could at best be described as flea pits. Another Goan owned the only eating-house in Kilindini, a mud and wattle establishment facetiously called the PALM HOTEL. When two friends, Mr Larkin and Mr Jones, went to eat at this shanty, '...Mr Larkin elected to dine in the first-class refreshment room, while his pal, Jones modestly entered the second-class. All that divided them was a sheet of americani stretched from one mud wall to the other, but it was sufficient to make the distinction – first and second. As the meal proceeded and each course was brought in to Larkin, he would inquire of his friend as to how he was faring on the other side of the partition, and was surprised to learn that they were being served exactly alike. He waited until coffee was placed before him, and finding that he had fared no better than Jones, took the Goanese proprietor to task for his deception. Why, demanded Mr Larkin, should he be charged more for his dinner than the gentleman in the second-class? The courses had been identical on both sides of the americani, and to make any difference in the price was sheer swindling! The proprietor, blandly smiling, explained that there was a decided difference in the two services. In the first place, there was a lamp on the first-class dining room table. The second-class table was only dimly lit by the same lamp shining through the partition. And the difference in the dessert too was worth noting. Oranges for first-class – bananas for second. Larkin had to be content with the explanation – the Goanese gentleman was so evidently sincere'[127].

The highway of the town was Vasco da Gama Street, a cosmopolitan hub with a constant hugger-mugger from dawn until late at night. The clatter of the two-wheeled carts, the clickety-clack of the hooves of the small Muscat donkeys and the penetrating cries of the hawkers and vendors added to the constant din. The rich and the poor and the high and the low, had to rub shoulders as they wove their way through a colourful throng and hazards of a different kind left behind by the humans and the animals. The street stank of filth which was mercifully kept in some check by the combined forces of brisk winds, torrential rains

---

[126] The first Hindu hotel in Mombasa was opened by Pundit Nathoo Lal in 1903 in Cranford Street

[127] Ref: p143 – Salvadori, Cynthia – *We came in Dhows.* Paperchase Kenya Ltd., Vol I. See insert: Preston (Genesis) p18

and the burning sun. Muslim women – Arab, Swahili and Indian – covered from head to ankles in black *buibuis* and *burkhas* flitted around like tents on feet, all looking like peas from the same pod. To the uninitiated that is, for the young bucks had no difficulty in telling a maiden from a matron. The peephole in the *buibui*, the owner's window to the world decorated with coloured thread and beads, often revealed the woman within. The darting eyes heavily laden with kohl, the hands tattooed with henna and the *'lachak'* in their walk were enough to give the game away.

Walking gingerly in *kurta*-pyjama or *lungi* and talking softly were the Hindu men, their wives bedecked in 22-carat gold nose rings and gaudy silk sarees and ill-fitting *chupples* shuffling along a good distance behind. There were the Swahilis in their long, nightshirt-like *kikos* and *Kanzus* intermingling with tall Somalis chewing *khat*. Walking just as nonchalantly behind were their willowy *bibis* (wives) with finely chiselled features and colourful cotton wraps with bold patterns. Every other person seemed to be chewing *paan*, a bettlenut sandwich laced with a red sweet dye called *katha*, and they spat projectile gouts of the juice onto walls and the pavement. One could not help but notice the carefree Gariama women with their bouncy walk and swinging hips – the movement exaggerated by their thick, short grass skirts. Their naked torso revealed perfect nubile mammae but women carrying a child on their back often showed a smaller or even a withered left breast. This was a result, no doubt, of pressure from the hammock strap across and above the breast, depriving it of its blood supply.

Walking up and down the street at a snail's pace was the Arab coffee vendor carrying a tall conical copper pot resting in a wire frame with a hot charcoal *jiko* underneath. The thick black brew spiced with a shake of ginger attracted people like children to an ice cream van. The call of the *muezzin* rising from the minaret of the Sunni mosque at the brow of the hill stopped the vendor clicking his thimble sized porcelain cups like castanets and his simultaneous cries of '*Kawa kawa*' – and caused a momentary lowering of peoples' voices. Tucked above d'Souza's shop were two dingy rooms of the venerable establishment, the MOMBASA CLUB, a precursor of a more august structure under construction in the shadow of Fort Jesus. Here, the *bwanas* met to raise their glasses to the great queen and to plot the future of the coolies, *babus* and the boys.

Further afield were the shanties where the newest materials – *mabatis* and flattened tin *debes* – were beginning to be put to use. Here, Swahili women sat outside their front doors soaking up the sun and raking each other's hair with wooden combs to scrape out the lice and nits. For the local prostitutes, the sight of so many youthful Indians was godsend and they beckoned them with exaggerated waves of their hands and calls of *'Aa ja o'* (Hindi for 'Come on in').

The street scene in Mombasa had not changed for decades but more recently a new mode of transport had been added. Eleven miles of a light narrow-gauge railway track had been laid along the more frequented parts of the island. This allowed the hundred and twenty or so Europeans to get around quickly and without breaking into a sweat. Small hooded trolleys ran on these lines and were pushed by Africans, some dressed in sailor's blouses and shorts. The *gharry* could carry four passengers, two in front and two behind, and once it got on the move down an incline, the African boys would hop on from behind. The system was part of the defunct railway brought in by a British company which had administered East Africa before the region officially became part of the empire. However, waiting in the wings was the real thing – a fire breathing steel dragon of awesome power, ready to strike at the heart of Uganda, the 'Pearl of Africa'.

Fakir Chand was appointed as a Station Master on 15 April 1898 by which time the construction had reached mile 150. Not much is known about his activities in his early days. By virtue of the fact that he was well-educated and spoke fluent English it did not take him long to become a Station Master. It is reasonable to assume that he may have worked as a *munshi* (clerk) for a short period of a few weeks between his arrival in Africa and his becoming Station Master. During this period, according to custom, he too may have sat cross-legged on the ground, worked at a low lectern-like desk barely a few inches high and kept records in Urdu.

The workers had precious little to amuse themselves with. A pack or two of dog-eared cards became a precious possession and helped to pass the evenings. Checkers was a favourite with many and the more highbrow indulged in chess. The athletic types took part in *kushti* (wrestling), *kabadi, charapas* (leap-frogging) and other pastimes imported from India.

There was no provision for the social, moral or spiritual welfare of the workforce. The sole aim of the IBEA Company was to build the railway and the majority of the workers had gone out to earn a living. There were those few, however, who wanted more than money and the pleasures of the flesh. Some of them were not satisfied with a silent prayer and they wished to improve the conditions for their brethren and spread the word of God. Fakir Chand was an ardent follower of Swami Dayanand Saraswati. One day at the railhead, somewhere in the bush, he felt an overwhelming desire to perform a *havan* (Hindu Vedic prayer). However, there was no *havan kund* to light the holy fire in. A partial solution was found by digging a square hole in the ground and packing it with kindling of dried-up twigs. With ghee from the cook and some dried wild flowers for *samagri* (incense), a few of the Hindus gathered around the holy fire and satisfied their spiritual needs.

The arrival of the rails in Nairobi presented Bauji with an exciting and long awaited opportunity to meet his good friend, Mathra Dass Kapila, who had been instrumental in goading him to Africa. An inevitable *havan* to give thanks was followed by a sumptuous vegetarian meal. A meeting with these fervent supporters of Arya Samaj made Bauji's spirit soar and he at once realised that the future of this Hindu reform movement was assured and the teachings of Dayanand would continue to conquer the hearts and minds of thousands of Indians as they made East Africa their home.

When the railway arrived on the shores of Lake Victoria at mile 581, a lot of work still remained to be done. The permanent installations were only completed as far as Nakuru. Fakir Chand was a Station Master somewhere along the line. He was transferred to Kisumu in circa 1902 and was immediately made a goods clerk, a job he held until he was appointed as the assistant SM in Kisumu in 1907.[128]

The area was inhabited by a friendly, good-humoured and co-operative Nilotic agricultural tribe named the Jaluo. They were naked, uncircumcised and lived in *bomas* of mud and thatch huts surrounded by a fence of euphorbia, bamboo or thorn. They were considered ideal for heavy labour.

---

[128] Ref: p446 Miller, Charles – The Lunatic Express.

Kisumu was laid out by a surveyor and geologist named Charles Hobley – 'Hobley Bobley' as he was known to his friends – became the first District Commissioner of Kisumu. The railway station, the dak bungalow and other important buildings were near the water. The Indian Bazaar and the railway landis were on a flat area higher up and on a bluff overlooking it all was the European area. A hut tax of *Rs*.3 was levied and those unable to pay could settle their account with a goat, chickens or crocodile eggs. How these were credited to the government coffers is unclear.

When nearly 500 natives were killed by Trypanosomiasis and plague, that was endemic in the area followed hard on its heels, Hobley offered one *pice* for each rat that was produced. These were barbecued to a cinder on an open fire, ten to a skewer. When the money ran out, so did the trapper boys, and the rats reigned supreme once again.

In 1905, Stephen Bagge, the new Provincial Commissioner, placed Kisumu in quarantine and issued a directive banning women from living there. When Ainsworth succeeded Bagge he quickly came to the conclusion that most English officers stationed in Kisumu became paranoid and developed a 'fear complex' about the climate. An assistant DC had committed suicide before his arrival, and a few months later, an Assistant Surgeon had shot himself. This was followed by the Provincial Treasurer who blew his brains out. Ainsworth observed that 'Kisumu was not, at this time, a place for a melancholy man'.

Ainsworth built Kisumu's first golf course simply to clear several square miles of malaria breeding swamp and its vegetation. Ainsworth personally loathed golf but it took him only a few rounds to develop a life-long passion for the game. The course was situated near the Indian landis and whilst it provided a good view, the women felt intimidated by strange *Mzungus* in their neighbourhood. On one occasion when the buttocks of a *babu's* wife became the target of a stray golf ball, the husband was not amused and he complained so vehemently that the golf course was moved to its present position on the other side of the bay.

The Indians too were susceptible to the same forces of nature and disease, but where the Europeans could pick and choose, the others had to accept the leftovers. Whereas the European Station Master was posted to *Maji Mazuri* (sweet water) the Indian counterpart had to be content with *Maji Ya Chumvi* (brackish water).

141

In 1901, Fakir Chand went to India on his first home leave. This was to bring to Kisumu both his wife and son, Umrao Singh[129], who was born soon after his departure to Kenya. However, he was destined never to see his first born who died a few days before his arrival in the village. He returned to Kisumu having spread the word that Africa had endless prospects and was the continent to be in.

Meanwhile, the Indian community in Kisumu began to thrive and put down deeper roots. Fakir Chand's organisational ability and command of English impressed the authorities and his good relations with businessmen endeared him to the Indians. By 1906, he was holding the position of Chief Goods Clerk.

In 1907, while the world was celebrating the abolition of slavery, the settlers were gloating at the meeting of Kenya's first Legislative Council. This was a political bone thrown to the Europeans by the British Government to keep the clamouring Europeans quiet. Kenya at that time was described by Sir Charles Eliot as 'practically an estate belonging to His Majesty's Government'. To that point, the Government held the land and it owned the railway. Minerals and all the forests were state owned and the labour flow was under Government jurisdiction. The settler could not cut timber on his property, draw water from a river flowing through his land, or indeed, sell his farm without state consent.

Indians too received a morsel or two but of a different kind. Bauji was appointed to the post of Assistant Station Master of Kisumu. This was an important post, for Kisumu was not only an important railway terminus but also a gateway to all lake traffic and the interior of Uganda. The Indian community was flattered and the news spread throughout the country like a grass fire.

The same year the gentry of Kisumu were all gathered at the railway station to welcome a young politician who in time would be hailed as one of the greatest Englishmen of all time – the Rt. Hon. Winston Churchill – then the Under-Secretary of State for the Colonies. Bauji was there.

---

[129] It was not uncommon for Hindus in Punjab to give their first born a Sikh name. The Muslim and Sikhs sometimes chose a Hindu name for their first child. Thus, Harjeet Kaur nee Johal's mother was given a Hindu name, Vidya Vati, by her father, Lal Singh. Seth Allidina Visram's first grandson is called by a Hindu name, Anil.

**Fakir Chand Mayor. First Station Master Kisumu.
Circa 1928. Courtesy of Dhruv Dhupa.**

Two years later, Bauji was appointed as the first Indian Senior Station Master in the Uganda Railway, a post he would hold until his retirement 22 years later.

The impending home leave was an exciting prospect for all Indians in eastern Africa. For some it was a return to India for good, for others an opportunity to renew ties with friends and family and often to take on a wife. Fakir Chand had another reason for he had become a recruiter for the authorities. His reputation in Punjab had escalated to such an extent that friends, acquaintances, in-laws and out-laws counted the days when he would return and provide an opportunity for them to sign up. These men came from the Soods of

Punjab, the *jats* from Doab and the Muslims of the Ludhiana area. They included the partially educated aspiring *babus*, farmers, fishermen, carpenters, stone masons, cooks, barbers and some village strays game enough to give the new life a go. The rest were gathered from Cutch and Gujarat on his way back to Africa.

Once in Africa, the newcomers had to be found appropriate jobs, which was not always an easy task. The Muslim butchers were settled in Nanga, an area on Lake Victoria, to start the fishing industry. The skilled and semi-skilled had little difficulty. The barbers had a ready clientele. A brace of chefs he brought back at each visit kept his family, friends and endless visitors fed and watered. Some cooks returned to India while others such as Guran Sethi and Ram Murti were settled into other jobs.

Some of the young men who showed promise were taught English at the railway station in the afternoons until they were fit for employment. Some of the close relatives were offered accommodation. They were woken up at five in the morning and taught to read and write or hone their English skills. Ebrahimbhai[130], who arrived as a little boy with his parents in Kisumu in 1931, recollected that arrangements were made for him to receive lessons in English from the Station Master until he was fit to attend at the Indian Government School.

Once the recruits had mastered the three R's, it was time to go to the railway school to learn Morse code, railway and office procedures and become a *'tar babu'*. Mr Ram Karan[131] writes *"Even in October 1920 there was a scarcity of jobs, I, though a telegraphist could only get employment in April, 1921 with the Post Office in Kisumu. During the inter period I gave training in telegraphy, Morse signal at Kisumu station, a facility provided by Mr Fakir Chand Mayor, to Messrs. Inder Singh Gill[132], Dharam Dev Mayor[133], Vidya Sagar Suda, Frangi Lal[134] and others who were looking for jobs and were unemployed"*. (sic)

---

[130] Ref: – p190 – Salvadori, Cynthia – *We came in Dhows.* Vol I, see insert

[131] Ref: p34 – Mayor, Ram Karan – *Memoirs of Ram Karan Mayor.* London, 1984

[132] Gill, Inder Singh – *The Industrialist.* Uganda & Kenya

[133] Mayor, Dharam Dev. Awarded MBE for Services to the Railways

[134] Farangi Lal. *'Farangi'* means English

144

B.S. Mohindra[135] was also a product of this 'School for Signallers' and was helped to find a job in the Post Office.

Those not so bright were trained to recognise symbols and given the job of stamping gunny bags and parcels and labels for wagons. Lila Vati recounts *"The approach of a white officer was so intimidating that these employees would hide in the wagons or behind a shed until all was clear".*[136]

The importation of personnel was not confined to railwaymen and civil servants. A well-known doctor in Kisumu was rescued from Lahore. A few days before his final MBBS examination he was held up at a street corner by a pro-independence rally. The principal of the Medical School, an Englishman, saw him and accused him of participating and of anti-British sentiments. All his pleas of innocence went unheeded and he was barred from appearing at the examination. Another year's expense was a body blow to an already impoverished family. As soon as he finished his examinations, Bauji brought him over to Kisumu, gave him furniture and 400 shillings and set him up in practice in the Indian Bazaar.

Kisumu was desperately short of good teachers, especially someone who could provide leadership and organise the boys' school. Accordingly, in the 1920s, Ravi Dutt Dixit, a young man with a degree from Punjab University, was head-hunted, brought to Kenya and started his career as a Principal at the Government Indian Secondary School, a position he held for many years.

The list of men recruited is endless. Once the new arrivals got established they brought their own friends and relations and the population began to mushroom. Ram Karan writes, *"Nearly 60% of Sood families who settled in east Africa came with the help of Mr Fakir Chand Mayor. He was most influential and commanded respect, regards and love from all the Railway and Civil Service officials and the general public." (sic)* [137]

In 1911, Bauji was allocated one of the two spanking new adjoining houses next to the landis. Shortly afterwards, he was given the other half too. This 'railway quarter' was more like an institution than a home. It was part school, part club and part hotel. The two

---

[135] Mohindra, Baldev Sahai. Awarded OBE for Services to Business and his work as the Director of Manpower

[136] Dhupa, Lila Vati. Personal communication

[137] Ref: p31 – Mayor, Ram Karan – *Memoirs of Ram Karan Mayor.* London 1984

Indian cooks and an African '*masala* boy' were kept busy all day. The railway provided free rations. On the days when the ship departed for Port Bell it was not uncommon for 30 or 40 people to partake in the evening meal. Some were fed at home and others had their food delivered to the steamer in tiffin carriers. Fakir Chand was always present in his official capacity to see the boat off just before dusk. These departures were more like a celebration. The pier was always crowded by the passengers and their well-wishers, and a brass band played to wish the travellers *bon voyage*[138].

"All the Sood families", writes Ram Karan *"were united and organised and had love and respect for each other. During the evenings all gents used to gather at the house of Mr Fakir Chand and discuss daily news of events and activities".* [139]*(sic)* People from other communities also dropped in unannounced for help, advice or just to pay their respects. A *hookah* was ever present and it was passed on from one senior member of the society to another, for it was impolite for young men to smoke in the presence of elders. Often the evening was spent in *'Shair O Shairi'* when the men would recite Urdu and Persian poetry, some of it classical, the rest their own compositions. There were so many members of the Sood clan in Kisumu that you could not do anything or go anywhere without bumping into a Sood. By the early 1920s the Indians of Kenya were calling the town *Soodanwalla*[140].

As the population of Indians increased and more amenities became available, Kisumu gradually became a very desirable place to live in and raise a family.

The Government built a good and adequately staffed hospital. The general practitioners were competent and healthy competition among them ensured that the population received excellent service. The various Indian communities were allowed to develop in their own way and at their own pace without any harassment. There was full religious freedom. Their leaders were men of integrity and they respected each other's viewpoint. Thus they were able to close ranks whenever their mutual interest was threatened. The social life and the sports facilities in Kisumu became the envy of other towns.

---

[138] Ref: p191 – Salvadori, Cynthia – *We came in Dhows.* Vol I. Quote: Dhupa, Dhruv Vrat

[139] Ref: p31 – Mayor, Ram Karan – Memoirs of Ram Karan Mayor. London 1984

[140] *Soodanwalla:* Sood town

146

The Soods had their own sports club. They were able to field an unbeaten Hockey XI from 1928 to 1935. They also produced outstanding players in cricket and tennis. Dyant Rai was one of the leading batsmen in Kenya and Walaiti Ram Bowry became one of the best-known tennis players. The Aryan Sports Club had a Volleyball team of considerable reputation. The Railway Institute had excellent facilities for outdoor and indoor games and a well-stocked library with the latest journals from England. The 'club' as it was popularly called, was open to the public upon payment of a small subscription.

It is no wonder the railway trainees in Kisumu dreaded the day when they would graduate from the 'school' and be considered fit to be posted to smaller stations along the railway line. Many a young man broke down and begged Bauji to have the posting cancelled, but the writing was on the wall. A sympathetic chat in the evening, a glass of hot milk and reassurance that they would remain a part of the family at large calmed their nerves.

Another sphere of his activity was Arya Samaj. This reform movement was started in Gujarat in 1875 by Swami Dayanand Saraswati and it had an even greater impact in Punjab. The young *babus* and like-minded people planted the seeds in the land of *Zanj* and carefully nurtured it until there were branches in every town and hamlet. The first branch was formed at the home of Kanshi Ram Bowry in Mombasa in 1905 and he was its first president. By 1908, the congregation had eighteen members who collected Rs 400 to buy a wattle and *Makuti* hut where they met every Sunday morning. In 1911, this was replaced by a stone and *Mabati* structure with generous donations from Nanji Kalidas Mehta, C.D. Patel and Murli Dhar. The first preacher did not arrive from India until 1913. That year a *Putri Pathshala* (girls' school) was opened and 25 students had their first lesson on the day of *Shivratri* celebrations. The Nairobi Samaj followed hard on its heels under the presidency of Mathra Dass Kapila. Then, in 1910, came the Samaj at Port Florence and Fakir Chand became its first president.

Sanatan Dharam[141] had, however, stolen a march when in 1894 an image of Lord Krishna and his consort Radha was installed in

---

[141] *Sanatan Dharam:* Orthodox Hindu Doctrine.
According to Agehananda Bharati, the distinction between *sanatani* and *Arya Samaj* has proper meaning only where there is a large group of Punjabi Hindus. In the Punjab, the people who did convert to Islam or embrace Sikhism during

Njugu Lane in Mombasa by a Gujarati named Lala Prasad. Three years later he brought a *Pipal* tree (*Ficus Religiosa*, a long-lived fig tree) from India and planted it in the grounds of this temple where it has been casting its benign shadow to the present day.

Unfortunately, there was considerable rivalry and bad blood between the two Hindu denominations. Preachers from India were brought to debate the different points of view. But, as time went on, the two factions learnt to live with each other. The younger generations were more tolerant and less dogmatic and inter-marriage gradually put paid to the attitudes of yesteryear.

Although the prospects of war had been kept alive in Europe during the first half of 1914, it was not expected that the European crisis would spread to East Africa. It was in Germany's interests, however, to extend the hostilities to Africa for it would divert large numbers of British troops from the European theatre where the decisive battles would be fought.

Both adversaries were ill prepared and ill equipped. The Germans, with their territorial force of 216 Europeans and 2,540 *Askaris* combined with 45 Europeans and 2,154 Africans in the police force were undoubtedly stronger. They were aware, however, that they would not receive any support from Europe because the British dominated the waterways. The German General, Paul von Lettow-Vorbeck, convinced since taking command in January 1914 that war was imminent, had toured the country to assess the resources at his disposal and to get to know his subordinate commanders, and consequently, was better prepared than were the British.

Both the British and the Germans were aware of the vulnerability of the Uganda Railway, which ran almost parallel to the Kenya-Tanganyika border. It was the one line of communication linking the two British Protectorates with the outside world. Von

---

the past four centuries, were the *Sanatanis;* then in the nineteenth century, the *Arya Samaj* engendered a fundamentalist Hindu revival in that area – accompanied by overt denigration of the *sanatanis* as those who had been lax and had not opposed conversion from indigenous religion to Islam. In East Africa, a few influential Gujuratis have joined the *Arya Samaj;* thus the distinction is no longer one that applies to an approximately even bifurcation between *sanatanis* and *Aryas* among Punjabis only; in a very true sense, this local, parochial Indian distinction has been de-ethnicised in East Africa. Here, one might say that every Hindu who is not an *Arya Samaji* is *ipso facto a Sanatani,* regardless of which particular sect or form of worship he favours.

Lettow-Vorbeck began his campaign against the British by instituting a series of attacks against the Uganda Railway. Patrols could not hope to protect the whole line nor to intercept all the attacking forces launched against it. Fortunately, miles of the dry, thick scrub made movement as difficult for the Germans as for the British so that the amount of damage done to the line was much less than expected.

The declaration of martial law in Kenya put an end to all rhyme and reason. Some of the Indians in Kenya became the innocent victims of the crossfire and had to suffer humiliation, harassment and hangings – all at the hands of the British. The Arya Samajists became the main targets.

The success of the Arya Samaj and its growing influence among the Indians became a source of jealousy and innuendo by other religious factions. In 1914, the Samajists launched the *Achar Sudhar Movement* against the consumption of alcohol and meat. This caused further friction. The upshot of the denominational infighting led to false propaganda and outright lies which eventually reached the already nervous military authorities who seem to have responded with a knee-jerk reaction.[142]

The first trouble arose when a military officer, Captain MacStead, tried to recruit Africans for the war effort by poaching Jaluo labourers who were employees of *Ramanand, Bhodraj and Company,* (RBC) an outfit located near Tsavo that supplied wood logs to the railway. When this failed, MacStead asked to meet Bishen Singh, a *jamadar* with RBC. Singh was accused of mistreating his labourers, and when the two disagreed, MacStead became violent, shook Singh by his beard and demanded to inspect all contracts and accounts. Singh was so petrified that he scarpered off into the bush. MacStead then met Lalchand, a staunch Arya Samajist and an employee of RBC, and Bodhraj, a principal of RBC, and the matter was soon resolved. Bishen Singh reappeared.

Soon afterwards, the Germans blew up the railway at Tsavo. RBC was suspected of collusion and its camp was searched. No incriminating evidence was found. A telegram from Lalchand to Bodhraj in Nairobi to inform him that all was well is said to have been intercepted by MacStead who is alleged to have changed it to

[142] Shastri, Anant – *History of Arya Samaj, Mombasa, 50 years.* New Delhi Press. New Delhi, India. Published in Hindi

read, "Come at Once" [143]. On arrival, Bodhraj was arrested and sent to a detention camp at Voi.

Meanwhile, on Monday, 17 August 1915, the army surrounded the Arya Samaj premises in Mombasa while a prayer meeting was in progress and arrested the participants. The building was locked up and taken over by the army and the men were taken to Voi. [144]

Bodhraj was tried, found guilty, fined Rs 300 and given fifteen lashes. Soon afterwards, he was rearrested and sent back to Voi. RBC's offices were searched and Rs 5000 confiscated. A Lieutenant Parker, a white anti-Indian, succeeded in bribing six Jaluo labourers to testify that RBC had helped the Germans to sabotage the railway line. Lalchand and Bishen Singh were arrested and taken to Voi. The confiscated money was distributed among RBC's labourers and two of the RBC's sub-contractors, Yograj Bali and Ganesh Das, and the Station Master at Mtito Endei, Sita Ram, were also arrested.

The initial charge of assisting and harbouring the enemy made against Bali and Das could not be proved as they were in Nairobi at the time the railway was blown up. A new charge was prepared and the accused retried. The defence advocate, Mr Shapley, was barred from the trial which opened at 9 p.m. The guilty verdict was delivered at 4 a.m. and the prisoners were shot at 7.30 a.m. following a short Vedic prayer. They were refused cremation and their bodies were dumped in a pit.

An attempt was made by the authorities to intimidate Lalchand to testify against the remaining detainees but he was incorruptible and refused to co-operate. All except Ram were charged with assisting and harbouring the enemy. Pandit Keshav Lall Dave and the founding members of the East African Indian National Congress were also accused of possessing seditious literature including copies of the Punjabi publication, *Ghadar*.

A court-martial was held at Voi on 3 December 1915 without the presence of a civilian lawyer. Three Africans testified that Bishen Singh had warned the workforce not to go outside their huts

---

[143] Ref: Professor Vishu Sharma. Personal communication.

[144] Some of the men arrested were: Babu Banshi Lal (President, Arya Samaj Mombasa); B.R. Sharma (Secretary); Kanshi Ram Bowry (Founder President, Arya Samaj Mombasa); Pandit Keshav Lall Dave (Founder member of East Africa Indian National Congress); L.M. Savle (Founder member of East Africa India National Congress); Purshotam Raval; Chagan Lal D. Bhatt; Dharamshi Bhai; Tulsi Dass; Chanan Ram; Bhanji Jivan; Babu Rala Ram and Lachman Dass

at night, thus making sure that there were no witnesses. Among the others who testified in front of the presiding judge, Colonel P.H. Dyke, and two other senior British Officers, was Sir Robert Hamilton, the Chief Justice for whom Keshav Lall Dave had worked for 24 years as Chief Court Clerk.

Ramanand, who at the time of the incident was in Nairobi, was acquitted. Kashav Lall Dave, Lalchand, Savle and Bishen Singh were all sentenced to death. The four men were roped together and sent to Mombasa. Bishen Singh was taken to the market place early one morning and hung before a silent and helpless, largely Indian crowd. The rest fared better mostly as a result of representations to the Chief Justice. Keshav Lall Dave and Savle's sentences were commuted to twenty years and subsequently to fourteen years each. Lalchand's sentence was reduced to ten years.

During the trial of B.R. Sharma, one of the men arrested by the army on August 17, 1915, which lasted ten nights, a signed statement by Multani Ram Verma was presented. It accused Sharma, who was the secretary of Arya Samaj, of preaching sedition in Mombasa. Seditious literature from Punjab allegedly found at his house was also produced in evidence, Sharma was found guilty and he received a prison sentence of fourteen years. Sita Ram was kept in prison without charge and he was eventually deported to India.

After the arrests, the Arya Samajists felt so afraid that many refused to participate in future religious and cultural activities. When a newcomer, Ram Nath Prinja, arrived from India in 1915 and re-started Sunday morning *Havan,* his housemates, Sant Ram Sharma, Lachman Das and Pandit Nihal Singh made him stop. All his books and literature were packed in a steel trunk and buried. But Prinja, a man of indomitable courage, could not be silenced for long. Within six months he moved to his own house, exhumed his books and restarted the prayer meetings.

The military's shenanigans included a raid on Arya Samaj Nairobi during which religious books and cultural paraphernalia were confiscated and the President, Mr D.D. Puri, was harassed. In spite of such intimidation and personal dangers, deputations from Kisumu and Nairobi, led by their presidents F.C. Mayor and D.D. Puri respectively, arrived in Mombasa to make representation and to give moral support to their friends. Leading citizens like T.M. Jeevanjee, President of the East African Indian National Congress, Abdul Rasul Visram and Suleman Virji also lent their support. Chief

Justice Robert Hamilton probably played a pivotal role in the clemency which was eventually accorded to the Indians.

The end of the war in November 1918 took the steam out of the whole unfortunate affair. In May 1919 after a review committee appointed by Sir Charles Bowring, the Acting Governor, had reported its findings, all the prisoners were released and their deportation orders were rescinded.

Many questions arise from this controversial episode in not so remote a part of the British Empire. Were the charges justified or were the accusations trumped up and a reflection of the anti-Indian sentiments of a large number of white settlers of Kenya? Was the trial fair? Were the Indians adequately represented?

Reverend Charles F. Andrews, an Indophile who investigated the matter soon after the war, came to the conclusion that the three Punjabis were executed without a fair trial, and he believed that they, and probably the others, were innocent[145].

With the passage of time and the fading of memories, and indeed, the disappearance from the world stage of those involved, the whole truth may never be known.

Once the hostilities were over and peace had descended on the world, the military authorities returned the keys to the Arya Samaj premises. A fresh beginning was made by a hastily convened meeting which raised Rs 300 for refurbishment and Narshibhai Patel, a Gujarati stalwart, was installed as the new President.

Mercifully, the Arya Samaj in Kisumu had continued to thrive unmolested under the presidency of Fakir Chand. On 21 April 1924 he inaugurated the building of *Arya Kanya Pathshala* (Girls' School) by placing a set of Vedic mantras under a granite foundation stone and tapping it into place with a silver trowel. The ceremony was attended by the leaders of other Indian communities and a great feast followed. The complex eventually covered a whole block in the heart of the town and consisted of a prayer hall, a rest house three-storeys high and accommodation for the teachers and a resident preacher. A large walled quadrangle served as a playground and a volleyball court. Another celebration followed the opening ceremony. This was performed by Lala Murlidhar Sood, who donated 500 shillings.

---

[145] REf: p151-152 – Gregory, Robert G. – *India and East Africa. A History of Race Relations Within the British Empire 1890-1939.* Clarendon Press, London 1971

In 1925, Fakir Chand became the President of the Arya Pritinidi Sabah, the supreme council of Arya Samaj in East Africa. This job and numerous meetings with railway authorities took him to Nairobi quite frequently. On such visits, his white uniform was swapped for a dark blue serge uniform. There was invariably a small crowd of Arya Samajists and railway *babus* to greet him at Nairobi Railway Station.

December in Kisumu was the month for the annual Arya Samaj convention. A large influx of Arya Samajis from all over East Africa came to the shores of Victoria Nyanza for this *jalsa*. For the leaders the convention was an opportunity to discuss the religious and political issues of the day, and for the others, to meet like-minded people. Activities included religious 'lectures', yoga and gymnastics demonstrations. The convention also afforded the 'Young Aryans' an opportunity to demonstrate a montage of literary, musical and other skills. The highlight at the end of the *jalsa* was a visit to Fakir Chand's farm in Kibos at mile 573. This was the opportunity for the Samajis to relax and let their hair down.

A special train delivered the visitors to the farm which lay directly under the shadow of the 'Monkey Stone'. This was a monolith jutting upwards like a jewel in the tiara formed by the crest of the Nandi Hills. For the young at heart and strong of limb, the challenge was to climb the mountain and have a picnic on this truncated obelisk which could easily accommodate up to 40 persons. The party of men would set out at first light and after a brief stop at the *Dadar Singh Shamba* for refreshments the real climb would begin. The porters, all cheerful *Jaluos*, unjustly described by one European administrator as 'strong in the arm and thick in the head', led the caravan. In the early days, each was provided with a loincloth stitched by my grandma, Mathra Devi, to cover their nakedness. They would march in a single file, into the heartland of the tough and sometimes truculent Nandi, carrying the day's rations, *debes* of water, *karais* (woks) and other utensils needed for the two chefs from Kisumu to prepare a mouth-watering lunch of vegetable dishes and fresh *jalabis* (sweetmeats). The panoramic view for those who made it to the top was the thrill of a lifetime. The scene boggled the mind and uplifted the spirit. For with one swoop of the eye, one could view an area from the undulating Mau Hills around Fort Ternan at mile 534, across the green of Nyando Valley and over the largest expanse of water in all Africa – simply *Nirvana!*

Those left behind at the farm had a good time eating mangos, guavas, pomegranates, paw paws, *jamans* (Java plum: *Syzygium Cumini*) and whatever else was in season. The fresh, cold sugar cane juice laced with ginger was a drink for the townies to die for. A few lucky children got a ride on a *ghori* (pony) which belonged to Fakir Chand's young daughter Lila Vati, the first Indian horse-woman in East Africa. This *ghori* was her pride and joy and she would carefully groom her and ride her to the neighbouring *'Macho Dogo'* farms on the Kibos River and the surrounding countryside.

By 1924, there were so many Sood families in Kisumu that Fakir Chand started *Sood Sabah* (Sood Brotherhood) of Kisumu. His lieutenants Dev Raj Mandal and Ram Karan Mayor were the secretary and treasurer respectively. The aims and objects of *Sood Sabah* were to look after the social, moral and financial welfare of its members. Soon the movement spread to other towns and hamlets, and in 1930, prompted a change in name to *Sood Sabah of East Africa*. Under its aegis, funds and materials were sent to India to support Sood families who had fallen on hard times.

Bauji's afternoons were spent in railway affairs and supervising a dozen or two of budding *karanis* at the railway school at the station. Here the young men were taught English, Morse code and railway procedures until they were proficient enough to take up various jobs in railways, the post office or branch out on their own.

He was always on the platform to meet the incoming passenger train from Nairobi and to see off the down train to the coast. The arrival and departure of the lake steamer was also an important event that needed his presence since this ensured attention to detail and a smooth and efficient running of the station and port facilities. It also kept the often-demanding white *bwanas* happy. This was not always an easy task, especially for the young recruits.

On one occasion, his nephew, a recent graduate, was sent to check the tickets of the first class passengers prior to the train's departure to Nairobi. The young man was fitted with a uniform two sizes too big and an equally ill-fitting pith hat. He approached a compartment where a couple of ladies were engaged in a rather animated tête-à-tête. *"Ticket please"* he asked politely. No one stirred. *"Ticket please"* he asked again, raising his voice a smidgen. Still no reaction. *"Your ticket please ladies"* he demanded, whereupon one of the *memsahibs* looked up disdainfully, picked up her parasol and began to thrash the young station assistant. The fellow was so humiliated that he burst into tears and came running to the Station Master. Fakir Chand went to the two ladies, accompanied by his nephew and enquired as to why they had resorted to violence. The woman apologised and said that she thought he was just an urchin out to cause annoyance. She sheepishly produced her ticket, which was clipped by the young man, and the matter was resolved.

Fakir Chand's evenings were as busy as the rest of the day. *"His home, a railway quarter, every evening was the meeting place of Soods. His advice and assistance was always acknowledged thankfully by each..."* writes Ram Karan in his memoirs.[146] He adds *"All gents used to gather at the house of Fakir Chand and discuss daily news of events and activities". (sic)* For years, his was the only Indian home with a telephone which was supplied by the railways and it was in constant use by assistants at the station seeking advice and instructions.

The visitors also included members of other communities and Khoja and Gujarati businessmen with whom he was a partner in a number of business ventures. Not much is known about these but they must have been profitable for him to maintain such a lavish lifestyle. Curiously enough, a special set of cutlery and crockery was kept aside for the Muslim guests as they were usually beef eaters. This discrimination was an acceptable practice at the time and no one seem to mind.

Fakir Chand was the first Indian to be invited to become a Freemason. He joined the Equatorial Lodge in Kisumu, made lifelong friends with some of the European officers and administrators, and became a Grand Master. Bauji had a taxing, if unique, lifestyle. His day would begin at 5 o'clock when he would wake up his nephew or any other of the young men who stayed with him from time to time and start them on their English lessons. While he was having his morning tea, Ganesa, a barber he had brought over from a village in India, would arrive and shave his beard and trim his moustache. Meanwhile, the houseboy had heated water in a copper *hamam* (oriental water heater) and this would be delivered to the bathroom in two large buckets. After a bath, it was time to check on the students. While he was having his breakfast, the servant would charge the *chilim* (tobacco burner) of his *hookah*. Bauji would then dress in a fresh, all-white uniform with his decorations

---

[146] Ref: p34 – Mayor, Ram Karan – *Memoirs of Ram Karan Mayor.* London 1984

155

and an enormous 22-carat gold chain and gold watch. A white crisp, turban completed the outfit. Meanwhile, two Jaluo boys would bring the rickshaw to the front door and the senior of the boys would come in and announce *'Tayari Bwana Gavana'.*

At lunchtime, the rickshaw would reappear at the station. The return trip along Station Road was much more arduous for the barefooted boys as it was uphill all the way. Once home, Fakir Chand would lay back in an enormous mahogany and cane chair with a two-tiered armrest, the lower part of which swung out to the front to form a rest for legs and feet. The houseboy would be ready and waiting to untie Bauji's laces and take his shoes off. After a brief rest, he would change into a muslin *kurta* and a cotton pyjama and tuck into a hearty lunch. Then it was time for a siesta on a *takhat posh* (divan) furnished with a thick cotton-filled mattress and half-a-dozen bolsters. While he puffed contentedly on his *hookah*, his brother-in-law would arrive, sit by his side and massage his legs and feet.

From the early days of the IBEA Company, there had been suggestions that Indian peasants should be settled in East Africa. In 1892, a director of the IBEA Company had written *"The climate and soil of East Africa are admirably adapted for the requirements of the Indian agriculturalist..."* The Indians had successfully established themselves in Zanzibar and mainland territories of the Sultan. By 1863, there were 5,000-6,000 of them and the entire trade which exceeded £1-1.5 million a year passed through their hands. In 1895, Jairam Sewji of Zanzibar proposed a settlement of Indians on the mainland funded by private capital. Schemes for such settlements in highlands and lowlands were proposed and supported by Sir Harry Johnstone, one of Uganda's first British Governors and Charles Eliot. "Indian trade, enterprise and emigration," wrote Johnstone in 1901, "require a suitable outlet. East Africa is, and should be, from every point of view, the America of the Hindu." Sir Frederick Jackson, Deputy Commissioner of IBEAC, F. L. O'Callaghan, Managing Member of the Railway Committee and Ainsworth were all in agreement. However, Eliot would subsequently make a u-turn and advocate the exclusion of Indians from the Highlands.

Of the 31,983 Indian coolies imported from India, 6,724 decided to remain in East Africa. There were those who advocated compulsory repatriation but this was unacceptable to the Government of India. It was suggested that even if such a drastic

156

and unfair action had been undertaken, it was inevitable that an influx of Indians would have occurred in East Africa.

Most of the Indians were hard working, diligent and law-abiding citizens, but without a doubt there were some bad apples amongst them. Eliot's indictment that 'Many hundreds of bad characters remained behind instead of returning to India, and became at first gamblers and loafers, and subsequently, thieves and animals' has been criticized by his own countrymen.[147] However, there were certain mitigating circumstances. The lax administration of the coolie camps encouraged vice and crime. Just as the expenditure on the railway declined, the winds of deflation began to blow. Furthermore, 70 dhows carrying trade goods worth £35,000, the original stock of many would-be Indian traders, were lost at sea in a violent storm. The Government showed no compassion or willingness to help the 5,000 Indians seeking a different way of life and left them to fend for themselves as best as they could. In marked contrast, the European settlers were handed free grants of 640 acres of land each in the Londiani-Molo-Elbergon district and Lord Hugh Cholmondeley Delamare was given 100,000 acres around Njoro for a paltry sum of less than £200 per annum.

Despite what had gone on before, in 1903 the Protectorate established a settlement of Indian farmers at Kibos. This was done and funded at the instigation of D.D. Waller, Acting Paymaster of the King's African Rifles in the Treasury, and compromised of 1,500 acres of a low-lying area of the Nyanza basin in the vicinity of the Kibos River, about six miles from Kisumu. Waller was instrumental in directing the land survey, allocating plots of land and obtaining financial assistance. His attempt to recruit farmers from the Indian provinces of Bihar, Madras, Bombay and Central Provinces was unsuccessful. This was because of the farmers' reluctance to go to a foreign land and due to official opposition from the Lieutenant Governor of Punjab. Parcels of land from ten acres upwards were therefore sold to the local Indians. Fakir Chand, who was a farmer at heart, was at the forefront when the 1,500 acres were divided among 30 aspiring farmers.

Many of these farmers were amateurs and totally unfit for the backbreaking work of taming the virgin land that they had taken on.

---

[147] Ref: p254 – Hill, M.F. – *Permanent Way.* Hazell Watson and Viney Ltd. Aylesbury and London

They soon found themselves in arrears in paying interest and taxes and subsequently went to the wall.

In 1907, only four Punjabi families out of the 30 'waifs and strays'[148] were still farming in Kibos. One of them was a young, newly married Sikh named Jagat Singh. He had worked as a coolie during the construction of the railway and it was somewhere in the bush that he met Fakir Chand. The two took an instant liking to each other and they became such good friends that Fakir Chand gave him 105 acres out of his own farm so that they would be perpetual neighbours.

Jagat Singh was a short, tough *jat* from a farming family in the Jullunder District and his small beady eyes earned him the nickname of *'Macho Dogo'*. His knowledge of land and grit was a sure-fire recipe for success. In time, he was supported by his sons, Gurdial Singh and Parduman Singh. Gurdial[149] recalls *"My father and the others had to make their own implements out of wood; there wasn't even iron for hoes and ploughs. They do the final shaping using sharp stones"* (sic) Jagat Singh became the first farmer to build a water mill on Kibos River for grinding white maize into *posho*.

Fakir Chand Mayor's farm was managed by Fakir Chand's illiterate brother, Shanker Dass who came to Kenya in 1900 at the age of twelve. By then, he had already been married for six years to Dropti Devi who was a year older than him. Shanker Dass was unfit to work for the railway as he showed no aptitude to learn. The farm was, therefore, a Godsend. Initially, it was a mostly wooded area but for a large salt lick towards the Nandi Hills where the Nandi traditionally brought their cattle. They were unhappy when their access to the mineral rich soil was suddenly cut off but no one seemed to care for African rights. The trees were cut down with *pangas* and the logs were sold to the railway for engine fodder. Then came the backbreaking job of extracting the stumps and breaking up the soil. A bungalow with a wide veranda was built with sun-baked bricks and grass thatch and the surrounding courtyard was covered with sand from the Kibos river valley to keep the black clay gumbo in check. A *boma* of thorn, bush and stakes was built at some distance to corral the cattle and as a safeguard from the marauding Nandi. The permanent Jaluo farmhands were accommodated on the farm where they built roundels of sticks, mud and thatch.

---

[148] Ref: p69 –Gregory, Robert G – India and East Africa

[149] Ref: p169 – Salvadori, Cynthia – *We came in Dhows.* Vol II

Once the land was ready for planting, *matama* and *wimbi* (millet) were the first crops to be sown and these were very successful. Wheat, rice, cotton, linseed and *simsim* (sesame) were all grown with varying success. Maize grew without difficulty. A small stream running through the farm fed a large pond besides which a market garden was planted. Aubergines, okra, fenugreek, potatoes, chillies and other vegetables grew in abundance. A special patch was reserved for mustard for making *saag*, a great favourite of the Punjabis.

The Great War of 1914 brought further hardship to already austere conditions on the Kibos farms. The Government seized all the oxen and the carts for a puny compensation, and what survived was returned well after the hostilities were over.

Various parcels of lowland were released to the Indians by the Government and private European individuals over the years that followed because the Europeans preferred the higher areas to the east of Kibigori around Chemlil and Muhoroni. Around 1919 a landowner named Creswell decided to sell his estate of about 1,000 acres at Buongo, an area adjacent to the farms at Kibos. Fakir Chand persuaded his relations and friends in Kisumu to buy this land. The new owners were nearly all Punjabis and 60 per cent of the acreage was purchased by members of the Sood clan, all of them railway employees.

Fakir Chand's farm at Buongo was managed by his youngest brother Ramji Das, an uneducated veritable rogue and farceur in his younger days in India. He had ostensibly stayed behind to run the family farm in Punjab but he soon let it go to wrack and ruin and frittered away all the funds sent to him from Africa. He was surviving by his wits rather than the sweat of his brow. When Fakir Chand's family visited the ancestral farms in Hiran they were horrified to find that the old crumbling house contained nothing that could be described as furniture and the sleeping arrangements consisted of a room half full of cotton wool into which one had to burrow like a mole. In later life, Ramji Das was fond of relating his escapades and how he survived by his wits, including by giving false evidence for anyone who was prepared to grease his palm.

On one occasion, he was in a witness box when the prosecutor asked the question, *"Does the road pass through the village pond or does it go around it?"* Ramji Das was unfamiliar with the area and the strange question stumped him. The lawyer repeated the question but the witness remained mum. Suddenly, the *kotwal* (police

159

inspector), another scoundrel and friend of the witness, interjected, *"Your Honour, Ramji Das says the road goes through the pond but no one seems to have heard him."* The witness nodded furiously and added, *"I suppose I will have to shout in future."* The prosecutor lost the case.

Once in Kenya, Ramji Das had no choice but to work for his living under the watchful eye of his brother. The whole process of taming the land in Kibos had to be repeated in Buongo. The *babus* were equal to the task and soon the land was green and gold with sugar cane and vegetable gardens. Small factories started to fill the air with wisps of smoke and steam and the sweet scent of *jaggery* and the African weald began to look more and more like Punjab.

***

The year 1928 was a year of great tragedy for the Mayor family for Bauji's only son, Shivan, developed severe malaria. Soon he was passing heme in his urine confirming that he was afflicted with the dreaded Blackwater Fever, a certain passport to death in those days. Bauji became very depressed and refused to go out, but a visit from an old Arab friend changed all of that. The two had met in 1914 on the pier on the day the *S.S. Usoga* was launched into Lake Victoria. During the celebrations, Bauji's daughter, Lila Vati, fell into the lake and it was this bystander who saw her lying underwater, pulled her out and revived her. The visitor prayed beside Bauji and implored him to return to work. *"Babu"* he said, *"Allah has at least left you with two daughters and a grandchild to bounce on your knee but he has taken everything away from me. Yesterday, my only son fell into* Ukerewe *and was taken by a crocodile. I have nothing, not even his dead body. Life must go on."*

S.S. Usoga alongside Entebbe pier, Lake Victoria, in 1946

The same year in August, the railway, too, received a heavy blow. Mr Christian Felling, the General Manager who was knighted in the Birthday Honours list, died as a result of a severe attack of malaria apparently contracted whilst attending a meeting of the Railway Advisory Council in Uganda.

Sir Christian Felling.

On 28 September 1928, Kenya was honoured by a Royal visit. A special train was placed at the disposal of the Prince of Wales when he landed at Kilindini. When he arrived in Kisumu, Bauji was introduced to him. On hearing of Shivan's recent death, he expressed his deep sympathy and commended Bauji for his long and loyal contribution to the railways. Ironically, the Royal Prince at the time was himself suffering from a bout of malaria. In a farewell speech in Nairobi, he spoke strongly of the need for anti-malarial measures to rid the country of this affliction.

In the prevailing culture at that time, a son was important to every Indian family and Bauji was no exception. His friends, daughters and especially his wife, Mathra Devi, encouraged him to re-marry. At her behest, he made a trip to India and married Prem Lata.

On return to Kisumu, the first child was born on the day when all Hindus were celebrating Divali. It was a girl and she was named Mohini (lovable).

Before the second child was due, Bauji's daughter, Lila Vati, gave birth to her second son, Dhruv. He was born in the same bed in Bauji's house as his brother Dev, two years earlier. It was therefore decided to deliver Prem Lata in the same 'lucky bed'. This confidence was not misplaced, for a boy, Bharat Bhushan, was born a few days later in 1930. The celebrations that followed were of, the like of which Kisumu had not seen before or since. After Bauji's retirement, the bed was taken to the farm in Miwani where it continued to uphold its reputation and deliver its promise! In 1933, Lila Vati's third son, Satya, was born and six years later, the family cat gave birth to five kittens in the same bed one night while the occupants slept unawares. They were all boys.

Fakir Chand retired from the railway in 1931 after a long career in Kisumu that had spanned over 30 years. During this period he had risen from a mere *Karani* to *Bwana* 'Governor', but at heart, he had remained a farmer and had made sure that there would be an active and fruitful second career waiting in the wings. Before he cast away his togs, however, there was one more job to do. *"In the last years of his service with the Railway,"* writes Ram Karan, *"Mr Fakir Chand was deputed with a special duty, was provided with a coach to travel and examine the position of the staff on the entire railway network with a view to re-organisation due to recession. This was a singular honour and he produced his report in 1930."* (*sic*) [150]

---

[150] Ref: p20 – Mayor, Ram Karan – *Memoirs of Ram Karan Mayor.* London 1984

Before Fakir Chand embarked upon this unpleasant, albeit essential assignment, his senior wife, Mathra Devi, pleaded with him. *"You may,"* she said, *"reduce their salary or demote them but don't take the bread from their mouth. Remember they are like our children."*[151]

Radical change was, however, inevitable and as a result, in the years 1931 and 1932, railway staff was reduced by 175 Europeans, 1,362 Indians and 7,461 Africans[152]. Severe reductions were made in the passenger train service: 38 of the older engines were repaired and laid up and eight of the new Garrat engines were not put into service. As a result of these and other economies, a saving of £300,000 in working expenditure was achieved with full effect expected in the following years.

In his Annual Report for 1931, the General Manager, Brigadier-General Sir Godfrey Rhodes wrote, *"Such an outlook forced a complete examination of each department with a view to re-organisation on a much-reduced scale. No more unpleasant or painful duty can be imagined...*

"Of necessity many members of the staff could no longer be retained because under the new conditions, there was no work for them to do..."[153]

---

[151] Ref: Dhupa, Lila Vati. Personal communication

[152] Ref: p476 – Hill, M.F. – *Permanent Way.* Hazell Watson and Viney Ltd. Aylesbury and London

[153] Ref: p503 – Hill, M.F. – *Permanent Way*

Sir Godfrey Rhodes.

    This was not a happy time for the Indians of Kisumu. It was the year of the 'Scattering of the Soods'. Not only the marginally employable men had gone to the wall but many others, fearing the loss of the 'umbrella' under which they had thrived, chose to retire voluntarily and seek jobs elsewhere or to go back from whence they had come. Those who chose to stay on with the railway were transferred to smaller stations along the line. The heydays of *Soodanwalla* were over.

Although he had a fully developed farm in Kibos, Fakir Chand decided to live in Buongo. He built a large house and an attached shop out of corrugated iron sheets and eucalyptus poles set on a high concrete plinth. To keep cool in the ferocious heat, the house had dropped plywood ceilings and a wide veranda in the back and front. At the back was a detached kitchen with adjacent storerooms for wood and a nursery for newborn calves. There was a massive sand covered courtyard back and front to keep vermin away – a hope against hope. The boundary in front was marked by a brisk stream with guava trees along its banks. Mango, pomegranate and other tropical fruit trees were strategically planted to provide shade and ambience. In the backyard stood a lone mulberry tree which provided fruit and acted as a post to tie the cows to at milking time. On one side of the kitchen was a vegetable garden and on the other three acres of eucalyptus trees. Well removed from the house was the jaggery factory. This consisted of a fuel storage shed and a larger shed to house eight huge vats to boil the cane sugar. Between the two was a crusher to extract the cane juice. The rustic buildings, surrounded by a sea of green and gold, lent the farm a unique charm of its own.

The sugar cane was crushed by metal rollers worked by teams of two oxen which went round and round, hour after hour – a scene reminiscent of the Persian wheel back home in Punjab. The juice was transferred by tin *debes* to the eight vats where it was boiled for three hours until it formed a thick brown syrup. The syrup was cooled in wooden trays and then poured into metal moulds where it solidified to form jaggery. Alternately, the syrup was constantly stirred in the cooling trays until it crystallised into brown sugar. Spices like ginger and cinnamon and almonds were added to the cooling syrup and scoopfuls were ladled onto outstretched sheets to make pralines – a mouth-watering favourite of young and old alike.

The boiling shed was a dangerous place with no provision for health and safety. It was not uncommon for the children or livestock to wander into this man-made volcano. Fortunately, no one lost a child but occasionally a stray calf fell into the vat and was boiled alive. The consternation of the farmer was not shared by the labour who became the recipient of glazed veal for dinner and syrup to make *pombe* (beer).

The cane husk, called *yugi,* was spread all over the yard to dry out in the sun and then used as fuel to boil the cane juice. If a sudden shower came down, a cry of *'yara yara yugi'* went up throughout the *boma* and every available man, woman and child rushed out to collect the drying husk and get it under the roof. Once the mission was accomplished, it was not unusual for the participants to break into a spontaneous *pas en masse.*

In 1920, an Australian named Eric Mayers came to Kenya to survey the land around Kibos and Buongo. He was very impressed with the potential of the whole area with the result that in 1922 an Australian outfit brought over a sugar factory. The railway built a station, a landi, a post office and a spur line to the factory. The area was renamed *Miwani* (Swahili for sugar cane) and the first batch of white crystalline sugar was bagged in 1924. The manager of the factory was an Australian eccentric with an enormous pendulous abdomen who was known to everyone as *Bwana Tanki* (Mr Tank). He would occasionally appear at the station with his wife and ten children – five boys and five girls. All the boys always wore similar shirts and shorts and the girls identical frocks.

With the advent of modern technology came the first signs of environmental pollution. The factory owners had no use for molasses and a constant stream of this thick brown syrup was allowed to run into a trench at least half-a-mile long. The stench from the fermenting treacle spread for miles and made life quite miserable. Repeated requests made to the factory owners and the authorities to stop this practice fell on deaf ears. The problem was only solved many years later when the original owners sold the factory to the Hindocha family who started making 'ether' from the hitherto waste by-product. This change, however, did not please the local Jaluos who lost their free supply of molasses to make domestic *tembo* (beer).

The majority of Indian farmers were semi-literate at best and they found the officialdom very intimidating. They lacked good advice, social contact with other farmers and opportunity to share their concerns and bargain collectively. Fakir Chand, who had acted as a counsellor to many of them, became acutely aware of a need for a representative body. He therefore started the Nyanza Farmers Association and carefully nurtured it through its infancy. Some of the farmers had reservations but after a few months even the

167

doubting Thomases threw in their lot. The 'syndicate' as it was popularly known, made representations to the Carter Commission in 1933, pointing out that very little land was made available by the Government and what was offered was at prohibitive prices. The Syndicate's offices in Kisumu provided a venue for the farmers to meet and secretarial support was at hand in filling forms and translating correspondence. The syndicate continued to thrive into the second half of the century when political pressures and the general milieu in Kenya changed to make life untenable for the small time Indian farmer.

Fakir Chand's lifestyle remained very disciplined even on the farm. He was up with the lark and after a bath and prayers he would dress up in immaculate white clothes and turban. He would then meet his *mianpara* (headman) and issue instructions for the day. After a hearty breakfast, he would set out sharp at 9 o'clock, stick in hand, and Motoro, his trusty African assistant, by his side. After an onsite inspection of labour and a visit to the jaggery plant, he would return for a late lunch. Then it was time for a rest and 40 winks. The late afternoon was spent reviewing farm affairs and receiving a progress report on the day's activities.

In the evening, the family would gather round on deck chairs under an enormous mango tree. The *hookah* was lit and one of the children was asked to read the newspaper while everyone listened. It was also time to bond, recite Urdu and Persian poetry and keep us busy in games. The neighbouring farmers would trickle along in ones and twos and it would slowly become a gathering of men only. The ever-present *hookah* was passed from one person to another while the farmers discussed their problems and sought advice. It was a time to translate their official correspondence and help them with form filling, tax returns and other government business – reminiscent of the gatherings in the old village of Hiran in Punjab. As the sun began to finish its daily trudge and dip below the western horizon, the *shambawallas* would return to their own families and replenish their energies to face another day.

All the farm labour came from the Kavirondo men from the Kano Plains on the south side of the rail track. They were hard workers and toiled all day, planting, weeding and cutting cane for a wage of around one shilling per day. Fridays were paydays. The entire labour force would gather round for the weekly event as the records were checked and payments made with hard cash and *posho* (white maize flour). The flour was measured with a tin *kebaba* (can).

The recipients watched the *jamadar* like a hawk to make sure they were not short-changed and there were constant requests for '*ungesha kidogo*' (add some more). Once this serious business was over, everyone felt happy and relaxed and ready to celebrate. Occasionally, someone would break into a song *"Jaluo pesa onge, Muhindi pesa nitye"* (Jaluos have no money, Muhindis have plenty) and the rest would join the chorus.

With cash in the pocket, it was time to head for the *duka* and spend, spend, spend. The Jaluos had long abandoned their tradition of wearing nothing but a layer of castor oil and taken to fashionable modern clothing in a big way. The merchandise in the shops consisted of cotton goods including cloth for shirts and shorts for men and gaudy dress materials for their *dakos* (women). Blankets were always in demand. Foodstuffs included flour for *ugali* (steamed *posho*) and *ugi* (runny porridge), many varieties of beans, *matama*, salt, sugar and boiled sweets. There was a steady call for knives, *pangas* and *makukis* (spears) and pots and pans. Luxury goods included shiny cheap baubles, bangles, beads, tobacco, cigarettes, matches and bars of bluish soap which were cut according to the customer's need.

Cigarettes were called *dawa* and were in great demand by men and women alike and these were sold in ones and twos. They were also handed out at the end of each sale as *bakshishi* (tip). A curious local custom was for the smoker to light his cigarette and then insert the lit end into the mouth, periodically parting his lips to let out whiffs of smoke. The object of this strange exercise was apparently to prolong the life of each *dawa*!

Each of the shops in Miwani had a resident African tailor. Once the choice of materials was made, the granite damsels would strip off in full view of other customers to have their vital statistics measured. Undergarments had not yet found a place in the wardrobes of any of them.

Once the shopping was done it was time to head for the nearby stream for a communal bath. This was a long drawn ritual of laughing, singing and uncontrolled pleasure. The final step to enhance the appeal of body beautiful was for each person to cover their body with a thick layer of soapy lather and to let it dry on the skin.

Fakir Chand was also consulted for matters affecting the mind and the body. Cuts and bruises from *pangas* while cutting cane and other farm accidents were common and soon cured by a dab of picric acid or iodine solution. Once in a while a labourer would sustain a snakebite and the whole labour force would down tools in a panic. The petrified victim would arrive at the front door of the sanative with half-a-dozen well-wishers with long faces. Bauji, the villagers believed, had the powers to cure snakebites – which he did. The 'doctor' and the patient would sit down facing each other while the others gathered around to get the best view. There was pin drop silence as the ritual began. Ash was strewn on the ground as the Vedic mantras were chanted to invoke the gods. The injured hand was then touched three times with an old leather slipper and with a hand on his head, the client was reassured that he would live to fight another day. He was then instructed to buy a pound of sugar and offer some to all the bystanders and anyone he met on his way home. The next day the whole labour force and the victim would turn up for work, smiling, singing and raring to go. The secret? The vast majority of the snakes in Africa are non-venomous grass snakes… a triumph for psychology.

Most of the farmers in Miwani, Kibos and the lowlands in the vicinity were subsistence farmers. Their needs were few, their lifestyle and food were simple, their knowledge was shallow and their ambitions were limited. Most wanted their children to plough the land or at best become *karanis* in the railways or civil service. The Jaluos were already beginning to close the gap and the future looked bleak.

The Africans were quick to mimic the Indian cultivators and to learn the rudiments of *biashara* (business). They started coming around the farms to sell fresh milk, eggs, chickens, and even the most Indian of Indian items – *ghee*. Each *debe* of milk had to be checked with an hydrometer as it was often diluted with water and every egg was floated in water to test it for freshness. Every household was increasingly becoming dependent on African made goods. They supplied *makekas* (reed mats) to sit on, *kipapus* for carrying goods and *matungis* for storage, cooking and keeping drinking water cold. It would not be long before they would start growing their own sugar cane, opening their own *dukas* and driving the Indian *shambawallas* and shopkeepers to the wall. In fact, the harsh economic conditions of the 1930s had already exposed the underbelly of many farmers and resulted in a couple of them to abandon farming altogether. Education would perhaps be their saving grace?

Most of the farmers had children of school age but there were no facilities for education and no prospects of a school. In fact, there were no schools anywhere between Nakuru and Kisumu. The farmers were too illiterate to teach their own children and too poor to send them to a boarding school of which there was only one in all of Kenya.

Bauji emptied a small *yugi* storage shed opposite the cane crusher and started a *madrassa* (school). The first pupils were his daughter Chander Mohini, his son Bharat Bhushan and the three sons of Shadi Ram Mohindra: Inderjeet, Raj and Munilal. Here Bauji taught the three R's to his fledgling charges. Soon children from other farms in Miwani, the sugar factory and the neighbouring hamlets of Kibos and Kibigori came flocking in, and before long, the school was bursting at the seams. Bauji had limited time to teach and the hullabaloo of a working farm was not conducive to good education. Bauji persuaded a Sikh farmer friend to donate two acres of his land upon which they built two rooms of corrugated iron sheets surrounded by a wide veranda. This spanking new facility was named Inder Singh Kala Singh Primary School and it opened its doors in approximately 1938. Surprisingly, this was the first purpose-built primary school building anywhere in Kenya.

The first full-time teacher was Mr Joshi. Others such as Mr Jagan Nath Sharma and Mr Kaur Chand were also hired from Punjab on two to three-year contracts and when these were fulfilled, they were slotted into the government school in Kisumu. Once the school was up and running, Bauji reduced his commitment to management and the teaching of English. Eventually, a committee of farmers took complete charge of the day-to-day affairs.

The Indian teachers brought with them Indian values, teaching practices and the tradition of corporal punishment. This included slapping of the face, caning of buttocks, strokes with a ruler on out-stretched hands and torture by the timeless cockerel position.

Painting of punishment in a classroom in Northern India, courtesy of Victoria & Albert Museum.

Such sadistic practices were by no means uncommon in other schools in Kenya and were accepted by many as the norm, but when the following incident took place, Bauji was forced to intervene.

One morning, Bauji's houseboy delivered a customary, complimentary brass tumbler of hot milk for the teacher and placed it on the table. As the glass was overfull, the teacher bent forward and had a slurp of the hot milk. This amused the children and one of them nudged his friend and said "*Ngombe*", meaning an ox. The teacher, who had managed to burn his lip and spill some of the milk, was so incensed that he tied the pupil's ankles with twine and suspended him from the ceiling. When Bauji received word of this incident that evening, he was compelled to act and disciplined the teacher. After this, some of the violence continued but to a much lesser degree.

Creepy-crawlies were part of life in Miwani. They often sought refuge in the cooler dark recesses of the house. It was not uncommon to find a snake curled up under the bed. Whilst it made the children shudder, my grandma would shoo it away with a walking stick and think nothing of it. The beds in the farmhouse were the high Indian style charpoys strung with local sisal ropes. Each long carved spindly leg often had to be placed in a *kebaba* full of water to act as a moat to stave off an attack by marauding ants. Above each bed was a *machar dani* (mosquito net) tied to the four posts. These kept the helicopter sized creatures at bay during the night – but not always. If one or two of the critters breached the defences the night was one of Chinese torture. All one could do was to lie still and wait for the telltale drone in the ear before the enemy landed on the face. This was the time to give it a quick swat. More often than not, it escaped and one ended by slapping one's own face. Just when one was about to doze off the buzzing resumed. The mosquito net was more for comfort than protection against malaria as the anopheles had all evening to bite the unsuspecting victim.

One evening, my grandma was making chapattis in the kitchen when she suddenly noticed a pair of large bright eyes piercing through the darkness outside. She soon realised that a cheetah had parked itself in the only doorway and seemed to be watching her every movement. There was no escape. Her heart missed a few beats but she displayed a remarkable presence of mind. She began to add fuel to the fire in the three stone stove until the rip-roaring flames began to singe her hair and sear her skin. The only protection was her flimsy cotton sari which she wrapped around her face. The heat also got to the visitor and caused the beast to retreat. Quick as a flash my grandma jumped to her feet and slammed the door shut. The startled visitor bounded into the night and was never seen again – a close encounter of the African kind!

Dogs, our early warning system, were often quiet when they were most needed. When the Nandi rustlers descended from the hills, both variety of *machungis*, human and hounds, would remain strangely silent until the perpetrators and the cattle had vanished. Wild boars did not seem to take much notice of the dogs either. During the time of drought they would appear in the dead of night and chew up the banana palms and anything else that was soft and chewy. Sometimes the night watchman would spend the whole night banging a tin *debe* to frighten the snorters and this kept the whole household awake until the break of dawn. Occasionally, the dogs themselves seemed to be the prime target of some creatures of the night and were found dead, badly mauled or absent without a trace.

The tussle between nature and creature was much more unequal in Africa of those days and more often than not, the grim reaper arrived early. In 1941, Fakir Chand developed a boil on his thigh and this quickly destabilised his diabetes. Deep in the Kano Plains there was no access to insulin or intravenous fluids and Penicillin was still confined to the hallowed halls of the Radcliffe Infirmary in Oxford. The nearest doctor was at a day's march in Kisumu. He quickly lapsed into a coma and died on the morning of 2 June. He was cremated in the late afternoon on open grassland beside the very rail track his friends – the *coolies*, the *boys* and the *bwanas* – had so painstakingly built nearly four decades earlier.

Due to the speed of events our family could not arrive in time for the last rites. We travelled on the up-train overnight as we had done on numerous occasions before. Our favourite 'TT' was accompanying the train. He was a short, rotund, bespectacled Englishman who would constantly whistle as he scurried along the corridor from one compartment to another. He always found time to greet us with a cheerful '*Going to see Grandpa Fakir Chand again*' and often handed out toffees from his pocket. The twice weekly train from Nakuru always arrived at Miwani in the small hours of the morning and we always depended on him to wake us up between Muhoroni and Chemlil. This time around he came quietly and tears welled up in his eyes as he conveyed his condolences to my mother and said, *"Fakir Chand was a good friend and a fine man."*

As usual, we piled out of the train at Miwani to be greeted by the Gujarati Station Master with expressions of sympathy. This time, however, there was no bullock cart waiting across the tracks and no one to greet us with a *'jambo mama, jambo mtoto'*. We handed our luggage to African *totos* and waited until the train disappeared westwards leaving behind a shower of red embers. The night was cool and all was quiet except for the chirrup of insects and an occasional sound of a bird preparing to welcome the dawn. This was a scene our bleary eyes had witnessed many times before as nothing much seemed to change in the village. But this time we had to walk past a huge pile of hot coals that glowed brighter with each waft of the gentle breeze. My mother took my hand into her uncharacteristically cold and clammy hand and we stopped for a moment. No words were spoken and nothing needed to be said but I knew that never again would I see the tall and handsome turbaned figure of *Bwana Gavana*, my Grandpa, again.

Fakir Chand Mayor, a farmer's boy from a small village in Punjab, had shunned the stethoscope and opted for adventure in a land little known to the people of North India. He not only helped in the construction of the steel spine of British East Africa but held the most powerful position that any Indian has been appointed to in the history of the East African Railways.

The role of Station Master in Kisumu, the gateway to the interior of Uganda, is difficult to imagine in this day and age. In a totally underdeveloped country a hundred years ago, however, it was a position of great importance and prestige. In those days, the railway had an absolute monopoly of all travel, all transport on the land and lakes and over all communications. For all practical purposes, the railway was the government of the territory. Fakir Chand held this pivotal rank for 30 years, which besides giving him an enviable record, afforded him an opportunity to develop his ideas and realise his ambitions and aspirations in other fields.

He recruited his countrymen from Punjab, Gujarat and Cutch regardless of their caste or religious beliefs and helped them in getting established on the new continent. He was an entrepreneur, an educator, a religious leader and a farmer, but above all, he was a friend, a guide and a confidant to all who came across him.

Tributes came from all directions, from *landiwallas, shambawallas, dukanwallas, Governmentwallas*. When news reached Kisumu, the bazaar was closed for a day. Ram Karan, in his memoirs, writes, *"Fakir Chand's phenomenal rise to the high position was a tribute to his remarkable ability, diligence and hard work. His qualities of character gained him respect and repute equally with fellow superiors in service and the public at large – Asian, African and European…"*

"Mr Fakir Chand was a man of many qualities. He was one of those who are not spoilt by high position but became humble with risen status. He loved to see others around him well established and on the path to progress. This was not all. He made deliberate efforts

to play his part and use his position constantly to see anyone known to him move to a better position…" (sic)[154]

Lall Chand Sharma who first met him in 1913 wrote, *"That day at the Arya Samaj satsang* (prayer meeting) *I was introduced to many persons including the President, Mr Fakir Chand, a noble person who was the Station Master at Kisumu. He arranged for me to learn the job of a train clerk from Mr Amir Singh, one of the staff members at Kisumu Railway Station."* (sic)[155]

[154] Ref: p18-19 – Mayor, Ram Karan – *Memoirs of Ram Karan Mayor*

[155] Ref: p25 – Salvadori, Cynthia – *We came in Dhows.* Vol II

Fakir Chand Mayor 1878 – 1941

Decades after his death, people still remember him fondly. In 1998, Manmohan Singh Shukla, a lawyer from Dar es Salaam, had a chance meeting with Dyal Singh a retired Sikh, in a village in Punjab. The old timer began to reminisce about his days in East

Africa and fondly remembered Fakir Chand as ' a kind and helpful man and a torch bearer for the Indian community'.[156]

A day after his death, an unknown engine driver stopped his train at night at the bridge near Fakir Chand's farm. When all was quiet, a long melancholic whistle reverberated through the still air from the Mau Hills to the lake, and from the Nandi escarpment to the Kano plains – a sounding of Last Post from one railway man to honour another.

MIWANI REVISITED

When an opportunity to visit this playground of my childhood presented itself in 1978, I jumped at the chance. The motor car had now become the king of passenger transport in Kenya so we approached the area along the new road at the foot of the Nandi Hills at the opposite end to the familiar railway station. A warm glow began to engulf my body at the very thought of meeting some old friends and the prospect of showing the community to my wife, Kusum.

We stopped the car at the very first farm that once belonged to my father, Durga Dass Dhupa. He had bought this farm as an investment and to keep my mother happy for she had a vision of retiring there, just as her father had done. I doubt that my father had any intention, however, of ever soiling his hands. The farm was of course there, but little else. We pushed forward through a thicket and came upon a heap of mud which looked like an anthill but for a few blocks of unbaked clay with specks of whitewash struggling to hold their shape against the ravages of time. These were the only clues that these were the remains of a once fashionable farm bungalow. The rest of the buildings had vanished without trace. The only deep well in the village which gave the farm its name, *Khu walla Shamba,* had long been filled in and ploughed over. Gone were the majestic mango trees and the *jaman* that stood next to the bungalow. Gone too, was our 'bird tree', a giant Gum Arabic tree with hundreds of elaborate, intricately woven nests of weaver birds dangling precariously from delicate branches. Where once one could hear the chirruping of the hungry fledglings a hundred yards away, there was now nothing but stony silence.

---

[156] Shukla, Manmohan Singh. Personal communication

As I cast my eyes over the rest of the farms, the feeling of nausea was only heightened at the realisation that all the farmyards had fallen prey to some devastating act of vandalism. It was as if a tornado had swept through the entire area selectively sucking up all signs of human habitation into its sinister funnel. Only one shanty of wood and corrugated iron was still visible down the road so we drove up to it and knocked on the cracked, ill-fitting door. We knocked again and again and eventually our persistence produced a belated response. The door creaked open and slowly a small, bent and dishevelled figure emerged, squinting at the midday sun like some creature of the night unhappy at the sudden exposure to daylight. The man was emaciated with bloodshot eyes and his thinning blotchy reddish hair badly in need of a cut and fresh henna. It took me some time to recognise that this was my old pal Inayat who had once shared my desk at school and taken part in our childhood escapades. He could climb a tree faster than a monkey and bring down the choicest of ripe guavas. The isolation and *pombe* had taken their toll and reduced him to a sad, bumbling idiot unable to recognise his buddies. I tried to jog his memory but it was an exercise in futility. The time was short so we wished him well and pressed on.

We left, anxious to see our grandpa's farm. The once elevated road, the backbone of our village, was now no more than two parallel grass covered ruts and eventually even these gave way to prairie. We soon realised we had gone past the farm and reached the spot where the school once stood. We pushed through tall grass and clumps of cane and there, in front of us, was our alma mater, or at least what was left of it. All we could see was the rusting but largely intact roof, for the rest of the structure was buried under a sea of sand due to repeated floods. An ignoble end to a fine institution. The topography had changed so much that the small brook that ran in front of all the farms was nowhere to be seen and the railway main line that lay on a high embankment seem to be in danger of being buried too.

We did not linger and backtracked a couple of hundred yards. The ancestral farm had suffered an even worse fate. The cannibalisation was so complete that not an iota of the farmhouse and the surrounding buildings was left, all having fallen under the plough. All we could do was to stand and stare in disbelief.

Suddenly, my eyes came to rest on a tall, rather forlorn palm standing head and shoulders above the surrounding sugar cane, and it brought back a flood of memories and a vision of the whole farmyard. Surely, this was none other than our old friend the *'khajoor'*. Years ago, a tiny strange looking sapling had mysteriously taken root under the plinth of the south bedroom. It had only avoided the chop of a *panga* because grandma thought it was a date palm and everyone began to hope that one day it would be replete with succulent dates. Its uniqueness was perhaps its redemption for it had somehow survived all adversaries that had laid everything else to waste. It had grown tall and proud and witnessed all the changes. It had the answers to all of our questions – alas, if only it could speak.

I could not resist the urge to go up to it and run my hand over its rough, dry trunk – a symbolic handshake, I suppose. As we were about to leave I noticed a half-withered stump and soon worked out that this was the remains of our mulberry tree. This was the only tree of its kind in the whole area and it had been lovingly brought over by grandma from Punjab and nurtured with mulch and tumblers of water until it was strong and tall. It had not only rewarded her by producing long, sweet purplish *shetoots* but also doubled as a post to which the cows were tied at milking time. Here we kids would stroke their wet muzzles and feed them supplements of salt, jaggery and leftover dough while the *toto* tied their hind legs and milked them. Occasionally, we would crouch beside him and he would direct the milk straight from the teat to the mouth. Delicious!

Our visit was now over. We drove away with a heavy heart and a moist eye. On reaching high ground I felt compelled to stop and take one last look. My spirits were rekindled as I surveyed the valley awash with the green and gold of hundreds of acres of sugar cane that had once grown in Punjab, swaying in the warm, gentle breeze. The houses and sheds were gone, but this, a living memorial to the brown men and women from a faraway land who had changed this virgin weald to a land of milk and honey, would go on forever.

Now those men and women had gone too. Some had departed to meet their maker; others had gone to the land from whence they came. All, however, had left one thing behind – their SPIRIT.

Chale aye un reh guzaron se JALIB [157]
Magar hum wahan kalb o jan chor aye.

---

[157] I have come away from those directions, Oh Jalib But I have left behind my spirit and my heart

Chapter 6

Landies and Landiwallas

Why they were called 'Landies' no one seems to know. Perhaps the tent pitched by Corporal George Ellis of the Royal Engineers in May 1898 and James Martin[158] a few years earlier on the same soggy landscape called *Engore Nyarobi* by the Masai and meaning *'a place of cold water'* was a landi. In 1902, a missionary from Sagala Mission Station wrote, *"...The shacks, or landis as they are called, lean into each other to join and shut out the light. It is a labyrinth place in which people and rats live together in a common squalor. The ground squelches under the feet like the crust over a morass and one treads with care around great piles of garbage and open gutters transporting night-soil to one or other of the big open cesspools."*[159]

There were landies where there was railway. In Mombasa, the rail men lived in Makupa and Kilindini landies; in Nairobi, in Sandiford (so named after a railway engineer who once found a leopard under his bed) and Nagara landies; in Kampala, they were called *Nasambia* landies and elsewhere, just railway landies. Usually, they comprised rows of identical terraced houses, called quarters, with eight to ten houses in each landi. Occasionally, just a pair of semi-detached bungalows merited such a designation.

In Nakuru and Kampala, and perhaps elsewhere, the size and location of landies reflected the status of the occupants. The *'white collar'* workers –clerks, goods shed men, guards, ticket examiners, senior engine drivers and senior *'loco-men'*– were allocated quarters in *wadi* (big) landies. The *fundi* class (artisans) were housed in *choti* (small) landies. The Africans were relegated to a separate area in even smaller landies. The Railway Police *askaris* for some odd reason lived in *'Police Lines'* under the watchful eye of an Indian

---

[158] Ref: p42 – Trzebinski, Errol – *The Kenya Pioneers.* Heinemann. London 1985
The area on the banks of Nairobi River called Nairobi River Camp came to be known as Martin's Camp after James Martin spent ten days there recruiting Africans to work for the railway
[159] Ref: p201 – Huxley, Elspeth – Nine Faces of Kenya. Collins Havrill. London 1990

police inspector who was allocated a detached bungalow in the same compound, but of course, at a *'respectable distance'*. The Europeans lived in detached bungalows in the best part of town surrounded by tall, well-manicured, ki apple fences. These were called *'quarters'* and never referred to as landies.

The dawn of my memories came in Nakuru where our family lived in a railway quarter – number 3. I was to live in railway accommodation until I left home in 1954 for higher education in the United Kingdom. That first hazy recollection is of our family making preparations for a three month trip to India, known locally as *'home leave'*.

Traditionally, almost all railway families visited India every three to four years as the ties with the mother country were very strong. This time round, our family had an added reason and that was to take my sister, Sudershana, for higher education in Punjab. She was, as her carefully preserved records show, a very bright and gifted young teenager. She was always at the top of her class and excelled at whatever she did. Sudershana's heart was set upon going to England and reading medicine – revolutionary thinking in those days.

My parents were in a quandary. Advice, mostly unsolicited, poured in from all directions and most people favoured marriage to education – for who in their right mind would send a daughter alone to live away from home. It so happened that the industrialist and educator, Seth Nanji Kalidas Metha, was visiting Nakuru as a patron of the Arya Samaj School. He was so impressed by Sudershana's achievements that he urged my father not to deny her higher education. My grandfather, F.C. Mayor, another stalwart of education, was also strongly in favour of further studies and he was prepared to offer financial support. All my parents needed was moral support, but sending their daughter to England was still out of the question. A compromise was reached and my parents had to promise Sudershana that after becoming a doctor in India, she would be sent to England for specialisation. It was 1938 when the family set sail from Kilindini aboard the steamship *Karagola*.

Hardly a couple of weeks after our return to Nakuru, our morning was interrupted by the knock of a *'telegram boy'* – a sure sign of disastrous news in those days. On opening the reddish envelope, my mother burst into an uncontrollable paroxysm of crying. Nothing was said but I had a sort of premonition that my sister was dead – my mother's firstborn and her only daughter. She had become the victim of a typhoid epidemic which had swept through the school in Jullundar City and decimated almost half of the girls in the dormitory.

The landies often reeked with snobbery. In most towns, the *wadi* landies were situated in better areas and on higher ground surrounded by greenery, away from the hustle and bustle of rail yards. The *choti* landies were a smaller replica, often buried into the shunting yards, surrounded by fuel depots and other railway *objets d'art*. Social contact with artisans' children, although unavoidable, was discouraged by the *babus* and there was no hobnobbing among adults.

Life in the landies was never dull. There was always something on the go and everyone knew everyone else's business. Most people lived in peace and harmony. There were endless celebrations of Hindu, Muslim and Sikh festivals and everyone joined in with great gusto. At *Lorrie*, celebrating the harvest, the Punjabis lit bonfires outside their homes and at night there would be a communal singsong and a dinner followed by the distribution of handfuls of special sesame seed candy called *reorian*. Everyone joined in the Muslim *Id* and Hindu *Divali* festivals and *thallies* (trays) of sweetmeats were exchanged between households. Then there were the religious rituals where everyone had fun except the principal players. Hindu boys had to suffer *Mundan Sauskar* and the ignominy of the hair on their heads being shaved off, and Muslim boys *Sunatan* (circumcision) where they were shell-shocked by the pain inflicted by mullahs armed with nothing more than a split cane and a cutthroat razor.

The epitome of celebrations and communal co-operation were the weddings. It was a busy time for everyone. Women, dressed up to the nines, would go from house to house to personally invite their friends to the wedding and related celebrations. Only women and children were invited to the pre-nuptial evening *sangeet* which was sometimes spread over several days. These evenings comprised of dancing and singing of popular and often bawdy songs with liquor, marijuana, and sex as principle themes. The approach of the wedding day was preceded by feverish activity. One team of volunteers would go from house to house collecting tables, chairs, crockery and cutlery, while another would get down to the task of erecting a marquee with tarpaulins invariably borrowed from the railway goods shed. Once this was accomplished it was the turn of the children to decorate this *tambu* and the *Vedi* (dais). Flags were shaped from coloured paper and hung from miles of string and festoon made from crepe paper. By the time the wedding day arrived the place was awash with bright and gaudy balloons and bunting.

These were the days when the priest often held sway. The old Indian traditions were still strong and the hallowed hour was decided by a *mahurat*. The wedding would start at this auspicious hour, often in the dead of night, and would last up to four hours. Halfway through the proceedings the bride was whisked away to change into a set of clothing brought by the in-laws. Later, the wedding ceremony was halted to allow the couple to march out into the cold night to view *Dhruv Tara* (North Star) to ensure that their union would be as permanent as the position of the polestar.

The overdressed kids usually slept through these events, curled up in piles like little puppies on the marquee floor beside their mothers, or wherever there was room to spare. The men hung around in knots shooting the breeze while the priest chuntered on and on. Only the women seemed to know or care what was going on and often lessened the monotony by periodically breaking into a spontaneous chorus of their repertoire of popular wedding songs.

Suddenly it would be all over and it was time to feed the *baraat* (groom's party). The banquet always started with sweetmeats – two, five, seven or eleven varieties, depending on what the bride's father could afford. The savoury dishes then completed the meal. No meat or alcohol was served at Hindu weddings. Important guests were honoured by serving their food in special trays called *pattals* which were piled up high to impress the guests, and God help the bride's father if someone important was left out.

According to custom, as soon as the formal ceremonies were over, the hosts were at liberty to tease and rib the guests. Such shenanigans included the stealing of the groom's shoes by the girls, which were returned only on payment of a ransom. Other pranks included serving cotton wool filled samosas, *paan* (betel nut) laced with green dye and whatever else the hosts could think of.

When everyone was satiated it was time for the bride and groom to play *kangna*. This was a series of games pitting the newlyweds against each other, all designed to get them to relax and to know one another. This was followed by the women imploring the groom to recite *chunds* (couplets) which are composed to flatter, tease and even flirt with the females of the bride's household. While this mischief-making was going on, a serious business was in progress elsewhere – the matter of *Daaj* (the dreaded dowry). If it

185

was *khula daaj* (open dowry) as opposed to *bund daaj* (closed dowry which is the norm these days), all the dowry and gifts from friends and relations were displayed for the whole community to see.

Then came the *Doli* and a chance for close friends and relations to say tearful goodbyes. Each person gave the bride a hug while at the same time pressing currency notes into her palm. Finally it was the turn of the parents to wish her luck and to whisper that she was now leaving for her own home and the only way out was feet first.

But all was not over yet. As the men began to dismantle the marquee, the ever-ebullient women started preparing for *Nishani*. Large trays of sweetmeats were loaded on the houseboy's head and distributed from door to door including to those who were not invited to the wedding.

As for the father – the poor man was left to sit back and ruefully count the cost, as the bills began to arrive and the debts began to mount. His only consolation, perhaps the old adage: *'To take is the daughter's right and to give is the parent's obligation.'*

Life in the landies was not glamorous or luxurious, but it was a remarkably good environment to grow up in. The children were happy, relaxed and well provided for and the nuclear family was stable and nurturing. The housing was heavily subsidised. Each quarter in a landi was large, airy and well maintained by the railway. Each had a garden in front and an open communal space behind. In Nakuru, roads around the landies were lined with shady pepper trees, ideal for climbing, and tall gravilias bearing flat, spiky, orange flowers laden with nectar. A typical unit had a large bedroom and a lounge with an enclosed verandah in front and back. On one side of the rear verandah was a common bathroom and on the other side a storeroom. A large courtyard separated the kitchen, a 'boy room' for the servant and a toilet. A high ceiling prevented heat from the corrugated iron roof barbecuing the occupants. The maintenance was carried out by the railway and the houses were painted every three years, all without charge.

The railway families were generally reasonably fed and clothed. The vast majority of landiwallas were vegetarians and garden produce was cheap. African *matumias* (women) sold vegetables from their *shambas* at the local *skoni* or from door to door, cutting out the middleman. During the 1940s, in Kampala, we could buy 100 oranges for a shilling and a bunch of bananas for 50 cents. Quite often the families would club together and bulk-buy foodstuffs such as ghee, lentils and wheat flour.

In spite of this, all was not always well, for the *babu*'s resources were often stretched to the limit. The average family was large and elderly parents also had to be looked after. It was also customary for the newly arrived young men from India to stay with friends and relatives until they could find a job. Yet another burden was the need to send part of the earnings to India to support the rest of the family. It was therefore not uncommon to see children with stunted growth and deficiency diseases like rickets, beri beri and occasionally kwashiorkor.

Our family was fortunate as we would receive additional supplies of staples such as fruit and vegetables from my grandfather's farms in Miwani and Kibos. He would also give my mother a present of 500 shillings after each one of our four-monthly visits to the farm. This was a very substantial amount as it was equal to my father's monthly salary.

Mercifully the weather was kind and the children needed simple clothing. Short-sleeve cotton shirts and shorts were the order of the day and these were more often than not sewn at home. Older children and adults had their clothes made by a *darzi*. We had at least one pair of custom-made leather shoes for school and plimsolls for sports. The *mochi* (cobbler) and the *darzi* were so accommodating that people often turned up at their homes after hours and they were always welcomed – free enterprise! Bata Shoe Co. took care of *'canvass shoes'* for sports and leisure.

In the late 30s and early 40s my father always wore a white pith helmet and he cut a fine figure dressed in a white suit. As he had a fair complexion the Africans often mistook him for a European and they would step aside and salute as he passed by. My brothers too had to don white pith hats. Before they went out he would make sure that their clothes were clean, their shoes laced up and that they carried a clean white handkerchief in their pocket. This was perhaps a reflection of his days in the military cantonment in Punjab. By the time I grew up, times had changed and I had to make do with a green trilby.

Dhupa brothers – Dev (right) and Dhruv – Circa 1937.

The furniture in most railway homes was sparse and rickety. A dining table was a rarity as most of the space was taken up by the Indian-style charpoys with long stick-like legs and the frame strung with tape or rope made from jute or local sisal. Although uncomfortable for the sleeper they provided an ideal hideout for Cimex *lectularius*. The bugs would emerge in the dead of night to feast on the blood of their unsuspecting bedfellow. It was a common sight on Sundays to see the beds being stripped and unstrung and the tapes and the joints in the woodwork washed with boiling hot water to get at the pesky bugs.

This was not the only vermin one had to share the house with. Cockroaches invariably occupied every nook and cranny in the kitchen and ran riot as soon as it was dark. Field mice were difficult to keep out and were regular raiders of the housewife's larder, often drowning themselves in a *sufuria* of boiled milk. A meat safe was an ideal piece of equipment but hardly anyone was lucky enough to own one. The fight against such adversities was a futile one for as soon as the house was fumigated, new armies found their way in from the neighbouring houses.

If this lifestyle of the landiwallas seems harsh, spare a thought for other Indians who fared even worse. Most lived in communal houses where they rented a room or two and had to share all the facilities. It was not uncommon for five or six members of a family to share a single room. Here they relaxed, studied, ate their food and produced even more children.

Many of these *Bazaarwallas* came to school in Nakuru in tatty clothes and bare feet. They took very little part in extra curricular activities for more often than not their fathers wanted them to help out in the *duka* and learn the rudiments of their fathers' trades. Going to school barefoot seemed such a funky idea that I decided to do the same. I would leave home smartly dressed but arrive at school without shoes, having deposited them with our cobbler, whose little shop was on the way to school. On the way home I would collect the shoes and arrive in a tip-top fashion, albeit with grubby feet. This fad lasted only a couple of days as my teacher, Mr Gopal Dass, let the cat out of the bag. My father was not amused.

The school age in Kenya was seven, so the Indian *totos* had many years to bum around and get into mischief. To stop the children from going wild, my mother, Lila Vati Dhupa, started a free *madrassa* (nursery school) at home in Nakuru. The neighbourhood kids would gather for three hours every morning and many of today's successful adults learnt the rudiments of the three R's sitting on a bare, cold concrete floor.

The rest of the children's time was spent horsing around. Children's books were unavailable and most of the toys were our own creations. A stuffed sock was our volleyball and a clothesline served as a net. Empty sewing thread reels were used as wheels for our toy motorcars and a discarded rim, wheel or motorcar tyre gave us hours of pleasure as a make-believe vehicle. Most of the games we played had their origins in India and none of these needed any specialised equipment.

The most popular pastime was *guli-danda*. *Guli* is a piece of cylindrical wood, the size of a cricket bail but with tapered ends. The *guli* is placed on the ground and made to fly up by striking one end with a *danda* (stick). It is again hit while still in the air. Whoever catches the *guli* gets a turn as a striker.

The other games were *kabadi, meeru daba, agar patta,* the universal game of *kiri kara* (hopscotch), and of course, *bante* (marbles). Bottle tops were used as currency and the value varied with their rarity. For weight lifting, we used a set of *moonglies* (Indian clubs) which were often fashioned in the railway carpenter's shop. A plethora of hardwood trees provided ideal conditions for climbing, swinging and a popular game called *chorel*.

We spent many an afternoon on mango trees eating green mangoes with salt and hot chilli powder. It was on such a tree in Kampala that I made my first acquaintance with tobacco. Someone produced a cigarette and this was passed around. Being the new kid on the block, I was the last one to get the spit laden, soggy fag end. This was a blessing in disguise for it was such an unpleasant experience that I never smoked again.

The raiding of the neighbourhood vegetable patches was a favourite pastime but the real prize was the railway doctor's extensive peach orchard. After a well-planned raid, the spoils were meticulously divided. The price of getting caught was a beating by the *shamba boy*, or worse still, the ignominy of facing the doctor himself.

The Indian *totos* in the landies were 'railway children' in every sense. Railways were the reason for their fathers being in Africa in the first place and many generations of Indians were born, lived and died in railway landies. My mother was born in a railway quarter in Kisumu in 1907 and continued to live in a railway house after her marriage, for a total of 55 years, spanning four generations. The railways touched every aspect of our lives. We were surrounded by the sounds, sight and the smell of railways. We had to walk across the shunting yards to go to school, the railway hospital and railway club. When we travelled, it was in a railway carriage. It is no wonder that many of the games we played were based on what we saw. All manner of rims and wheels were our pretend trains and engines and these were brought forth by the proud owners who polished and cherished them much like cars at a vintage rally. Names of real engines like 'Uasin Gishu' or 'Karamoja' were given to these and could not be used by others. Strategic points around the landies were named after railway stations and most kids wanted to emulate their fathers.

It was not long before these childish pursuits were discarded in favour of 'real games' such as hockey, cricket and volleyball. Before we could graduate to the railway club there was work to be done, so the open barren *maidan* between the landies became our sports ground.

Here stumps were drawn with charcoal on the wall of the end house of a landi which acted as a butt and wicket keeper. This, however, caused endless problems. The housewife complained of the constant *thump, thump* against her bedroom wall, the budding wicket keeper was unable to hone his skills and there were constant disputes as to whether the ball had struck the wicket. The proverbial tin *debe* came to the rescue for there was never any doubt when the *boom* of leather on tin declared that the batsman's defences had been blown asunder.

Football and volleyball were the first two team games to catch our imagination, most likely because they were cheap and a large number of players could participate. Football needed a ball and a couple of stones at each end to act as a goal post, and for volleyball, we could use the same ball and a clothesline for a net. An old threadbare sari doubled as our net for the more important games. It was, however, 'East African Rules' volleyball that was to grip the Indian sports community and hold sway during the Second World War and for a few years that followed. Volleyball clubs sprang up in villages and hamlets from Malindi to Mwanza and from Dar to Dodoma. Teams such as 'Aryans', 'Hindu Union' and 'Sir Ali Muslim Club' developed intense rivalries and huge followings, and local heroes like Tappu, Pedu and Meru from Nairobi became household names. A Sikh primary school teacher, Masterji Ranjit Singh, was the most feared serviceman in East Africa in spite of a withered leg, for which he had to wear an enormously high leather boot.

The cream of the East African volleyballers invaded Kisumu every Christmas for the annual 'Gold Cup' Tournament. This was a magnificent gold trophy presented by Mr Kanji Naranji of Nairobi. When the Aryans, a team from Nairobi, won it three years running, it was replaced by a similar cup presented by the industrialist Inder Singh Gill. During the week, the Indian population of Kisumu almost doubled and the fans had a field day. The tourney also attracted the hooligans and other unsavoury characters who, incensed by their team's poor performance and with their own high level of alcohol, started fights which would sometimes disrupt the games.

The Sikh community with their tradition of service and hospitality not only produced a first-class set of volleyball pitches but served complimentary ice-cold sherbet to all the players and thousands of their fans. The tourney always ended with a parade with the victors dancing on an open lorry. The whole event engendered such fervour and energy among the Asians of East Africa that it is safe to say it has never been equalled. The bubble burst soon after the end of the Second World War when sports equipment from abroad was available once again and the opportunities to play internationally recognised sports, coupled with the ease of travel, changed the sporting scene forever.

Nineteen Forty-eight heralded the era of international competition when the Indian hockey players arrived in East Africa for a Pre-Olympics Games tour. The visit proved to be more of an exhibition of Indian prowess than a true contest. The local players were in awe of famous athletes such as Dyan Chand, Babu and Manna Singh, who mesmerised the opposition with their athleticism and stick-work. I watched them slaughter the Uganda XI by 22 goals in Kampala and by eighteen goals in Jinja. The other teams did not fare much better. However, there was disbelief when news came that the minnows from Nakuru had managed to hold the visitors to a 0-0 draw. Were the Indians human after all?

The Indian Hockey team with the Mayor of Nairobi – 1948.

The answer was not long in coming, for the standard in hockey and other sports began to improve in leaps and bounds. Local heroes like Surjit Singh of Nairobi and Baldev Singh of Kampala soon began to emerge. In 1953, I was asked to captain a Kenya Schools Hockey XI against Pakistan International XI at the National Stadium in Nairobi. We lost, 1-2, but not before giving the Pakistanis a run for their money. The sports scene in Kenya was becoming alive and fans were beginning to turn up to matches in the thousands. Curiously, however, their loyalty to local teams could not be guaranteed. During the same tour, our Kenya National team was leading the Pakistanis by a goal with a few minutes to full-time when some of the Muslim fans were seen to go on their knees and pray for Pakistani success. This kind of misplaced loyalty and bizarre behaviour was perplexing for the young Kenya-born generation and a sure-fire recipe for events of the ugly kind. Luckily, the match ended in a 1-1 draw. The star of Kenyan hockey continued to rise and in 1964 the amateur players of Kenya surprised the Indians and the sports world by becoming the first team to trounce India XI in India.

The European institution of sports clubs was to become a very important part of social life in eastern Africa. They were a template for all the other clubs. 'When two Englishmen meet they form a club', an old adage which is almost true for the club in Mombasa. When George Whitehouse disembarked at the Old Port in December

1895, a handful of Europeans had already formed the Mombasa Club. This was situated above M.R. da Souza's shop in Nadia Ku, one of the two narrow streets of the town. It had two rooms, one of which was occupied by the mess and the other which had a bar and a billiards table. The proprietors were Messrs. Boustead and Ridley[160], general merchants who had come from Zanzibar in 1892. The Europeans could also chill out in the three nearby hotels – The GRAND HOTEL CECIL and The AFRICA, flea pits all of them, but The AFRICA owned by an Indian was 'little more than a hovel and the food execrable'[161]. A cricket pitch had already been laid out not far from the Government House, an unprepossessing corrugated iron structure along the crest of the bluff.

A spanking new offspring to the old club was already under construction in the shadow of Fort Jesus and it opened its doors to members in 1896. Married couples were automatically excluded as residents and women were allowed on the premises at certain hours to read newspapers, but they had to leave when the bell was rung at 7 pm. They were not permitted to be members.[162]

The railway club was perhaps one of the most important institutions created for the Indian workers. Although based on a European model, they were quite puritanical, for no gambling or alcohol was allowed until the 1940s. Here women fared even worse than their European counterparts. No bylaws were needed for their total exclusion – the husbands took care of that.

The emphasis was totally on sport. The subsidised facilities were excellent and most clubs catered for modern outdoor and indoor games including billiards for the more esoteric members. Most had excellent reading rooms and modest libraries. All had a radio room where the less active men and those with a political bent congregated to listen to news from the BBC and the All India Radio. The sporting activities helped to focus the minds of the upcoming generations on wholesome activities and away from less healthy pursuits. Group activities instilled a community spirit and kept a lid on provincial differences and religious bigotry.

The railway clubs, in turn, acted as a model for other Indian groups who formed their own clubs. Some clubs, such as the Civil Service Club and the Suleman Virjee Indian Gymkhana in

---

[160] Ref: p12 – Trzebinski, Errol – *The Kenya Pioneers*

[161] Ref: p67 – Trzebinski, Errol

[162] Ref: p67 – Trzebinski, Errol

Nairobi were run on a secular basis and everyone was welcome. Others were based on provincial lines and these included the Goan clubs, Patel Clubs and Kathiawar Club. In larger towns, many of the clubs drew their strength from religious factions and these included Sikh Union, Hindu Union, Muslim clubs and Aryan clubs. The Muslims fragmented further into Aga Khan clubs, Bohra clubs and Ithanasari clubs. Larger groups such as the Soods had their own club in Kisumu which functioned very successfully for many years until its bubble burst as a result of the 'scattering of Soods' after the retirement of F. C. Mayor in 1931.

Another significant contribution of the sports clubs was their role in breaking down racial barriers. The straight jacket of apartheid prevented competition in all sports, and ironically, its effects were felt most acutely by the Europeans who, because of their small numbers, were often hard pressed to raise more than one team. An occasional fixture created a chink in the pigment barrier and gradually opened a floodgate of regular matches between the Indians and Europeans.

The Africans had to wait for many more years to become a part of this equation as they did not have the benefit of such facilities. Their participation, or lack of it, unfortunately did not cause much concern to either of the two other races. As children, however, we had no such constraints. Regular football matches were held between the brown and black *totos* of Nasambia landies in Kampala. There were no organisers, no referees, no spectators and no restrictions on the number of players. The game stopped when it was time for lunch and the victors walked away with the trophy – a teacup and saucer – which they got to keep until the next contest.

Tennis was perhaps one of the first sports to overcome the colour bar. In the early 30s, Yakub Khan, a railway clerk in Nakuru, became the darling of the tennis fraternity in Kenya. He went on to become the Kenya Champion. I can remember a large, standing-room-only crowd on the raised verandah of the Railway Indian Institute in Nakuru. Most of the spectators were European men and women and all were there to admire this fine athlete. Kenya may have produced better tennis players in the years that followed but none as stylish and as popular as Yakub. Even in the 50s in Mombasa, when no longer in the prime of his sporting life, he would attract large numbers of fans who came to admire his legendary grace and technique. His most ardent fan was the Provincial

Commissioner who would send his car and driver to pick up Yakub from his home so that the two could play together.

Yakub Khan (Far left) Kenya Champion Circa 1940 Railway Institute – Nakuru. Courtesy of Hamda Khan.

Cricket also played an important role in bringing down the pigment curtain. It was inevitable that a whole weekend spent in each other's company would lead to certain affinity, warmth and even friendship among the opposing players, whatever their colour. Lord Cranworth, years earlier, had applauded Ainsworth, the Nairobi District Commissioner, for arranging competitions between the two groups. He wrote, *"It is manifestly impossible to feel a lasting rancour against a man with whom you have but lately fought an enjoyable game of football or polo".*

Asian cricket in Kenya owes much to Mr Burjorji Commissariat, a Parsi, who came to Mombasa to work as a clerk in the National Bank of India around 1907. His enthusiasm was infectious and he formed a 'Burjorji XI' and promoted the game, not only on the coast, but in the rest of Kenya and East Africa. When he retired as the head cashier in 1937, he was elected an honorary life member of the all European Mombasa Club, an honour accorded to no other member of the Asian community. Such was his passion for the game that he encouraged Parsi youths by giving a gold sovereign to any Parsi player who scored a century.

196

During the 1927-28 season, the Railway Indian Institute, confident in its players' ability, made overtures to participate in the Country Cup matches but the Europeans rebuffed this attempt. In 1932, Mr E.P. Nowrojee, the son of Pheroze Nowrojee, a Parsi engine driver, who was a lawyer in Nairobi and a cricketer of distinction, wrote to the Kenya Kongoni Cricket Club asking for an 'annual international fixture of a three-day match between the Europeans and Asiatics of the country'.[163] The gauntlet was picked up and the first match was held in 1933. The game was won by the Europeans.

Some of the players of that era, such as Jaswant Singh, Karam Chand, Yakub Khan, Gurcharan Singh and Nowrojee became household names. Karam Chand's sixes became legendary. On one occasion, he is said to have hit the ball with such force that it sailed over the railway pavilion and landed in the cricket ground of the neighbouring Civil Service Club.

The Parsi passion for cricket in Kenya had its roots in Bombay where they were the first Indian community to take up this 'game of gentlemen, played by gentlemen'. The result of the first contest in 1890 against the English was however different from the one in Kenya. In this match, the Parsis defeated a visiting English team by four wickets, prompting a Parsi elder to remark that *'the imaginative and emotional Parsi youth felt for a day or two that he was the victor of Waterloo'*.

The British, too, associated nationalism with cricket. A major complained that the crowd was 'more attractive to the artist than the administrator'. *'The faces of those who composed it wore, in too many cases, an ugly expression'*. When the winning runs were scored, recalled the Major, the spectators *'conscious that in some particular or another, the black man had triumphed over the white man'*, ran *'hither and thither, gibbering and chattering and muttering vague words of evil omen'*. In the tent of the whites-only Byculla Club, the head of one of Bombay's largest British firms remarked: *"I know nothing of cricket, and I care less, but I could have collected a lac of rupees on the ground to prevent this, if money could have prevented it."*[164]

---

[163] Ref: p165 – Salvadori, Cynthia – *We came in Dhows.* Vol III

[164] Guha, Ramchandra – *A Corner of Foreign Field.* Picador

Asians vs Europeans. 4th Test Match Nairobi 1936.
1st Row. C.V. Braimbridge (U) Gulamali, Karamchand,
Malik, Mohanlal, Mullick, Yakubk Khan,
Sir G. Rhodes (U).
2nd Row. Jaswant Singh, Narowjee, Gurcharan Singh,
(Capt.) Karachiwala, (V.Capt.) G.N. Shah.

In 1948, my class fellow Dilbag Singh Kular was promoted to the first XI in a game against the Kampala European Club. The undiscovered fine athlete batted so well that he became an instant hero. A week later, the Chief Inspector of Schools, Mr Snoxall, was visiting our school. He came into our classroom and began to examine the 'black book' that was kept on the teacher's desk. This was used by the teachers to record the names of mischief-mongers. Three strikes and one had to go to see the principal, Mr Lall Singh, who was rather liberal with his cane. The inspector read the entries and without looking up asked Dilbag Singh to stand up. The teachers had accused him of 'making noises like a camel'. Dilbag stood up. The inspector asked him to make camel-like noises. Dilbag remained silent. *"Have you ever seen a camel?"* the inspector inquired. Dilbag, petrified and tongue-tied, shook his head from side to side. Mr Snoxall then looked at Dilbag straight in the eye and asked, *"Are you the young fellow who scored all those fours against us last Sunday?"* Dilbag nodded sheepishly, unable to articulate any sound. *"Stick to your cricket, son,"* said the inspector with a wink as he turned around and left the classroom, with the bemused teacher scurrying behind him.

Not long afterwards in 1949, my father was transferred from Kampala to Mombasa. I was mortified at the thought of leaving my friends and severing my sports ties. However, lady luck was on my side and the move turned out to be a blessing in disguise.

A month after my arrival in Mombasa, I managed to score a century in my very first game for the Railways Second XI and suddenly my services were in demand. I was catapulted into the First XI and asked to open the innings in a prestigious game against the Mombasa Club. This was a daunting task at best but it was made worse by the fact that a visiting county cricketer from England was making a cameo appearance for the European team. Mercifully, no-one thought of mentioning this to me. So, on a warm sunny Sunday morning, I took the crease totally oblivious of what was in the offing. Prior to this our captain had approached me in the changing rooms and asked me if I was wearing a 'box'. I was not, but I was too embarrassed to admit that I did not know how to do up the ties, so I just nodded. I can just remember the red shiny missile leaving the bowler's hand and bouncing off the coconut matting. I went on my back foot to present a straight bat and then, there was darkness. When I opened my eyes I was in the pavilion and the captain's face was peering down on me. *"I thought you were wearing a box,"* he asked. I remained silent. We were all out for 75 runs and my contribution – '25 runs, retired hurt'. At the close of play the bowler came up to me, his face beaming, and handed me an abdominal guard saying, *"Here is something for the crown jewels."* My place in the First XI was assured.

The year 1942 saw the scattering of our family. My two brothers, Dev and Dhruv, had to leave home for secondary education in Nairobi. As there were no boarding schools for Indians, they had to live with my uncle Kartar Chand. My father had brought him over from India in the late 20s and supported him financially until he became a police inspector in Nairobi. Now it was his turn to help his younger brother. Little did my parents realise that henceforth, one child or another would always be away from home in pursuit of higher education in Nairobi, India or the United

Kingdom, and it would be 28 years before the whole family of five would all meet under one roof.

Meanwhile, my father had built a large house in the *Sikh Colony* area of Nairobi. This had three self-contained apartments, one for each son. He planned to live in the penthouse with his youngest. This was a calculated risk which did not come to fruition for no one could have foreseen the social, financial and political uncertainties that lay ahead. The 'old faithful' more than fulfilled its promise, however, for it continues to provide rental income to this day.

One 'advantage' of my brothers' departure to the big city was that I became the sole owner of their battered 'penny farthing'. After endless falls and grazes, I mastered the machine. Being the only bike in the landies it conferred upon me a certain status among my peers. Everyone wanted a ride and for the price of a 'gob stopper' I would let someone stand astride the back wheel with his toes precariously hugging the hub-nuts. Soon I was carrying bodies on the crossbar and handlebar. The inevitable happened and a friend of mine came off and broke his arm. We conspired to blame it on football and his unsuspecting mother banned him from taking part in this dangerous sport, fit only she claimed, *'for kalas and fundis.'*

The popularity of the bicycle among Indians varied from one town to another and there seems to be no rhyme or reason for this. In Kampala, the bicycle was so popular among the Bugandans that it was practically used as a beast of burden. Sultani, a cycle merchant who came to eastern Africa as a clerk to Seth Allidina Visram, made a fortune selling bicycles to Africans. Yet he did not succeed in convincing his fellow Indians of its advantages. By contrast, in Mombasa, almost everyone in the landies had a bike.

In 1950, Vishnu Bowry, a member of the Sood clan, was appointed manager of the new Municipal Stadium at Tononoka. He introduced bicycle races and soon it became a very popular sport. This was the first multi-racial event and competitors and a large number of spectators came from all races. Only everyday standard dirt bikes were used as anything more esoteric was unaffordable and unsuitable for the coarse and bumpy cinder track. The grand prize at every meet was a new Raleigh and for the first few years every one of those was won by Peter, an African clerk in the PWD.

My success came in short distance races and after I had accumulated a sufficient amount of vouchers, which were given out in lieu of cash, I decided to buy a new Raleigh and retire my battered old Humber. My father volunteered to pick up the bike from the dealer and bring it home. All afternoon I waited with a heightened sense of anticipation. My father came an hour late and he was walking. On his way home, he had stopped at a corner shop and as he turned his back a thief grabbed his opportunity and all my father could do was to watch the back of the stealthy larcenist.

One of the popular events during the 'Race Sunday' was a novelty needle and thread race. After two laps a thread was handed to a partner who threaded a needle and then completed a third lap. My regular partner was Marlene Bates, a lovely girl with blond hair. At the end of one exciting race, which we won, Marlene gave me a hug and a kiss which prompted loud whistles from the crowd. By the time I got home, the bush telegraph had already informed my father of my wayward ways and my cavorting with a white girl. A simple gesture and youthful exuberance, misinterpreted by a spoilsport as a step down the slippery slope of depravity. The informant, a landiwalla, registered his concerns that such behaviour would set a poor example for the rest of the Indian boys and girls and was sure to lead to loose behaviour, drinking and sexual liaisons. My father was not impressed by such puritans who, he said, 'were out to steal the youth of the upcoming generations' and he advised *vogue la galere*. Ironically, I was never to see the fair maiden again, for my days in Mombasa were over and I had to leave for Nairobi to pursue further education.

Marlene Bates, (far left)
The first cycle meet in Mombasa – 1950

201

Because of such narrow-minded attitudes it is no wonder that there were few, if any, organised sports for the developing Indian damsels until the late 1940s. When *Arya Samaj* in Nairobi first included women in their annual sports meeting, the more conservative elements in the Indian circles shook their heads with disapproval. Many a matron declared in solemn tones that the girls were running a risk of their innards turning topsy-turvy and thus compromising their future prospects of childbearing – and who would want to marry such a girl. The female physique, they argued, was designed for gentler pursuits such as sewing, knitting and home-making.

Although sports played a very important role in the lives of the landiwallas both at home and at school, the athletics scene in Asian schools was a dismal one. The Asian High School in Nairobi was an exception, for it had a long tradition of competitions between the four houses – Romans, Trojans, Spartans and Grecians – into which the school was divided. The highlight of the annual Sports Day was the crowning of the best athlete as the *Victor Ludorum*. Unfortunately, this fine tradition was wiped out in one fell swoop in 1953 when the Headmaster, Mr G.S. Amar, decided against it.

The Duke of Gloucester School, Nairobi. Hockey X1, 1953.

A protest meeting confronted Amar in the new science lecture room which was filled to the rafters, but the Headmaster refused to change his mind. As I was the spokesman, I was summoned to the office the next morning and threatened with expulsion. As a punishment, my nomination as the Head Prefect in the coming year was cancelled. I was allowed to continue as the captain of the Hockey XI and the Cricket XI for a second year but we were reduced to begging and borrowing sports equipment.

While this turmoil was going on in Nairobi, Mombasa was taking steps towards a sustainable programme of athletics. However, the Annual Empire Day celebrations in 1954 were marred by a bizarre incident. The festivities opened with the raising of the Union Jack, inspection of the Guard of Honour and the usual speeches and tub-thumping. All went smoothly and Bristol fashion until the start of the 10,000 yards (now metres) event. Mr Eddie Soares, a young newly recruited teacher at the Allidina Visram High School, was astonished to find that the contestants were made to run in their respective lanes with obvious advantage to the runners in the inner lanes. He writes, *"I yelled at the runners in the outer lanes to run in the first lane closer to the kerb. Some of the runners looked puzzled, a few ignored me and three waved in acknowledgement, under the impression that I was cheering their efforts… I then acted impulsively. I got into the main stand and shouted at the runners not to run in the lanes… Who is the Clerk of the Course, I shouted, he doesn't know how to run the race."* The young Indian was arrested immediately and locked up in the equipment storeroom. During the tea interval, the Provincial Commissioner and Mr Hatfield, the Provincial Education Officer, 'drifted towards the window' of the storeroom, and instructed Soares to appear at Mr Hatfield's office on the following Tuesday.

At this meeting, Soares was made to stand throughout the proceedings. After a period of 'silent treatment' his presence was acknowledged and Soares explained his actions and mentioned that he had organised athletics meetings at the Bombay University. Suitably impressed, Hatfield invited Soares to a meeting with the P.C.

"You are not expected to speak, can you remember that."
"Yes, Sir."

"Just keep silent. I will inform your Headmaster to give you leave of absence."[165]

The meeting, a post-mortem of the recent Empire Day Sports, was chaired by P.C. Desmond O'Hagan. Col. Mackenzie was once again nominated as the Clerk of the Course and asked if he would accept. The Colonel, a huge man with florid features and a handlebar moustache, stood up ponderously. *"Gentlemen"* he said, *"I will not stand. For years I have been guilty of not being aware of how to run the long distance races. On Saturday, it was brought to me rather vividly by a young man on the field. For his pains I got him arrested. I have consulted the Engineer and the Surveyor… I was told in no uncertain terms that I was not only completely wrong but had deprived many a long distance runner in the outer lane of a medal. I would now like to apologise to this body and not accept the nomination. I do not know who is the young man and I offer my sincere apologies to him."* Hatfield would have none of that. He stood up and said, *"In view of the long and dedicated service, I ask him to accept. I will suggest to Col. Mackenzie that this young man be co-opted to be his assistant. Do you agree Col. Mackenzie?"[166]*

"I certainly do," replied the Colonel.

This started a long lasting and fruitful friendship between Soares and the Colonel. Soares remained a part of the Kenya Athletics scene from 1955 to 1985.

---

[165] Ref: Soares, Eddie. Personal Communication

[166] Ref: Soares, Eddie. Personal Communication

Eddie Soares – Teacher A.V. High School – 1965.

A great hiatus in our education was the arts. The focus at school and home was on the three R's and sports. The result was a plethora of excellent scholars and good athletes but a paucity of aesthetes. The reason perhaps was that most of the coolies were themselves a culturally deprived group and their struggle for existence in a dark and distant land was not conducive to the development of artistic talents. Be that as it may, it is fair to say that many, if not most of us, grew up in a cultural desert.

Many of the Indian *babus* seemed to suffer from a phobia that music might become a corrupting influence on their growing

205

charges. Many carted off their phonograms to India and carefully stored them, fully intending to rescue them when the family was all grown up or when they returned home after retirement. My uncle, a doctor in Kisumu, kept his Marconi in a locked glass cabinet as a centrepiece in the lounge. This was unlocked only for the BBC Overseas News and the All India Radio broadcast which followed on its heels. Every evening his cronies would gather in his living-room and wait for the hallowed hour when the cabinet was unlocked with great panache and the knobs twiddled to get the sound just right. The signature tune was the signal for the listeners to take their leave and for the radio to be locked up in its cell until the news on the next day.

If the societal attitude towards music was so old fashioned its stance against dancing was even more entrenched. A young woman singing in public could purport to be modest by wearing plain attire, shun make-up, cast her eyes towards the floor, remain expressionless and cover her hair for good measure. But dancing involved *mudras* (hand gestures), gyrations of the body, eye movements and facial expressions to convey the performer's innermost feelings.

The Gujarati dances, *Garba* and *Ras,* with or without men, were very popular and generally acceptable because of their association with folk dancing and religious festivals. Here, the elders could keep a watchful eye. Punjabi women danced the *Gidda* in women's gatherings only. Punjabi men did not dance at all. Bhangra, the most popular dance among Punjabi men and women today, had not been invented.[167]

Agehananda Bharati, a don in anthropology at the University of Syracuse, studied the East African scene first-hand in 1964 and wrote, *"Now a good percentage of the wealthier adolescents, boys and girls, are both admirers and performers of such alien imports as the Twist, the Frug, and Rock 'n Roll: it takes an American*

---

[167] Ref: p257 – Singh, Gurcharan – *Studies in Punjab History and Culture.* Enkay Publishes Pvt. Ltd. New Delhi
Bhangra owes its ancient roots to Sailkot district now in Pakistani Punjab. In 1952, Gurcharan Singh, a novelist and educator, saw a performance by three young *bazigars* who had left Sailkot and settled in India. Gurcharan Singh was so impressed that he encouraged the troupe to perform at various places. The first 'Bhangra team' was formed in 1954 at Mohinder College in Patiala. The springboard for modern Bhangra came following a performance at the Republic Day celebrations in Delhi.

choreographic creation less than a year to get firmly established in East Africa. These are tolerated by the elders. Paradoxically, it appeared as though the Twist and similar dance forms, as well as jazz and Indian filmi music, caused less anxiety among the conservative and the parent generation in East Africa than the potential pursuit of classical Indian dance and music. In trying to elicit some response about this lack of culture import, I suggested that culture had to be bought, and could be bought, by wealthier Asians. Though this was admitted, there were after-thoughts: "We do not want that our daughters should dance and sing like professional musicians; if we did, who would marry them? No-one wants to marry an artist." Translated into culturally explanatory language, the statement means something like this: in India, the professional singers and dancers were the baiji (prostitute singers and dancers) and the barwa (music and dance instructors and procurers) throughout the centuries since Muslim rule. The South Indian bhagavtar and devadasi had direct ritualistic significance, but the Asians of East Africa know nothing about it, there being no South Indians among them. Hence, any woman who sings might be likened to a baiji, and of course, nobody marries a baiji. [168]

Many Indians of East Africa regarded sex, alcohol and gambling as the three sins – mortal or venial, depending on their background. Drinking was least objectionable of these pleasures. Usually it was a solitary activity carried out in the privacy of their homes. Only the 'down and outs' went to public bars, the entrances of which were always shielded by heavy wood screens to keep out prying eyes. No concession was usually made to social drinking – thus, either a person was a teetotaller or a drunkard.

Many Arya Samajists, a large number of them Punjabis, tried to deny themselves of as many of the 'five enjoyments'[169] as they could, denying the fact that *Mamsa* (meat), *Matsya* (fish) and *Madya*

---

[168] Ref: p253 – Bharati, Agehananda – *The Asians in East Africa.* Nelson Hall Publishers. Chicago USA

[169] Ref: p222 – Parrinder, Geoffrey – *World Religions: From Ancient History to the Present.* Facts on File. 460 Park Avenue South, New York, NY 10016
Stages to supreme bliss can be attained according to a person's spiritual capacity. The stages are: *pashu* (beast), *vira* (hero), or *divya* (divine). The stage of hero has the ritual of 'Five Ms': *pancha makara* in which he successively partakes of wine *(madya)*, fish *(matsya)*, meat *(mamsa)*, parched grain *(mudra)* and sexual intercourse *(maithuna).* At the highest stage the aspirant becomes dead to the world and its antinomies, liberated while yet in the flesh.

207

(wine) were freely used in India for many centuries by those who could afford such things.

The Sikhs were notorious for their uninhibited drinking and usually imbibed whiskey by the gallon. Some of the professional men in Mombasa (and perhaps in other places), recollects Manmohan Singh, would often leave town at the weekends and meet at a secret rendezvous for unrestrained indulgence. Others would gather at a friend's house and binge drink late into the night while their womenfolk huddled together in the kitchen trying to keep the food hot until the men got hungry or the booze ran out. Convention dictated that their wives did not eat until the men had been served.

For Muslims, drinking was often a covert activity. Many were partial to a tipple but swore in public that not a drop had ever passed their lips. Even the Khoja Ismailis, a group of Shia Muslims, ritually and ideologically most removed from orthodox Islam, would not admit to the use of alcohol. On a visit to East Africa, the late Aga Khan was invited to a sumptuous dinner for the top echelon of the Ismaili hierarchy. When word got out in the press the next morning that the hosts had invited two white girls to sit by the side of His Highness – 'wenches, not ladies of any name' – and that he was offered the best French champagne to drink, there was a hue and cry. A letter was published a day later to refute this. It explained that the community had indeed offered the Aga Khan a bottle of best bubbly to show that only the best would do – but that the champagne turned into water the moment it touched His Highness's lips. [170]

Alcohol consumption by Indian women was hardly significant. An occasional woman might drink for 'medicinal purposes'. There was a general relaxation of attitudes in the mid-twentieth century, but most women did not indulge. The more modern women did not think that drinking was bad and often joined their men for a *chotta* (small) peg or two. Those who were ultra modern or those who had been to schools abroad drank at parties and sundowners. In most cases, women started to drink after marriage due to encouragement from their husbands. Many of the women who drank in public camouflaged their rum and whiskey by mixing it with Coke. Two Hindu-Punjabi ladies, both known as Mrs. K, became well known in Nairobi as connoisseurs of Scotch. The younger one was a celebrated beauty in her day and years ahead of her time. Her

[170] Ref: p204 – Bharati, Agehananda – *The Asians in East Africa.* Nelson Hall Publisher. Chicago

socialising and drinking became as legendary as her beauty. Alcohol, however, eventually took its toll and in her twilight years she became a familiar figure at the hospital due to her dementia tremens. The two ladies emigrated to Canada, established a reputation as 'whiskey experts' and lived to a ripe old age.

Gambling was vindicated as a justifiable pursuit. Betting on horses had become a common habit since the early days of the colony. Playing the stock market, it was argued, helped to augment the family coffers, essential for bringing up the family and to educate the children. Playing cards for money was thought to be quite innocuous and was a major activity at some of the Indian Clubs. The age-old tradition of gambling at *Divali* helped to confer instant respectability on such activities.

In East Africa the subject of sex was a taboo. Sex was never discussed in Indian homes, schools or elsewhere. Segregation of the sexes was the hallmark of decorum. An invisible line separated the males and females at home, in schools and in religious places.

Young people deprived of opportunities to intermingle and interact with the opposite sex became very frustrated. When a rare meeting of the girls and boys took place, they felt awkward, embarrassed and shied away. The boys often over-reacted by showing off or becoming rather boorish. By contrast, in Uganda where the schools were co-educational, the attitude between sexes was much more relaxed and their behaviour more natural. The Ugandan children not only had formal education together but participated in joint sports, dramatic arts and other extra-curricular activities. The cast-iron mould of separate education in Kenya was eventually broken in 1953 when four young women were admitted to the A level programme at the Duke of Gloucester School. This change was in fact forced upon the authorities because of the lack of laboratory space and paucity of trained teachers. Thus Hilda Fernandes, Rosemary, Musarat and Ms. Kent became the first girls to walk through the hallowed halls of the 'Duke' and became the vanguard of generations of young women who 'went to the dogs'. The initial stir caused by this sea change lasted only a few weeks for soon the wolf-whistles stopped and the swish of the skirt and female silhouette ceased to turn male heads.

In Hindu *mandirs* and Sikh *gurdwaras* men sat on one side of the hall and women on the other. Muslim women did not go to the mosque at all. The Sunday prayer meetings at the Arya Samaj were usually all male affairs. God help the mister who was suspected of looking at the women. On one occasion, a young single railway man was seen to be glancing repeatedly towards the ladies during *Divali* celebrations. He was accused of ogling and the matter was reported to the elders of the community. When the young man came to *babu* Fakir Chand's house where the Soods met every evening, he was censured in the traditional manner by the withdrawal of his *hookah* and *pani* (water) privileges. It is said that the young fellow realised that he had wronged and begged for forgiveness on bended knees.

The growing children in such a setting had no role models and no chance to learn from parental guidance or behaviour. They did not see any tender moments or witness any flirtation. There was no kissing and cuddling, no sideways glances, no exchange of smiles and not even hand-holding. Any congress, and there must have been some in view of the large number of children in each family, was assigned to the hours of darkness when the children, who slept in the same room as their parents, were asleep – or so the parents thought. Often they were either woken up by the amorous parental encounters or had just pretended to be asleep.

The next day was the opportunity for the kids to compare notes amidst much mirth and laughter. Thus it was common knowledge among the landi boys that the Sethis always called out their children's names to ensure they were asleep and if there was no response, lit a candle and got on with the job. In Mr Shah's house, one night the charpoy could not take the strain and the couple landed on the concrete floor – not one of the ten children heard a thing!

The fantasy world of movies, the main if not the only entertainment for the Asians in East Africa, had considerable influence. The films often dictated fashions, customs and social behaviour. The yuppies had advance tickets for late night Saturday shows, very much like season tickets for sporting events in other countries. Films were discussed with much seriousness and excitement as if they were a literary work. I was visiting Kampala in 1964 when Raj Kapoor's movie – *Sangam* – was causing a great commotion in East Africa. A young Gujarati fellow rushed into a barber's shop where I was having a haircut and declared, "*Best movie of all time, yar – ema kiss kareche (*there is kissing)." The barber nodded and carried on. The young man could not contain himself and he stood up and blurted, "*Arre moda uper* (on the

210

mouth). *First time, I tell you.*[171] A lot of the conservative families regarded movies as a bad influence unless they were based on a religious or historical theme. Whole neighbourhoods would then turn up to watch movies, such as *Ram Raj* or *Sikandar*.

The boys talked a lot about sex but hardly ever saw any action. This was usually confined to literally standing at the corner and watching all the girls go by. This might be outside the Arya Girls School at Nagara in Nairobi, but the favourite haunt in most cities was the *Khoja Khanna*. Here, every evening, the western clad Ismaili girls[172] were sure to provide a glimpse of the ankle for the sex-starved guys to drool over. See but not touch was the general rule of the day.

What could a young fellow do if not resort to solitary satisfaction? But this too, was a minefield of dangers. *"Masturbation is a vice"*, said the older boys, *"punishable by the gods with impotence and infertility". And what was more, it might lead to poor performance at sports.* The first was not true, the second was too remote to cause any concern, but to fail in sports was a real cause for concern.

Such forebodings were not surprising when sex and sexuality has been surrounded by ignorance, misinformation, myths and religious and social interference. For centuries, the Indians believed that the supplies of semen were limited, and by inference, that the wasteful scattering of seed was wrong. The Chinese thought that masturbation caused weakening at all levels. The West held that such wastefulness was an appalling sin. Sinbaldi, who in 1642 produced the first of Europe's standard works on sexuality, the Geneathopia, threatened gout, constipation, a hunched back, bad breath and a red nose. Ellen White, founder of the Seventh Day Adventists 200 years later, claimed that a vision had revealed to her that masturbation would turn a man into a cripple and an imbecile. Even doctors, 50 years later, were claiming that the reward of "self-

---

[171] A kiss on the lips was first shown in a classic Indian movie, *Shakuntala*. In the 1940s, the Indian Board of Censors banned kissing. Foreign films continued to be shown uncensored.

[172] This was a result of a *firman*, a canonical injunction to a community, by the late Aga Khan, who ordered that women of all ages should wear western dress on almost all occasions but particularly for their domestic chores.

abuse" was blindness or epilepsy.[173] The Indians in Kenya could be excused for their quirky thoughts.

Dating among Kenya Indians was, of course, unheard of and marriages were all arranged.[174] Love, however, often finds a way to circumvent such strictures. In the early 30s, two Sood sisters in Kisumu took a shine to a couple of young Sood men who were sharing a room at the Arya Samaj boarding house. They exchanged letters for a few months before one was intercepted. This was a matter of grave concern for the girls' father, so an emergency meeting was held at Fakir Chand Mayor's house and it was decided to marry the girls off as soon as possible. The two young men were summoned the next evening and ordered to get their nuptial plumage ready. A major scandal was thus averted and the honour of *Sood Baradari* (brotherhood) was saved.

This respite, however, was temporary. The third sister, waiting in the wings, would see to that. The *'hussy'* got the Punjabis in a tizzy and tongues began to wag when she was seen cavorting in public and riding pillion on her boyfriend's bicycle on Government Road in Nairobi. All appeals to curb her behaviour fell on deaf ears. The *coup de theatre* came in 1944 when she eloped to Nakuru. The couple were ostracised for good.

By contrast, when a Hindu Punjabi girl was whisked away from the railway landi in 1951, it hardly caused a ripple in the waters around Mombasa. The young man, a local hero, had played his cards right. He had approached the respective parents but the girl's mother was unrelenting. On the *'auspicious day'* as he explained later to his friends, he went to the local temple and in the presence of the priest, prayed for courage and blessings. After a handsome donation to appease the gods, and no doubt the priest, he armed himself with a large saffron *tilak* on his forehead and nervously set out on his mission. Under cover of darkness, he approached the back door where his beloved was waiting with a traditional red *chuni* (scarf) draped around her shoulders and a gold bangle on her wrist.

---

[173] Ref: p343-344 – Tennahill, Reay – *Sex in History.* Stein and Day, New York, 1980

[174] Most Indian marriages in more enlightened circles these days are either love marriages or by introduction, where each party is free to say yes or no. Unfortunately, they continue to be called 'arranged marriages'.

Dating during the 50s remained a covert activity. The forward types met the girls on late Saturday mornings after school and made a beeline for KB's Café for *'cake and coffee'* in a curtained booth. The majority went to the 'schools show' at the Regal Cinema on Harding Street for a canoodle in the back row of the balcony. The show also attracted European boys from the Prince of Wales School and girls from Loretto Convent School, and as a result, a few inter-racial liaisons began to blossom. Some of the rich boys, usually the sons of businessmen, who had access to a motor car, would drive their girls out to the quietness of Nairobi Arboretum.

By the early 60s, the younger generation was much more affluent and mobile. Their favourite haunts were the drive-in cinemas where, the privacy of the motor car, the surrounding darkness and the paucity of older Asians at English films provided a perfect venue to take your date. The college students were also into drinking and dancing parties. Curiously, the girls did not want to be seen smoking and they would slip outside into the dark to have a quick drag. Smooching was rare in the company of others as the young women were afraid of getting labelled as slappers.

Pre-marital sex among Indian girls during the first half of the twentieth century was very rare indeed. The girls were usually confined to the house after school and they were chaperoned when away from home. Occasionally, someone 'got lucky' but the consequences of being discovered were severe.

When Narbada, a Gujarati girl, had a brief but tempestuous affair with a young student at the Arya Samaj *Ashram* in Nairobi, her parents locked her indoors until arrangements were completed to send her away to another town. A Hindu Punjabi girl, Sarla, had the misfortune of getting pregnant by a Muslim young man in Nakuru. The whole community seemed to go into mourning. The parents abandoned their daughter and she was never heard of again.

Sali adhi ghar wali is a Hindi proverb meaning 'wife's sister is half a wife'. Mild flirtation with the sister-in-law is not uncommon and it stops there – but not always. That is exactly what happened in the sleepy village of Miwani. The father of the girl, a sugar cane farmer, insisted on importing a suitable Sikh boy from the same area of Punjab as his first son-in-law. He was successful but only partially. While the prolonged search was on, the prospective bride fell in love with her *jija* and became pregnant. He took her as his second wife.

213

The chances of any worthwhile relationships between Indian boys and girls were remote. The boys, however, had more opportunities for sexual adventures. More often than not, their first experience was with a Bantu or Swahili woman. On the coast, a large number of *Shili Shili* (Seychellois) girls were available as *filles de joie*. They were very popular as they were light skinned, invariably beautiful and not too expensive. Even so, they were beyond the means of most young men unless they had a job. 'Brown experience' in East Africa remained a rare commodity except for a few young men who had a chance to visit India or Pakistan and had their initiation in the *Rundi Bazaar* (red light area).

Sometimes the peace and harmony of the landies in Nakuru was shattered when a group of women known as the 'fighting mamas' tried to settle their differences in public. They would come out in the open space and shout and swear until the air was blue, and sometimes, physically set upon each other. The children, the Africans and other women would gather around in a large circle and watch these gladiators go hammer and tongs.

The combatants were given Swahili names by the African servants much as one would name the fighting cocks according to their peculiar traits. Thus there was a mama *Matata* (quarrelsome); mama *Khelele* (loud mouth); mama *Fitina* (mischief-monger). Some women were labelled according to their physical attributes. For example mama *Matiti* (big tits); mama *Matako* (big arse) and mama *Maradadi,* for she always wore heavy make-up and jewellery. The hostilities would cease suddenly as the afternoon wore on and it was time for the husbands to return from work. This temporary truce was often short-lived and the shindig was resumed the next day.

Some of the women resorted to *Jadu-Tuna* (witchcraft). People would sometimes find strange objects and potions at their back door and the neighbours were quick to interpret their dire significance. When I was five with long flowing tresses a woman from a neighbouring landi cut off some of my locks. She, of course, denied all knowledge – a child's word against that of an adult. The neighbours came up with numerous theories ranging from the woman's desire to have a boy to her desire to cause me grievous bodily harm. I survived the evil spell and am still around to tell the tale. One hopes that she got her boy.

The fertility of women, or lack of it, has always been important in all cultures and in a fruitless union, the finger is invariably pointed at the female of the species. The ability to produce a child of the right sex imposes an added burden. The underlying cause of this is greed. Traditionally in India, the groom's parents expect a dowry, whereas in Africa, by contrast, the bride's father is the recipient of a dowry. A claim to cure barrenness has brought lucrative rewards to people all over the world. The charlatans often do better than the *bona fide* practitioners and Kenya was no exception.

While crossing the Uganda-Kenya border at Busia in 1964, I met the local medicine man at the bus stand. His stall was full of neatly laid out twigs of many varieties, bits of dried chicken parts and strange paraphernalia which he kept wafting with his white cow-tail whisk. All the while he kept muttering to himself. He told me that he could cure thirteen diseases although he was at a loss to name more than a couple of them. Infertility was at the top of his list. Could he help with the sex of the child, I enquired. *"Kabisa"*, (certainly) he replied, with half a smile. He was not the only one so gifted.

Now, I had an aunt called Biran Bai who was a widow and she lived in Kisumu. She could not only guarantee a child, but a boy. When she came to Kenya in the late 1920s she brought with her a bag of *golies* (pills) made with a secret recipe which a 'sage had developed in Punjab'. Word soon spread and the demand for the magic pills continued to grow. Women who conceived rewarded her with expensive gifts and those who bore a son were even more generous. Those who were unsuccessful – well, there was another *goli* waiting for them.

Years later, Biran was running out of her pills, so she asked her brother if he could send her back to India so that she could replenish her supply and fulfil her wish to bathe in the holy waters of *Ganga*. As she was getting on in age and there was no one available to accompany her, my father came up with a brilliant solution. He suggested to her that she might consider mixing the remaining tablets with the best jaggery from his farm in Miwani and make a fresh supply, which she did. As far as bathing was concerned, he convinced her that all the water from the Ganges mixes with the Indian Ocean and that some of that water was at our doorstep in Mombasa. This did the trick. She spent the week rolling her pills and taking the water at Nyali Beach. Biran Bai was happy and so were her clients – at least half of them. Only the doctors frowned!

The king of the railway landies was the railway doctor. In Nakuru, he lived in a large, plush, detached bungalow surrounded by a peach orchard. He was the only rail man to have a car. His services and medicines were dispensed without charge. No one regarded him as a railway employee and people fell over each other in order to keep on the right side of *dacterji.* They showered him with gifts at the slightest excuse.

The first doctor that I can remember from my childhood days in Nakuru was Sukhdev Bharadwaj. He was a tall, friendly compassionate man with dark hair which was beginning to turn salt and pepper. He tended me through two life-threatening illnesses – first typhoid, and then osteomyelitis of the left femur. As his youngest son, Bharat, was my *pukka* friend, I spent as much time at his house as mine and before long, I began to regard myself as a part of that family.

Bharat was fascinated by motor cars and the two of us would sneak into the garage and twiddle the steering wheel and various knobs for hours on end. We often used the main road outside the hospital as our playground, waving at the very occasional car that went by. The road, a narrow strip of tarmac, joined the European area and the Show Grounds to the main road that formed the spine of our cow town. It was said that it was built by the municipality as a sop to the *memsahibs* who constantly complained of dust getting into their clothes. One day, while larking around, Bharat persuaded me to stop an oncoming car by both of us lying across the road. The rickety little contraption putt-putted to a stop a few yards from where we lay and down stepped an elegant lady in an all white flowing frock and a wide brimmed hat tied under her chin. She ordered us to stand up and asked where we lived. We pointed to the doctor's house and left the scene giggling. Soon all was forgotten.

That afternoon, the hospital assistant came to the house and asked us to accompany him to the doctor's office. Anticipating a treat of some sort we bumbled into the office. There, to our great surprise was the lady we had met earlier, gracefully occupying a large chair. She sat expressionless as we received a right ticking-off. We apologised to her with folded hands and promised not to play on the road again. As we slinked away, we were at a loss to know how she knew who we were. Bharat Bharadwaj never lost his love for cars for the last I heard of him was that he had become the Director of the now famous Kenya Safari Rally.

The arrival of Dr Sirmukh Singh, who replaced Dr Bharadwaj in 1945, took Nakuru by storm. Not only did he have three beautiful daughters but each one rode a chestnut Arabian. Nakuru had never seen an Indian horsewoman before and suddenly there were three –

all goddesses – in their pink coats and jodhpurs, turning heads wherever they went. Their memory must have been so deeply etched in the minds of the young landi boys that they were a topic of conversation at the Annual Reunion Luncheon of the Railwaymen in London some 57 years later.

The doctor, it was said, had been sent to Moyale on the Kenya-Abyssinia border as a reprimand, following complaints by the general practitioners in Kisumu that he was delving into dentistry and optics for which he was not licenced. At this remote out-post, the indomitable man responded by adding other strings to his bow and made a lot of money by becoming a horse trader and acting as a *bureau de change*. This led to further jealousy among his peers and an equally vociferous clamour for his withdrawal from this border station. On arrival in Nakuru, Dr Singh was an instant success. His 'one stop' government hospital not only provided all these services without charge but he was also in great demand as a veterinarian.

If the doctor was popular, his compounder was even more so – at least with the railway kids– for he was ever ready to supply them with picric acid and sticky plaster for cuts and bruises. He would also dole out generous quantities of sulphur powder and a crystalline substance that we called 'potash'. These two, when mixed in the right proportions, made excellent *barood* (gunpowder) for our Bangalore torpedoes. The fundies in the loco-shed were forever willing to make the hardware from metal water pipes and rods. At *Divali*, the Hindu festival of lights, the children would bring out these potentially lethal contraptions and the loud bangs could be heard well into the night. These 'bombs' also enabled us to pretend that we were soldiers in the Indian National Army ready to fight for the freedom of India.

During the 30s and 40s there was a groundswell of anti-British feelings among the Indians in Kenya to coincide with the freedom movement in India. Events in India were followed very closely and religious festivals were used as an excuse to give vent to Nationalistic sentiments. All denominations of Hindus were drawn together in this common cause. The temple halls were plastered with images of Gandhi, Nehru and Subash Chandra Bose. Speeches extolling the virtues of freedom would end with shouts of 'Quit India' and 'Jai Hind'. For a few years Jai Hind (victory to India) replaced the customary greeting of *namaste*. At such meetings, the partisan crowds would link arms, sway to music, wave the Indian

217

Tricolour and sing *Vande Mataram*, *Bharat Desh Azad Hoga* (India will soon be independent) and *Bakri Gandhi Di* (Gandhi's goat).

**Popular photo of Gandhi
and Pandit Nehru**

During the run-up towards Indian Independence and the imminent creation of Pakistan, the East African supporters of both causes became quite unsettled. There was a realignment of loyalties by many Muslims, and in Kampala, they started their own sports club. The secular nature of the Indian constitution was not generally understood and most people viewed it as a simple Hindu versus Muslim conflict. Mercifully, the daily news of rape, pillage and murder failed to incite them to duplicate the mindless folly of their brethren on the Indian subcontinent. In many towns there were separate independence celebrations but the citizens of Kampala set an example of good sense and tolerance by holding a joint celebration. The President, a Muslim, ushered in independence at a massive gathering at the Recreation Cricket ground by proclaiming, *"Pakistan-Hindustan Zindabad; Hindustan-Pakistan Zindabad."*

At the time, my two brothers were at college in Jullunder City in Punjab, which was a hot bed of Hindu-Muslim conflict. With grandma, they had to witness the mayhem on the streets from our ancestral *haweli*, a relic of the past, which had stood in *Chownk Soodan* (Sood Square) for longer than anyone could remember. The stone dowager had massive outer walls pierced by a dark, narrow, labyrinthine passage, guarded by heavy wooden doors designed to keep marauding horsemen out. In the event of a dacoit managing to breech the door, he was sure to lose his head in the dark alley.

In actual fact, the fortalice had never been tested by anything more than a clap of thunder or an odd hailstorm. Now in its dotage with crumbling plaster and beams ravaged by woodworm, it was called upon to resist an assault by the departing Muslim neighbours who doused the entrance doors with kerosene and set them alight. The boards proved equal to the task and withstood the ram and the flame, vindicating the faith of the long-gone builder, great grandfather Ram Dhan. Life for this *haweli* had, however, come full circle and soon after peace had descended on the land, its timbers buckled and it came crashing down – all except its façade, which continued to defy gravity and pretend to the outsiders that nothing was amiss.

A handful of *babus* who came to Kenya in the 1920s onwards had little intention of pursuing a long career with the railways. They merely wanted to use their job as a stepping-stone to a learned profession. A few tried but even fewer succeeded.

Mr Sham Lall Gajree, a young single minded *Karani*, started at the very bottom. He first read for London Matriculation and then accountancy. He had a long and successful career as an independent accountant until he became a casualty of the changing political climate and was forced into joining the exodus of Indians to the United Kingdom. The most outstanding of this select bunch, however, was another bright-eyed Punjabi teenager who arrived in Kenya in 1923.

This was economically a difficult year for Kenya and for Indians in particular. The Railways, the chief employer of Indians, had reduced their wages by a whopping one-sixth. The job market was chockfull and for immigrants there was precious little chance of finding employment. It was amid such austerity that Chanan Singh, a fifteen-year-old, arrived in Nairobi.

His father, Daulat Ram, a carpenter by trade, was determined to educate his only surviving son, but during Chanan Singh's time at school, the sword of Democles was hanging over his head. It fell in 1921 when his father pleaded poverty and withdrew him from school. Chanan Singh decided to seek his fortune in Kenya but while marking time he was married off to a damsel named Bhagwanti.

The first few weeks in Nairobi were excruciatingly long for the couple had no money and no prospects of a job. Chanan Singh's luck changed when he met a 'kind Indian' at Arya Samaj, who helped him to get a job as a locomotive fitter at 120 shillings per month. The aspiring *'karani'* had to work as a *fundi*. His ego was bruised but his spirit unscathed. It was a matter of *marta kya na karta* (any port in a storm). However, before he could start he had to demonstrate his ability by making a hexagonal iron nut. Chanan Singh, who could not even handle a file, was beaten, but an old fitter took pity on him and produced a nut and Chanan Singh got the job.

The Locomotive Fitter Class 'C' struggled with nuts and bolts for seven months before he was given clerical work, but on the books he remained an artisan. The arrival of a new European foreman from West Africa changed all that. The two were drawn together by a common interest in Omar Khayyam and Tagore. A word in the right ear and Chanan Singh was made Clerk Grade 'C' at a salary of 120 shillings per month. [175]

Although his parents were orthodox Hindus (Sanatanists) Chanan Singh followed the teachings of Arya Samaj. In 1926 he was sent to Nakuru, where he became the first secretary of the newly established Arya Samaj. My father, Durga Dass Dhupa, remembers the single mindedness of his friend who would spend all his spare time burning the midnight oil. One or two of the other railway men tried to follow the same path. *"But while we succumbed to the rigours of everyday life, Chanan Singh continued unabated,"* recollected Daulat Ram Khanna. [176] In 1940, he obtained a degree in Economics from the University of London. Four years later, he was called to the Bar by the Honourable Society of Lincoln's Inn. In 1945, the Railway lost its 'Senior Clerk, Special Grade' and Chanan Singh embarked on his third career as an Advocate of the High Court of Kenya.

---

[175] Ref: p108 – Bharati, Agehananda – *The Asians in East Africa.* Nelson Hall Company. Chicago

There appears to be no truth in the statement that Chanan Singh sold clothing and other merchandise 'from house to house'. I have checked this with many sources including Joginder Bhangu, his son-in-law.

[176] Khanna, Daulat Ram. Personal communication.

220

The practice of law did not consume all his energies. He became the editor of RAILMAN, SOL and FORWARD. He wrote editorials for the COLONIAL TIMES, a radical weekly newspaper whose courageous publishers and editors such as Mr Girdhari Lal Vidyarthi, Mr D.K. Sharda and Mr Haroun Ahmed were sent to prison for speaking out against the injustices of the colonial system. He wrote articles for the AMRIT BAZAAR PATRIKA and the HINDU. He was the author of the Immigration Bill and wrote: A SHORT HISTORY OF THE GANDHI MEMORIAL ACADEMY SOCIETY.

As an advocate, he was involved in many celebrated cases. He acted on behalf of Makhan Singh, the fiery father of Trade Unionism in Kenya, and stopped the government from deporting him. During the Second World War, regulations were passed by the Kenyan Government which prevented entry into Kenya without a permit. Those who had a permit had to do a specified job for a specified employer. After the war, a new Immigration Law was, however, passed and the wartime regulations lapsed. Under the old regulations, a young educated Indian was allowed into the country to work as an artisan. After the war, however, Makhan Singh was found to be working as a clerk with a local bank and he was prosecuted for contravening the wartime regulations.

Chanan Singh argued that the power to punish for infringement of the old regulations died with them. He quoted decided cases arising from laws passed during the Napoleonic Wars of the early nineteenth century and the laws passed during the First World War. When a permanent law is repealed, the infringement of it can be punished after the repeal under the general law of the country, but a law that expires by the effluxion of the time leaves nothing behind. At the end of the argument, the Magistrate remarked, *"This has been a veritable law lecture"*. Makhan Singh was acquitted.

Around 1950, Chanan Singh inflicted a stunning defeat on the Colonial Government when ex-Senior Chief Koinange was prosecuted and acquitted for his third attempt at growing coffee on his farm.

In another case, Chanan Singh had to lock horns with the police. Four Indian children were charged with stealing spent bullet cases from the scrapyard of a local firm. A large number of these shells had spilt out of bags which were lying against a fence and slipped into a drain. The children playing in an adjacent field had found and collected them.

221

The police charged them with theft alleging that they had taken handfuls of the cases from the bags by passing their hands through a gap between the ground and the fence. The children insisted that the police story was a lie. The most damaging witness, as far as the defence was concerned, was the European Assistant Superintendent of Police who stated that there were no bullet cases lying about and that the boys must have stolen them from the bags lying against the fence inside the scrapyard.

During cross-examination, Chanan Singh asked the officer when he had last visited the area. He replied *"This morning."* There was every risk now that the children would be found guilty and flogged or fined. Chanan Singh decided to forego lunch and as he could not afford a car he had to walk to the scene of the crime to confirm that his young clients were telling the truth. When the court assembled in the afternoon, Chanan Singh made an application that the court visit the scene. The Magistrate could not see the point of the application when a senior officer had given definite evidence. The application was denied but the Magistrate promised to reconsider the application if it was made before the court adjourned at the end of the day.

A re-application was granted and the court travelled to the scene. The Magistrate was terribly angry when he picked a handful of shell cases from the railway line and saw a large number lying in the drain. He stated that he could never have imagined that a senior police officer would lie. He announced at the scene that the boys could consider themselves acquitted and that he would give formal judgement the following morning.[177]

As a political entrepreneur, the former railway *babu* served the nation as a member of the Legislative Council of Kenya from 1952 to 1956. In 1960, he became the Founder President of the multi-racial Kenya Freedom Party, which campaigned for immediate independence on the basis of one-man-one vote. He was re-elected to the Legislative Council in 1961.

Following independence in 1963, he became a Specially Elected Member of Parliament and was appointed as the Parliamentary Secretary to the Prime Minister, *Mzee* Kenyatta.Since, however, the Africans did not want an Asian to hold such a high post, he was promoted to a Judge in the Kenya Supreme Court.

---

[177] Ref: Chanan Singh papers (unpublished)

Justice Chanan Singh.

Some newcomers, such as Anderji Odhavji Nathwani and Mahasha Inder Singh Gill, used the railway as a spring-board to launch themselves into business and made a great success of it. In fact, Nathwani used the railway as a refuge when his first flirtation with business failed. This was a recycling enterprise, the first of its kind in East Africa, which depended on buying empty bottles, *Chupa Tufa* and old gunny sacks and reselling these at a profit.

Young Nathwani moved to Nairobi at the turn of the century and joined the railway as a cashier. He was fond of reminiscing that everything in Kenya was Indian. The Governor of Kenya was also the Governor of Bombay, the currency was the Indian rupee and the first bank to arrive was the Bank of India. The first private medical doctor in Nairobi was an Indian from Goa. Dr Rosendo Ayres Ribeiro set up his practice in a tent on the very site where the famous Whitehouse Bakery was later built. Soon he was in great demand by the sick of all communities. The tubby doctor became a familiar sight in Nairobi as he did his daily rounds atop a tame zebra. Eventually he moved into the Indian Bazaar (now Biashara Street) in premises built out of packing cases in which drug supplies had been sent from England. When bubonic plague broke out in 1902 it was Dr Ribeiro who arrived on his zebra and declared *hic incept pestis* (here is beginning of the plague) to confirm the diagnosis in two Somali men.[178] The Medical Officer of Health panicked and ordered the evacuation of Indian Bazaar and had it burned to the ground. As a result, Dr Ribeiro lost his surgery, but he received a domestic plot near the station as compensation. There he built a spanking new *Dak bungalow* on stilts from which he conducted his practice. In 1903, the Government gave him a concession of sixteen acres behind Victoria Street (now Moi Street) in recognition of services rendered over his report on the plague.[179]

---

[178] Ref: p44 – Trzebinski, Errol – *The Kenya Pioneers.* Heinemann. London 1985

[179] Ref: p44 – Trzebinski, Errol *The Kenya Pioneers.*

**Dr Rosendo Ribeiro on zebra
making his rounds in Nairobi – Circa 1905.**

The railway provided Nathwani with a steady income but it did not satisfy his yearning for trade. Throughout this period he kept his eyes open and had both ears to the ground. He forsook the railway as soon as an opportunity knocked at his door and he opened Nairobi's first petrol station. The project turned out to be a gold mine and it remained the busiest petrol station in Kenya for many years.

Success in business gave Nathwani an opportunity to devote a lot of his energy to religious and community welfare. In 1950, he was elected the President of the Arya Samaj in Nairobi, and ten years later, he became the President of Lohana community. The octogenarian never forgot his humble beginnings and as a reminder of his earlier struggles he kept *Chupa Tufa* (empty bottles) as his telegraphic address until his death in 1966.

Inder Singh Gill, another landiwalla who reached the pinnacle of his profession, had arrived in Kenya only a year earlier than Justice Chanan Singh. They had uncanny similarities in their younger years.

Both came from a dirt-poor background and a small village near Ludhiana in Punjab. Both were lucky to have received a good education for those days in Arya Vedic Schools and both had no difficulty in passing Standard B (third middle). Although they were both named Singh, neither of them were Sikhs. They were, in fact, Arya Samajists. In each case, they found employment with the railways at 120 shillings a month. Both were married as teenagers before leaving for Kenya.

Inder Singh Gill found a job as a teacher in his village of Jundali at Rs 13 a month. Eager to improve his lot, he wanted to follow his uncle, Nahar Singh, to Kenya but he was advised to cool his heels until the right opportunity presented itself. This came when he met Mr Mathra Dass, an accountant with the railways in Nairobi, who promised to take him along to Kenya at the end of his home leave. In fact, Nahar Singh and Mathra Dass were great friends and leading members of Arya Samaj in Nairobi.

With a loan of Rs 300 from his father, Inder Singh met his companion at Ludhiana Station and the two set out for East Africa. The trip as a deck passenger was rough and uncomfortable but that was how most Indians travelled in those days – a small price for reaching the Promised Land. Inder Singh arrived unannounced at his uncle's house in Nairobi in 1922.

Like for many other young men, a career with the railroad was Godsend. He came under the wing of Fakir Chand and was accepted as an unpaid trainee telegraphist. His mentor was Ram Karan Mayor, a very bright young nephew of Fakir Chand, who was working for the Post Office while waiting for a better job with the railways. He wrote "...*I gave training in telegraphy, Morse signal at Kisumu station, a facility arranged by Mr Fakir Chand Mayor, to Messrs. Inder Singh Gill, Dharam Dev Mayor, Vidya Sagar Suda,*

Farangi Lal and others who were looking for jobs and were unemployed".[180] This training was undertaken in his spare time and without remuneration. Once the Morse signal was mastered, Gill and others were hired as assistant station masters at 120 shillings a month and posted all along the line. In 1925, Fakir Chand sent his bright *charge d'affaires*, Ram Karan, who had by now joined the railways, and Inder Singh, on a 'special duty' to Kampala. This was to clear up a perennial problem of horrendous congestion of goods during the busy cotton season.

Inder Singh served at Molo, Elburgon, Gilgil and Njoro stations, which many other Indians tried to avoid. For here, the settler presence was strong and their manner was too often abrupt and their demands unreasonable. During Inder Singh's posting at Njoro, Lord Delamare was impressed by his easy manner and efficiency and the two developed a friendship. *"Yes, we knew each other,"* recollected Mr Gill modestly many years later. Little did Delamare realise that the young jat with a white turban and a flowing black beard would one day become a principal player in the economy of East Africa.

Inder Singh's big break came in 1926 when he was posted to Nsenji Station in Uganda. This was a railway man's goldmine for a lot of produce, especially cotton, was loaded onto railway wagons here. The ginners rewarded the station master handsomely for his co-operation in getting the rolling stock in time and prompt dispatch of their precious crop. So lucrative was this posting, and such was the clamour to go there, that most station masters were only allowed to stay for a maximum of two to three years. The ebullient young man was soon delving into saw milling and cotton ginning. He had such a good nose for business that within a few years he became economically almost at par with Seth Nanji Kalidas Mehta of Lugazi and Mulji Madhvani of Kakira – two of the most prominent businessmen in East Africa.

To judge a man purely by his financial success is vulgar. Inder Singh possessed wealth but he did not allow it to possess him. He was kind, generous and full of humility – and he never forgot his past. He was proud of his Arya Samajist education. At one of his visits to Arya Samaj in Nairobi he was introduced to the congregation as Sardar Inder Singh Gill. He reminded the speaker of

---

[180] Ref: p34 – Mayor, Ram Karan – *Memoirs of Ram Karan Mayor.* London 1984

his Arya Vedic educational background and said that he preferred to be called a Mahashay.[181]

In 1948 he built 'Gill House', a five-storey building occupying a whole city block. This skyscraper became a landmark in Nairobi for many years to come. The diversification of business interests showed his foresight, for in 1972, along with the rest of the Indian population of Uganda, he was expelled by the despot, Idi Amin. Inder Singh lost more than 70 million shillings. Life for the millionaire landiwalla had come a full circle, for he returned to Nairobi, where he had arrived half a century earlier, with nothing but a twinkle in his eye. He acknowledged to his last day *"It was all because of my uncle, Nahar Singh that I am what I am today. I still keep his portrait in my office".[182]*

Another group of railway men were those whose education in India was cut short for a variety of reasons and circumstances forced them to emigrate. Not uncommonly, the sole breadwinner had to share his meagre pickings with his parents, friends and relations who followed him to Africa. However, men such as guard Naginder Singh, station master Chain Singh, locoman Din Muhamed, Durga Dass Dhupa and numerous others had a dream and a desire to provide for their children what was so cruelly denied to them. They led a frugal lifestyle. Not for them the pleasures of mundungus, booze, *charas* or even a cheap movie. They saved every cent in order to send their children abroad for higher education.

Education and a professional qualification, however, did not guarantee a job on return to Kenya. The *bwanas* controlled everything and were unwilling to cede an inch of ground. Meritocracy was a mirage and the yardstick was still the colour of one's skin. When Dhruv Dhupa returned from Birmingham in 1962, after a period of fourteen years, during which he not only became the first Kenya born person to become a Member of the Royal College of Obstetricians and Gynaecologists, but was also voted the 'Surgeon of the Decade' at Dudley Road Hospital, he discovered the truth. He had merely crossed the moat of the colonial fortress – the ramparts, tall and strong, still barred his way.

---

[181] Personal communication with Dr. Dhruv Vrat Dhupa who was present at the time.

[182] Ref: p187 – Salvadori, Cynthia – *We came in Dhows.* Vol I. Paperchase Kenya Ltd

When he applied to join Kenya Medical Services, the then Director, Dr Fendal, told him *"Kenya did not need any specialists".*[183] This was *déjà vu,* for his elder brother, Dev Vrat, was given the same excuse when he returned from Edinburgh after he became a dentist in 1955. Dr Fendal advised Dhruv Dhupa to pursue general duties at the Mombasa General Hospital.

Luckily for Dr Dhupa, one arm of the East African community, Tanganyika, had already achieved independence a year earlier, and at the behest of Professor Rendel-Short of Makerere University, he joined Tanganyika Medical Services as the Chief Consultant to the Dar es Salaam group of hospitals of Muhimbili and Ocean Road.

His appointment facilitated the return of Tanganyika students as interns after their training at Makerere and in time he made a significant contribution to the establishment of the Medical School at the University of Dar es Salaam. Due to his organisational skills and proficiency the number of deliveries at the Ocean Road Hospital increased from 6,000 in 1962 to 23,000 in 1972 with hardly any additional facilities – 'nothing short of a miracle that reasonable standards still persisted'[184]. Muhimbili became the only hospital in the sub-Sahara, excluding South Africa, where radium was available for treating cervical cancer and patients were often referred from Kenya. This prompted a Kenyan politician to raise a question in the Parliament of Kenya seeking justification 'for a Kenyan specialist's invaluable contribution to Tanzania's medical services' while Kenya badly needed experts.

The black politicians in Tanzania did not always appreciate a good thing when they saw it. They were just as prejudiced as the colonialist masters they once complained against. The arrival of a black Tanzanian doctor with a specialist degree, but experience only as a registrar in England, changed the equation. He was appointed as a consultant and soon afterwards was unashamedly made to leapfrog over senior specialists who had no inkling of these changes until they arrived at work on Monday morning to find the door signs changed. Although Dr Dhupa was not affected by this upheaval, the writing was on the wall. The harassment of Asians and

---

[183] MEDICUS: November 1996. Magazine of the Kenya Medical Association, Vol 15, No 1

[184] MEDICUS: November 1996. Magazine of the Kenya Medical Association, Vol 15, No 1

nationalisation of their property was the last straw. He crossed over to Kenya by car with nothing but a shirt on his back to embark on a career as a private obstetrician and gynaecologist in Nairobi.

It did not take him long to build a large consulting practice because of his reputation of caring for his patients 'with a religious fervour'[185]. He had an unflinching zeal to better the lot of the medical fraternity and when he was the chairman of the Kenya Medical Association he initiated his schemes for the welfare of doctors' families and medical insurance for all physicians. As a trustee of the Arya Samaj and as a Rotarian, he devoted much time to charitable projects and to uphold the Rotary's motto of 'Service Above Self'.

Two other locally born and raised landiwallas distinguished themselves in the field of politics. They were Gurdial Singh and Shafiq Arain. The two had remarkably parallel careers. They were both at the heart of turmoil in Uganda for almost three decades and both achieved the distinction of representing their country as diplomatic agents of the highest rank.

Both were born in 1933 and came to Kampala as a result of their fathers' transfer to Uganda from Kenya. Gurdial's father, Chain Singh, became the station master at Mbulamuti while Shafiq's father, Din Mohamed, worked as a locoman in Kampala. Both young men had their high school education at Government Indian High School in Old Kampala.

Life for Gurdial, away from home at the tender age of fourteen, could not have been easy but he thrived in spite of this. He shared my desk at school and I remember him as a self-reliant, confident young fellow with an intense desire to excel. His intelligence, affability and organisational skills made him very popular with his peers. He loved organising sports events and making speeches. At a trophy presentation in 1948 he spoke so well that it prompted my father to observe, *"This young man will go very far"*. No-one was surprised when he graduated from school with first grade and five distinctions in the Senior Cambridge examination and chose a career in law. Gurdial Singh returned to Uganda in 1958 after being called to the bar at Lincoln's Inn, London. He set up his shingle in Kampala and was soon dabbling in politics.

Shafiq Arain was a good sportsman. He distinguished himself in Field Hockey and Cricket and played for Uganda Asians in the

---

[185] MEDICUS: November 1996

prestigious Triangular Cricket Tournaments. He too went to England to study and obtained a degree in journalism from the University of Nottingham.

In 1958, a number of like-minded radical Asian intellectuals such as Gurdial Singh, Shafiq Arain, Rajat Neogy, Natoo Karia and Dr Muljibhai Patel, formed the Uganda Action Group (UAG). Later, these 'Young Turks'[186] as Sir Amarnath Maini called them, in association with militant Africans, were instrumental in the formation of the Uganda People's Party (UPC) and Apollo Milton Obote's rise to power. Gurdial Singh and Shafiq Arian worked tirelessly with Obote to put forward UPC's demands for a common roll and universal adult franchise.

Both Gurdial and Shafiq reaped generous rewards for their support for the President following Uganda's independence in October 1962. Both served on many statutory bodies as advisors, chairmen, ministers and representatives of the Government. In 1971, Gurdial became the deputy Mayor of Kampala. Shafiq served as an MP from 1962 to 1971.

Obote's regime was, however, beginning to come apart at the seams. His relations with Major-General Idi Amin were on a collision course. He managed to antagonise the Israelis who were training his army and police. The British, too, wanted to see his downfall because his socialist posture and foreign policy ran counter to British interests. His government's resolve to expel all Asians holding British passports made matters worse. On 25 January 1971, Obote was deposed by Amin in a *coup d'etat* while he was out of the country attending at a Summit Conference of Commonwealth leaders in Singapore.

The Annual General Meeting of the Uganda Law Society on 19 February 1972, over which Gurdial presided, was to prove a very decisive hour for him. It would test his principles and the strength of his spirit.

Mr Felix Onama, a West Niler like Amin and his co-conspirator in bringing down Obote's Government, wanted to inflict a *coup de grace* on the fallen leader. Onama got an Indian Advocate, Anil Clerk,[187] to bring a motion welcoming the *coup d'etat*.

---

[186] Ref: p113 – Gregory, Robert G. – *Quest for Equality: Asian Politics in East Africa 1900-1967.* Orient Longman Ltd. New Delhi 110 029

[187] Clerk, Anil was murdered by Idi Amin

Gurdial was aware of a whispering campaign in the Law Society and the country at large accusing him of treasonable intent of sabotaging the motion. It was imperative that he seize the opportunity of exonerating himself of such grave allegations. Gurdial, a man of principle, asked the question: *"Was the law Society, as a Law Society, competent to accept or reject, welcome or unwelcome, a Government of Uganda? If it was, then where was the legal authority or precedence for that competence?"*[188]

It turned out that there was neither legal authority nor precedent for it. In any case, argued Gurdial, the mode of ascent of Amin's regime was known, but its policy was yet unknown. The motion was never carried. Gurdial ruled it out of order. He informed the meeting that the Law Society could still pass the motion subject to voting him out of the chair. When that motion was brought, it too failed.

The sound of the warning had hardly died down when Amin's *modus operandi* was unveiled in a manner never to be forgotten. Outstanding advocates such as Godfrey Binaisa QC, Wilkinson QC, John Kazzora and Chris Mboijana, fled the country. *"As a result of the stand I took,"* writes Gurdial Singh, *"I made a judgement in my own context and left Uganda a few days later being the first Asian to leave Amin's Uganda well before eighteen months when Amin expelled all Asians from Uganda in August 1973"*.[189]

Why did Amin decide to expel the Asians from Uganda? One of the reasons, it has been suggested, was that he was spurned by an Asian girl. Secondly, he was unable to put right any of the eighteen points given as the reasons for overthrowing Obote, so he turned on the only community with money and property that he could plunder to give to black Ugandans. Thirdly, the failure of Asians to integrate socially with Africans made them a popular target. Lastly, Asian reluctance to become Ugandan citizens rankled the blacks and by expelling these British citizens from Uganda, Amin would, as he later put it, *'be teaching the British a lesson they would never forget'*.[190]

---

[188] Proceedings of the Uganda Law Society. Annual General Meeting, 19 February, 1972

[189] Personal letter from Gurdial Singh to the author, dated 30 July 2003

[190] Ref: p93 – Mutibwa, Phares – *Uganda Since Independence.* Hurst and Company. 38 King Street, London WC2E 8JT

As a result of their expulsion, 70,000 Asians not only lost money and property running into billions of shillings, but were subjected to groping, beatings and the snatching of their personal effects as they proceeded to various points of departure. This exodus was followed by an unholy scramble to grab their shops and houses by jubilant Ugandans including top officers in the civil service, and sadly, even the teachers and professors at the University of Makerere.

While Obote was cooling his heels in Tanzania and plotting his return under the benign shadow of *Mwalimu* Julius Nyerere, both Shafiq and Gurdial continued to support his cause. The three of them returned to Uganda from Dar es Salaam on 27 May 1980. Obote won the subsequent election and on the evening of Saturday, 11 December 1980 he was sworn in to his second presidency of Uganda.

For their unflinching support, the President rewarded them handsomely. Gurdial Singh was made the High Commissioner for Uganda to India and Shafiq Arain was appointed as the High Commissioner to London.

President Obote with Gurdial Singh and Shafiq Arian at Bushenyl – Ankole. May 27th 1980. Day one on return to Post – Amin Uganda from Dar-es-salaam.

Gurdial Singh presenting credentials as High Commissioner of Uganda to Honourable SanjivaReddy, President of India – February 1981.

Shafiq Arain, High Commissioner for Uganda on his way to present his credentials to the Queen at Buckingham Palace. February 18th 1981.

Some of the non-railway Asians were so involved in the Railway Institute activities that they came to be known as 'honorary landiwallas'. Only one woman managed to earn this designation. She was Sugrabai, the wife of Haider, the grandson of Seth Allidina Visram, the uncrowned 'King of Uganda'. She and her husband came regularly to play tennis at the club in Kampala. Since the men

236

were reluctant to play with a woman, it fell on teenagers like Shafiq Arain and myself to become her tennis partners.

I remember Sugra as a vivacious, self-confident woman. She would play tennis dressed in a simple white sari but still managed to turn all the heads. Quite simply, she was the most beautiful woman in Uganda. She was a socialite who took a very active interest in women's issues and their well being. She became the founder member of the Uganda Council of Women, the Muslim Women's Association, the YMCA and the Family Planning Group.

It was inevitable that she would be wooed by political leaders to join their party. In the 1950s when Uganda was heading towards independence and the Asians were deeply involved in the political fervent, the Baganda King asked for her help. She endeared herself to the Baganda people by addressing a large crowd in their own *Luganda* dialect. They made her a member of the *Mamba* Clan and she was co-opted as a member of *Lukiko*, the Kabaka's Parliament – an honour never bestowed on an Asian before. She joined the Kabaka Yekka Party in 1962 and was elected to the Ugandan Parliament the same year. A coalition government followed with 'King Freddie' as the President and Milton Obote as the Prime Minister.

In 1967, Obote introduced a new constitution which vested power in the office of the President. He then tried to dragoon the MPs into accepting a one-party parliament. *"He called a parliament session"* relates Sugrabai, *"where he asked each and every MP to swear allegiance to his new constitution. One by one, these politicians gave in until it came to my turn. I refused to join the UPC, which by then was facing allegations of misappropriating large amounts of public funds. I told Obote that he should go to the people and ask them before trampling on our constitution"*. She then walked out amid loud cheers and vowed never to return to parliament. Later that year, Obote abolished tribal kingdoms and the subsequent uprising was put down by Obote's commander, Idi Amin.[191]

.

---

[191] Ref: Visram, Sugrabai. Personal communication

237

Sugra Namubiru Visram.

The coup in January 1971 merely replaced the despot Obote with a blood-thirsty brute – Idi Amin. After killing thousands of members of tribes loyal to Obote, he turned his attention to Asians who he accused of 'milking the nation'. After announcing that all Asians were to be expelled, he changed his mind and decided to spare those with Ugandan passports. Sugra who was a Ugandan citizen fully intended to stay, but a dramatic incident changed all that.

"One day in 1972," says Sugrabai, *"he (Amin) ordered all the Asians in Uganda to come to a mass registration at the airport. We went out of fear. We lined up and Idi Amin with his six-foot four-inch frame, postured around in a physically intimidating way as his people counted these petrified families. He saw me and turned on his heel. 'You,' he said. 'I've been looking for you and your husband.' My heart sank and thought this was it for me. But he spared us with a menacing look and walked away. On that night we decided to leave. I was 49 years old".* [192]

---

[192] Ref: Visram, Sugrabai. Personal communication

Idi Amin – President of Uganda.

At heart, Sugrabai remained a Ugandan and vowed that one day she would return – *inshalla*. This came to pass in 1994. The new President, Mr Museveni, invited her to meet him. There was a spirit of reconciliation on both sides and when he asked her to become his advisor and help him in rebuilding the country, she was only too happy to accept.

Sugrabai and I met by chance at a luncheon at a mutual friend's place in Surrey in 1997, almost 50 years since I had played tennis with her in Kampala. She looked slimmer than I had imagined and her face looked longer and leaner. She cut a fine figure in a simple sari and was as charming as ever. She was quite keen to talk about her life in Uganda but was at some pain to give credit to her late husband with whom she had fallen in love at a tender age, and for whom she and fifteen members of her immediate family had changed their religion from Ithnasheri to Ismaili. *"He was my best friend and advisor and stood behind me at every curve and bend and supported me through some difficult times in Uganda."[193]*

Mrs Sugrabai Haider Ali Visram now lives in Putney.

---

[193] Ref: Visram, Sugrabai. Personal communication

Sugra and her husband, Haider Visram, with Freddie the Kabaka of Buganda.

Many of the young men who started at the lowest rung of the ladder had long and distinguished careers. With their diligence and tenacity they managed to rise through the ranks until they reached the top of the hierarchy and were awarded 'European Grades'.

Mr R.N. Dhiri worked at various wayside stations where he impressed his superiors with his efficiency and pleasant manner, and in the late 1940s, he was promoted to the post of Station Master at Nairobi. He returned to Chandigarh in India where he became the founder and editor of SOOD SANDESH, a popular newsletter in Punjab. Mr Abdulla Mir, a *karani*, worked his way up the ladder until he became the Chief Clerk at the headquarters in Nairobi. Mr D.D. Mayor who started his career with a thrashing from an English *memsahib* at Kisumu Station, ended his days in Mombasa as the first Indian Traffic Superintendent.

Both Mr Mir and Mr Mayor received an MBE for their loyal services. Mr Ram Karan Mayor, who showed promise from the beginning, retired as the Chief Goods Clerk. He also devoted a lifetime to the good of the Hindu community and promotion of Arya Samaj and its religious and educational activities. He became the first and only railwayman to publish his memoirs and that, too, in English.

Ramkaran Mayor– 1901 to 1997.

The majority of the landiwallas were ordinary folk. Most had only been as far as the next village before setting forth to a distant land, oblivious of where it was and what they would find. There, with shouts of *Harambee*,[194] to co-ordinate their efforts, the men used the strength of their minds and bodies to undertake the gargantuan task to move the trees, rocks and rails until they had built a steel spine to unite the land from the coast to the core of Africa. They, along with their black and white brethren, are forgotten, unnamed, untraceable and unsung men who had ventured out to build a railway but ended up in building a nation. Heroes, all of them.

---

[194] *Harambee.* Derived from Hare Amba, an Indian goddess. It is said that the coolies would invoke her name as they co-ordinated their efforts when moving the rails and other heavy objects. It has come to mean 'pull together' and *Harambee* was used as a rallying cry by President Kanyatta.

Later, *Harambee* was adopted by self-help movement as a money-raising system for local self-help projects such as schools, dispensaries and community centres.

The concept was abused by some ministers, officials and individuals to bully businessmen, colleagues and even neighbours in order to extract funds for their own benefit.

Chapter 7

The Killing Fields

**But here at the end is only a hide,
a horn, and a carcase...**

Winston Churchill[195]

To the primitive man, hunting was, and still remains, a way of survival. It is a means to fill his stomach, cover his body and provide shelter for his family. His very survival depended upon his skill and ingenuity to trap, capture and kill the quarry. The animal had a sporting chance to escape and the hunter a chance to kill or be killed. This duel between man and beast did not alter the balance of nature as man was just one of the factors in the constant cycle of life and death in the vast wilderness. The invention of gunpowder, however, changed this equation forever.

The closing of the nineteenth century and the dawn of the twentieth century brought a hunter of a different sort to the shores and the hinterland of British East Africa. This was the 'White Hunter', a licensed killer, often masquerading as a sportsman. No more were the 'big five' and the great herds faced with a snare, spear or speeding arrow but a killing machine with weapons of mass murder. The purpose of the hunt was not the need to survive or to compete for land, or even the lure of the wild, but a lust for trophies and ivory. The halls, corridors and lounges of rich homes from Africa to Europe to America were filled with stuffed animals, skulls and heads mounted on wooden shields.

Ironically, hunting increasingly became the preserve of the rich in Europe and America. In India, too, the kings, *nawabs* and landed gentry safely sat in their tree houses or *howdahs* on elephant backs while the beaters drove the game towards a hail of cartouche. They got their sense of machismo by slaughtering the innocent before retiring to their hunting lodges amid cries of *shahbash* (bravo).

---

[195] Ref: p12 – Churchill, Winston – *My African Journey.* Hodder and Stoughton. London 1908

In Africa, however, it was also ivory that fuelled the desire to decimate the elephant herds.

Maharaja of Gwalior

Ivory, with its reward of gold, was a temptation that few could resist. In 1900, the price was £1,000 per ton.[196] The finest ivory came from the Protectorate and Zanzibar was the great centre of this trade. The blacks joined the whites in their grisly safaris and delivered the booty to middlemen who sold it to Balauchi, Arab and Swahili traders.

The most notorious (some say famous) of the elephant hunters was Arthur Neumann, who came to be called Bwana Nyama (Swahili for meat) because he always tied it in a fly-proof muslin cloth whilst out in the bush, a precaution which puzzled the Africans.[197] He set out of Mombasa on a journey to the north of Mount Kenya with an entourage of 50 Swahili porters. He returned in triumph three years later with his porters jumping, dancing and showing off tusks to the crowd lining the narrow streets. All

[196] Ref: p25 – Trzebinski, Errol – The Kenya Pioneers. Heinemann, London
[197] Ref: p171 – Meinertzhagen, Richard – *Kenya Diary 1902-1906.* Eland Books. London 1957

returned safely except for his personal servant, Shebane, who was killed by a crocodile, and his gun bearer, Square Face, who was mauled by a lion.

Another hunter was Karamoja Bell, who hunted in the Karamoja area on the Kenya-Uganda-Sudan border where the country was black with elephants. He is said to have shot a thousand elephants and returned 'with over 14,000 lb of ivory – all excellent stuff'.[198]

The quest for ivory did not stop with the killing of elephants. Many natives were murdered in the process. Two South Africans, Smith and Vincent, who were denied land in Kenya, turned to ivory and persuaded a Dr Atkinson to join them. The three of them were also supplying the Africans with gun powder, bullets and caps for guns, known to Africans as *'Fataki'*. During a bargaining session in the north of Kenya which was not going his way, the exasperated Dr Atkinson gathered the Rendile around a keg of gun powder giving the impression that it was full of Maria Theresa dollars, the Abyssinian currency. He lit the fuse and walked away as if to relieve himself. The blast killed most of the unsuspecting Africans. The perpetrators left the scene of carnage with the ivory which was carried by their 200 porters. The three were arrested and charged with dacoity and murder.

The African witnesses refused to give evidence for fear of repercussions. The all-European jury, according to Jackson, 'would not convict the men; the plea was fixed "because they feared they were going to be attacked"'.[199] Atkinson retired to his land at Karura. Smith and Vincent were deported to Bombay and once again India was saddled with British East Africa's white dross.[200]

The killing of game was not without its opponents. Many Hindus regarded this practice as demonic. Ptolemy, King of Egypt, tried to persuade the elephant hunters to refrain from killing by offering great rewards, but failed. Sir Charles Eliot held unfashionable but frank opinions in his dislike for hunting. He wrote, *"The temper which makes a man who sees a beautiful antelope walking in its pride across a plain long to bring his rifle up*

---

[198] Ref: p271 – Bell, W.D.M. – *The Wanderings of an Elephant Hunter.* Neville Spearman. London 1923

[199] Jackson, Frederick – *Early Days in East Africa.* Edward Arnold. London 1930 (Jackson to Hill 4.8.1903.F.O.3/720)

[200] Ref: p145 – Foran, W. Robert– *Cuckoo in Kenya.* Hutchinson. London 1936

to his shoulder and convert it into a bleeding mass of lifeless flesh seems to me devilish".[201] The Protectorate Government eventually put an end to the ivory hunters by restricting the number of elephants each man could kill. The end of this era, however, saw the beginning of a period of killings of another kind.

Safaris suddenly became all the rage. Rich men and women began to hire experienced white hunters to shoot game for pleasure rather than profit. During the pre-war period, Kenya was replete with dignitaries who came to 'bag a lion' or mounted scientific expeditions to collect specimens for museums. The Kenyan authorities were cock-a-hoop and their welcome for the visitors was hotter than the Kenya sun, for these safaris not only generated enormous amounts of wealth and employment, but gave Kenya's need for a higher profile abroad a tremendous boost. As well, the locals hoped, that all the activity would result in inward investment. They were not disappointed.

On 17 March 1906, Nairobi was all dolled-up like an Indian bride and looked gorgeous, with arches and colourful bunting, for a very special occasion – the unveiling of a statue of Queen Victoria. The streets were lined with Masai and Kikuyu warriors to welcome the guest of honour, the Duke of Connaught, and his daughter, Princess Patricia.

The statue and magnificent surrounding gardens were a gift from an Indian named A.M. Jeevanjee to the town of Nairobi. Jeevanjee was a merchant, steamship owner, contractor and philanthropist. He is said to have built every railway station between Mombasa to Nairobi and beyond. He was a courageous man and a formidable opponent. In 1902 he started his own press and newspaper, the AFRICAN STANDARD, when no other paper would publish his reply to an insulting letter about Indians published in the local European press by a settler woman. His purpose achieved, he sold the newspaper – but kept the press. 'Jeevanjee remained a staunch supporter of the anti-colonial activists and his press was used later by Manilal Desai, Harry Thuku and Sitaram Achariar'.[202] Jeevanjee's political and anti-colonial activities took him to England and other countries and brought him in contact with

---

[201] Eliot, Sir Charles – *The East African Protectorate.* Edward Arnold, London 1905

[202] Ref: p12 – Salvadori, Cynthia – *We came in Dhows.* Vol II. Paperchase Kenya Ltd

Royalty, the Governors, General Smuts and Mahatma Gandhi in South Africa.

The organisers of the Duke's visit got into a bit of a tizzy when they realised that the Princess would be faced with a large number of naked Africans, for the Masai wore nothing but a *shuka*, a shift of americani tied over one shoulder. Accordingly, the Africans were provided with a red blanket each. The effect was excellent and would have taken care of any embarrassing moments but for a shower of rain just as the Royal party was taking their leave for the Government House, when every Masai automatically threw the blanket over his head to keep it dry.[203]

The Connaughts were the guests of a settler named Jim Elkington, who had made sure that his servants were up to snuff. All went well until the party moved into the garden to sip the best coffee that Kenya had to offer. Suddenly, out of nowhere, a tremendous Masai gentleman appeared – tremendous because the Masai typically tie a brick to their manhood during childhood to make it longer – bearing a note for the host. The Duke retrieved the situation by leaning over to Elkington and remarked, *"The Elkington livery I presume"*.[204] In fact, the Princess was not that naïve or squeamish and only a couple of weeks earlier she had spent a whole afternoon in Muhoroni photographing naked Kavirondo. Meinertzhagen, who was accompanying her on this photo shoot, thought of her as a 'particularly nice girl, with no frills and full of fun'.[205]

The Duke went out shooting on the Athi Plains and wounded a wildebeest which was not recovered. The Duke was very keen on securing the head, and as he left Nairobi the next day, he asked his companion Harrison to send him a wire telling him whether the beast had been recovered the next morning. Harrison wired to say that it had been found dead and that its head had been brought in. 'As a matter of fact, no trace of the ducal wildebeest could be found, and Harrison had to kill another, which is being sent to Clarence House as the ducal wildebeest'.[206]

---

[203] Ref: p122 – Trzebinski, Errol – *The Kenya Pioneers.* Heinemann, London 1985 (From a recording made by Freddy Ward about life in Nairobi from 1904)

[204] Ref: p122 – Trzebinski, Errol – *The Kenya Pioneers.* Heinemann, London 1985 (From a recording made by Freddy Ward about life in Nairobi from 1904)

[205] Ref: p289 – Meinertzhagen, Richard – *Kenya Diary 1904-1906*

[206] Ref: p301 – Meinertzhagen, Richard –*Kenya Diary 1904-1906*

A year later, Winston Churchill came to Kenya on a fact-finding tour in his capacity as the Under Secretary of State for the Colonies. He was a young man of 31 and his meteoric rise was without a doubt due to his political connections. His hosts were anxious to impress him, as they were with every high profile visitor, and what better way than to provide him with a lion.

Young Winston could not resist such temptation and his up train to Nairobi was shunted into a siding at Simba Station. He shot a *kifaro* (rhino) in the shadow of Mount Kilimanjaro. This 'unprovoked assault with murderous intent on a peaceful herbivore', left him cold and full of remorse and revealed the softer nature of the great man. He wrote, *"But here at the end is only a hide, a horn, and a carcase, over which the vultures have already begun to wheel"*.[207]

On arrival in Nairobi, Churchill soon discovered that the whites were obsessed with lions and politics. Their hospitality and the reputation of their adopted country somehow depended upon providing a lion. 'How to find, and having found, to kill a lion is the unvarying theme of conversation; and every journey is judged by a simple standard – lions or no lions'.[208] Churchill went looking for lions in the Embu district around Mount Kenya but failed to find any, his reward, a couple of wart-hogs.

Churchill found Kenya a cauldron of political and racial discord. The white man wanted it all. Only the brown man stood in his way, and he had the temerity to demand equal rights and challenge the usurper at every step. The black man had lost it all and neither the white man nor the brown man really cared.

The coolie was, in fact, in a position to legitimately challenge the master. His thrift, industry and sharp business acumen were enough to a large extent to 'clear the white man, as surely and as remorselessly as the brown rat extirpated the black from British soil'.[209]

Churchill conceded that 'it was the Sikh soldier who bore an honourable part in the conquest and pacification of these East African countries. It is the Indian trader who, penetrating and maintaining himself in all sorts of places to which no white man would go or in which no white man could earn a living, has more

---

[207] Ref: p11 – Churchill, Winston – *My African Journey*

[208] Ref: p16 – Churchill, Winston – *My African Journey*

[209] Ref: p33 – Churchill, Winston – *My African Journey*

251

than anyone else developed the early beginnings of trade and opened up the first slender means of communication. It was by Indian labour that the one vital railway on which everything else depends was constructed. It is the Indian banker who supplies perhaps the larger part of the capital yet available for business and enterprise, and to whom the white settlers have not hesitated to recur for financial aid. The Indian was here long before the British official. He may point to as many generations of useful industry on the coast and inland as the white settlers – especially the most recently arrived contingents from South Africa (the loudest against him of all) – can count years of residence. Is it possible for any Government with a scrap of respect for honest dealing between man and man, to embark upon a policy of deliberately squeezing out the native of India from regions in which he has established himself under every security of public faith? Most of all must we ask, is such a policy possible to the Government which bears sway over three hundred millions of our Indian Empire?"[210]

The safaris were usually grand affairs often reflecting the wealth and status of the visitor. Between 80 and 100 porters were needed for just two hunters – some for the sole purpose of carrying the supply of whiskey. Goan cooks were in great demand and an essential part of the entourage to provide the *bwana* and his party with the finest morsels for the eight-course meals deep in wildest Africa.

In 1909, ex-President Theodore Roosevelt rolled into Kenya on a scientific expedition to collect specimens for the Smithsonian. His was the most lavish safari ever undertaken. His outfit had 500 porters excluding gun bearers, trackers, personal servants, skinners, tent boys and cooks. The guns never stopped blazing and the great man personally killed 296 animals including 9 lions, 8 elephants, 13 rhinos (including a rarer white) and 6 buffaloes. In all, more than 1,000 animals of 164 different species were taken during ten months of a march from Mombasa to the upper Nile. Four tons of salt were needed for curing the skins. Even the rare and elusive antelope, Bongo, was not spared. Kermit, the President's son, shot a pair of them. Such wholesale devastation shocked the hosts and prompted Lord Cranworth to ask, *"Do those nine white rhinoceros ever cause*

---

[210] Ref: p34 – Churchill, Winston – *My African Journey*

ex-President Roosevelt a pang of conscience, or a restless night? I, for one, venture to hope so ". [211]

The fashionable pursuit of hunting according to a well known pioneer, Jack Riddell, 'was recognised as a perfect anodyne for those crossed in love. Then there were the unmentioned advantages. If getting away from it all meant leaving the wife at home, those men with a mistress could safely take her on a safari and the discretion of the white hunter escorting them could almost be guaranteed'.[212]

The Prince of Wales also joined in this carnage. He arrived in Kenya in 1928 with great aplomb and much fanfare. He was accompanied by his mistress, Gwladys Markham, a divorcee due to unfaithfulness on both sides. The Prince was immediately at home with the members of the Muthiaga Club, a den of iniquity notorious for alcoholism, adultery and the outrageous behaviour of the in-crowd. *"One night"* recollects Derek Erskine, *"Edward P was dancing with my wife and he suddenly lost his temper with the records which he said were the wrong kind, and I very much regret to say that aided and assisted by my wife, they picked up all the gramophone records and threw them through all the windows of the old ballroom... ".*[213] At another party at the same club, Greswold William, a well-known drugs dealer, was thrown out of the room for offering drugs to the Prince at the dinner table.

The Prince's safari was outfitted by the Ahmed brothers, Alibhai and Ahmed, who had vast experience in supplying such expeditions with uniforms which were churned out at short notice in their *duka* in the Indian Bazaar. This entitled them afterwards to carry the Royal feathers over their door with great pride.

While on safari near Arusha, His Royal Highness first met the white hunters Bror von Blixen and Denys Finch Hatton who helped him to bag his first lion. The expedition had to be abandoned at Dodoma in Tanganyika when the Prince was suddenly summoned to London due to the unexpected illness of his father Edward VII.

Poor Gwladys was abandoned in Kenya where she married the rich and powerful widower, Lord Delamare, three years before his

---

[211] Ref: p156 – Miller, Charles – The Lunatic Express. The Macmillan Company, New York, 1971

[212] Riddell – *The Duke's Safari*. Blackwoods Magazine, no 1533, July 1943

[213] Ref: p27 – Fox, James – *White Mischief*. Penguin Books, 1984

death in 1931. His wealth and connections catapulted her into the social and political mainstream and she became the Mayor of Nairobi. Like many Europeans in Kenya at the time, she was a racist. She claimed *"...to be in a measurable distance of an Indian coolie is very disagreeable"*. Even worse, she claimed that the Indians were so unhygienic that they constituted a health hazard.[214] She led the members of the Muthiaga Club to bar the Aga Khan. She also publicly insulted a member named Sybil Martineau for 'having African blood'.

Edward P returned to Kenya accompanied by another mistress, an American beauty named Thelma, a two-time divorcee. She fell in love with Kenya and wrote, *"This is our Eden, and we were alone in it. His arms about me were the only reality ... his words of love the only bridge to my life. Each night I felt completely possessed by our love, carried ever more swiftly into uncharted seas, and I felt content to let the Prince chart the course, heedless of where the voyage may end"*.[215]

It ended in tears – for Thelma – for the heir to the throne had another paramour, Freda Dudley Ward, a married woman who had been the love of his life since 1918.[216] The two ladies shared his life equally when Prince Charming was not having other brief encounters. Thelma was cast aside when Edward accused her of having an affair with Prince Aly Khan while she was on holiday in America, which she denied. Poor Freda did not even get to speak to the Prince. She had to suffer the ignominy of being informed by the house servant, when she telephoned, that he had orders not to put her through. As the twenties came to a close, the Prince would meet the all-consuming love of his life, Mrs. Wallis Simpson, and devote the rest of his living days to her.

Then there was a British Subaltern, Richard Meinertzhagen, a strange cuckoo who had volunteered for service in Africa. On his arrival from Burma in 1902, he was attached to the King's African Rifles. When he was filling an official form which asked his religion, he wrote *"To all religions which recognise the unknown*

[214] Ref: p480-1 – Miller, Charles – *The Lunatic Express.* The Macmillian Company, New York, NY 1971

[215] Ref: p48 – Parker, John – *King of Fools.* St Martin's Press. New York 1988

[216] Ref: p69 – Parker, John – *King of Fools.* St Martin's Press. New York 1988

God".[217] During his five year stint in the East African Protectorate, as the present Kenya was then called, he embarked on a slaughter of huge proportions. He admitted to being *'obsessed by an unashamed blood lu*st'. He shot 19 lions, 7 leopards, 5 cheetahs, 16 rhinos, 7 hippos and an untold number of other animals. *"Hunting"* he wrote *"is a man's primitive instinct and I indulged it to the full".[218]*

He was equally nonchalant as far as human life was concerned. He stated that he had no belief *'in the sanctity of human life or in the dignity of the human race'.[219]* In 1905, during a confrontation with the Nandi, he arranged a rendezvous with the *laibon* Koitalel and his men. When the unarmed *laibon* arrived holding a tuft of grass as a gesture of truce, Meinertzhagen shot him in cold blood. The fracas that ensued resulted in the killing of 23 Nandi. Opinion remains divided as to the exact nature of events but it led to Meinertzhagen's downfall. In spite of being exonerated by three successive military courts of enquiry, the Colonial Office remained unconvinced and ordered his recall.

In spite of these shortcomings, which some may attribute to the culture prevalent at the time, Meinertzhagen exhibited a softer sentimental side to his character and much foresight. In his old age, he admitted to being shocked at reading his own records. Curiously, he did not kill any elephants claiming *"They are such wise animals… and to kill them for the fun of killing, or for the momentary gain of their ivory, is to my mind immoral. It is a pity that an intelligent animal like an elephant should be shot in order that creatures not much more intelligent may play billiards with balls made from its teeth".[220]* He championed the cause of game and argued along with Charles Eliot, the High Commissioner, that game should be preserved for posterity.[221]

---

[217] Ref: p94 – Meinertzhagen, Richard – *Kenya Diary 1902-1906*. Eland Books. London 1957

[218] pv – Meinertzhagen, Richard – *Kenya Diary 1902-1906*. (Preface to 1983 edition by Elspeth Huxley)

[219] pix – Meinertzhagen, Richard – *Kenya Diary 1902-1906*. (Preface to 1983 edition by Elspeth Huxley)

[220] pix – Meinertzhagen, Richard – *Kenya Diary 1902-1906*. (Preface to 1983 edition by Elspeth Huxley)

[221] Ref: p157 – Meinertzhagen, Richard – *Kenya Diary 1902-1906*. Eland Books. London 1957

In 1902, when two medicine men were publicly hanged at Fort Hall, after a revolt, Meinertzhagen observed, *"The Kikuyu are ripe for trouble, and when they get educated and medicine men are replaced by political agitators there will be a general uprising".*[222] He also believed that the country *'belonged to Africans and that their interests must prevail over the interests of the strangers'.*[223] He predicted that *'someday the Africans would be educated and armed; that would lead to a clash'.*[224]

In October 1903, when 5,000 square miles of uninhabited land on the Uasin Gishu Plateau, in the eastern province of Uganda (now in Kenya), was offered to the Jews as a homeland, Meinertzhagen wrote, *"I hope they refuse it for it is just asking for trouble. In the first place, the Jews' home is in Palestine, not in Africa. The scheme would only add to political confusion, and God knows there will be enough trouble here in 50 years when the natives get educated".*[225] He was out by one year.

Many other people, too numerous to mention, took part in ivory poaching. Even Robert Foran, the founder of the Kenya Police,[226] and Mama Ngina, the President's spouse, were involved in this seedy business.

The Indians of East Africa were no paragons of virtue. Many of the well-known businessmen such as Cowasjee Dinshaw of Zanzibar, Allidina Visram and his son Abdul Rasul, Suleman Virjee and Jeevanjee in Kenya were involved as middle-men in the buying and selling of ivory. Baluchi hunters brought back ivory from Abyssinia by donkey transport and sold it in Kenya. It would be naïve to believe that the Indians did not encourage the hunters and poachers by funding their safaris as they had done for the slave gathering expeditions. During the 1950s and 1960s, a significant number of Indians – Hindus and Muslims – were making money hand over fist by running small factories in Nairobi, which churned game into consumer goods for the up-market clientele.

Indian Maharajas, Nawabs and landed gentry had shown the same disdain to the sanctity of wildlife as their European

---

[222] Ref: p41 – Meinertzhagen, Richard – *Kenya Diary 1902-1906.*

[223] Ref: p31 – Meinertzhagen, Richard – *Kenya Diary 1902-1906.*

[224] Ref: p31 – Meinertzhagen, Richard – *Kenya Diary 1902-1906.*

[225] Ref: p117 – Meinertzhagen, Richard – *Kenya Diary 1902-1906.*

[226] Ref: p67 – Salvadori, Cynthia – *We came in Dhows.* Vol III. *Memoirs* by Shamsu Din, the owner of Sportsman's Arms – Nanyuki

counterparts. Their opulent hunting lodges and old paintings and photographs present ample testimony to this. What then was the reason why the Indians of Kenya did not take much part in this popular pastime?

A large number of Indians were railway or government employees or *dukanwallas* who were kept busy eking out a living under difficult circumstances. Most were too poor to buy a gun, let alone go on a hunting safari. Those who accompanied the Europeans into the wilderness did so as cooks, gun bearers and other support staff. Many of the pioneers were Hindus and Jains who were vegetarians and who abhorred the killing of all animals. The meat eating Indians, largely Sikhs and Muslims, tended to eat only chicken or goat's meat. Only occasionally did their gastronomic adventures extend to deer or other antelope.

Many of the Indian hunters in the pioneering days were men who had served in the Indian Police or the Indian Army. Some of them were seconded to the Kenya Police; others came over with the Army to enforce law and order during the various hostilities. Besant Singh was in charge of the Nairobi Police Station until 1904 when he was relieved of his position by a newly arrived recruit named Robert Foran. He wrote, *"The Sikh Inspector accepted being deposed with a friendly smile, which I thought did him immense credit .... The staff of the police station consisted entirely of Indian and African police. All the records were kept in Urdu by the Indian police writers...".*

"The splendid Sikh... was a great shikari, *a brave man and worthy of the highest traditions of the gallant Sikh units in the Indian Army – which he served with honour before transferring to the Indian Police and then coming to British East Africa. Besant Singh had killed 24 lions during the advance of the railway to Nairobi, making a habit of hunting them with a .303 rifle, for which he possessed only .256 calibre ammunition. To make these cartridges fit for his rifle, he wrapped them around with paper. This intrepid Sikh sportsman was a first-class shot but there are not many who would have dared tackle lions with ammunition that did not fit the rifle. Certainly I would not...* "[227]

Bishen Singh was another brave Sikh and an inspector in the Railway Police. He volunteered to accompany Smith, a section engineer, to recover Henry Ryall's body after he had been snatched

---

[227] Ref: p102-6 *passim* – Foran, Robert – *A Cuckoo in Kenya*

by a man-eater at Kima on 6 June 1900. Parenti and Huebner, the two men involved in the incident and Remington, the Postmaster-General, who was returning to Mombasa from a duty visit to Nairobi, were too scared to help. Smith, armed with a heavy rifle, Bishen Singh with a revolver and a sword, a gun bearer and the cook armed with a meat chopper, went out into the wild and recovered the almost intact body within about a quarter-of-an-hour.

Abdul Wahid, a Pathan from Amritsar, was a small time hunter who developed a passion for the conservation of game. He joined the new railway in 1901 at a salary of 85 shillings per month. The guards in those days were armed. Majid Cockar, his grandson, recalls the old pioneer telling the family that when he saw an impala or some similar animal he would signal for the train to stop so he could shoot it and carry it with him in the guards van.

Wahid left the railway and started a very lucrative business of supplying wood-fuel for the engines. His fascination for wildlife led him to start Nairobi's first zoo on Plot No.1,422 off Ngara Road. He also started exporting game with the profits and built himself a splendid mansion on Ngara Road. He was a dour man who lived a very westernised lifestyle. He was popular with the Europeans and was awarded an OBE, perhaps because he opposed his own people when the Indian Congress called for non-co-operation with the Colonial Government. During the war, I can remember playing among the dilapidated buildings in Ngara which was all that was left of the animal enclosures. On the way to the Coryndon Museum from Ngara one had to pass under the perimeter wall of Mr Wahid's palatial residence, and we looked forward to picking fruit from the branches of loquat trees that over-hung the wall.

The realisation that game was progressively being driven towards extinction by the need and greed of man began to dawn on some people. The land was increasingly falling victim to the plough and harrow. In a mere ten years, from 1905 to 1915, the acreage of European farms had increased fourteen fold from 368,165 acres to 5,275,121 acres. The Indians too were clamouring for land and were given some in the lowlands. The increasing population inevitably was burying good land under bricks and mortar. It would not be long before the swish of the antelope tails, the thunder of the rhino hooves and the roar of the lions would disappear from the once teaming savannah. Tourism, however, was dependant on game and the nation was becoming more and more dependant on it.[228]

In 1978, I visited the TREETOPS HOTEL in Kenya and saw animals galore, both in variety and in numbers. The antics of the elephants in water, the power struggle between the bull buffaloes and the bull elephants and an attack on a female buffalo all in front of the visitors was a sight never to be forgotten. On a subsequent visit in 1989, the situation had changed. On the distant horizon, one could see a few roof tops, a sign of territory increasingly compromised by human intrusion and a sad omen for the animals. As for the game, it never arrived. It proved to be an all night vigil of frustration. The inventory in the book of daily sightings at breakfast painted a totally different picture – a result of imaginative accounting no doubt.

Hunting of big game by Indians appears to be a mostly post-war phenomenon. The second and third generation Indians had more confidence, more disposable cash and were increasingly adopting western ways. The need to survive and make money was no longer a paramount aim. Their horizon was becoming wider and their lifestyle more varied.

Mr Niaz Mohamed and Mr Abdul Hakim developed their love for the outdoors, open skies and hunting after they served in the Kenya Army. They had remarkably similar careers. They both arrived from Punjab in 1940, and after cooling their heels for some time, they joined the army in 1943 and served until they were demobbed at the end of the war in 1945. Niaz Mohhamed found a job with Kilembe Copper Mines and Hakim joined the Post Office. It is during this period that they engaged in their passion for big game hunting. On retirement they made their home in England and both embarked on a third career with the Social Security Department and Customs and Excise Office respectively. They both died in the month of January in their early 80s.

---

[228] 350,000 visitors came to Kenya each year between 1972 and 1982. They generated $20 million in foreign exchange.

Niaz Mohamed.

Abdul Hakim.

There were a number of East African born and bred Asians who went hunting. Most confined their activities to duck and antelope and very occasionally big game. Iqbal Mauladad and the Sheikh brothers of *Mulango Kuba* in Pangani became well known.

There were others but their names have faded into the mists of history.

A large number of Punjabis and Gujaratis of Kenya were Hindus and Jains whose religious beliefs often prevented them from killing innocent animals. The elephant in particular had a special place in the Hindu hearts. They respected its intelligence[229] [230] and it was worshipped because it was the nearest thing to a cloud. In the Hindu pantheon, Ganesh, a mixture of elephant and man, is special for he is the remover of all obstacles and depicts a union between man and animal. He is the deity worshipped by other gods as their teacher since a glimpse of him brought happiness and made them laugh. The moral basis of the entire Jain discipline is *Ahimsa* or non-violence. All killing is prohibited, as all life is sacred and inviolable, even that of unfortunate beings who are born as animals. The Arya Samaj, a powerful Hindu movement in East Africa during the first half of the twentieth century, held sway over a wide swathe of the population. It promoted vegetarianism with the slogan *'Hinduo tum pete men kabrain banana chor do'* (Hindus stop turning your stomach into a graveyard). With such combined forces against all killing it is no wonder that hunting and shooting was looked down upon by a majority of East African Indians – but not by all.

Kuldip Rai Moman, a Hindu by birth, was a young man with scant respect for such strictures. He arrived from India in 1937 and found a career with the Post Office. His job took him to many places, big and small, and in each venue he found something of great interest. Unlike most of his colleagues, he was a bibliophile who loved poetry and the finer things of life. He enjoyed anything new and was especially attracted to adventure and nature.

Although not a solar-topeed 'huntin' and shootin' type, he could not resist the temptation when an opportunity to join an elephant hunt came his way. The party of friends arrived in the sleepy town of Masindi in an old beat-up Anglia where they engaged four porters with the help of the local chief.

The rag-tag party had hardly set foot in the wilds when one of the porters decided to 'visit the *bundu*' and that was the last they saw of him. They readjusted their loads and marched into the unknown, but before long a tropical rainstorm got the better of them

---

[229] Among the land mammals, the only brains larger than those of men are in the elephants.

[230] Ref: p 44 –Heathcote, Williams – *Elephant.* Jonathan Cape. London

and their hurriedly built a grass and sticks hut and spent the night in a soggy morass.

On the next day, they set forth with firm determination but the novices had under-estimated the formidable opposition of the elephant grass and the heat of the midday sun. Their bodies were soon dripping with warm sweaty brine and their spit turned into salve. When they called for water, *"Lete maji"*, back came the reply *"Hakuna maji, quisha sahau"* (no water, forgotten it). They were at their wits end when someone spotted elephant spoor and large footprints besides it where water had collected in small puddles. Faced with Hobson's choice, every man decided to go on all fours to sip this brackish elixir![231]

With spirits revived, they pressed on. The sun had lost its fire and the rim of the orange disk was about to kiss the grey horizon when they suddenly came upon a herd of nearly 300 elephants. They hurriedly selected a fine large bull and fired. A shrill piercing shriek arose to disturb the stillness but the bull was still alive and it took a second shot from a nearby tree to deliver the *coup de grace*. Fearing the creatures of the African night, the party decided to retreat but not before staking their claim, according to the age old custom of the forest, by cutting off the animal's tail. Lady luck had another surprise for the parched but happy hunters. As they were stumbling through the head-high grass, they almost fell into a stream of clear fresh water.

That night, sleep did not come easy to Kuldip. *"I wanted to sleep"*, he recalls, *"but the calls of the animals and the beauty of the surroundings kept me awake far into the night... The glory of a rising sun in the midst of the Nyika is a thing to be felt and a sheer delight to behold"*. The next morning, 'with the song of the birds and the sun on the hill' they relieved the tusker of his upper incisors. Another solitary innocent life sacrificed to give one man pleasure but a life silenced to deny all men pleasure.

Eventually all killing had to stop but this was not an easy aim to achieve. It would take nearly four decades from the time Col. Mervyn Cowie managed to persuade the authorities to reserve a small but game-rich area as a sanctuary for wild life which resulted in the announcement of the Nairobi National Park in 1946. The Tsavo National Park followed two years later. All hunting was

---

[231] Ref: Moman, Kuldip – POSTGEN – 'On the trails of the elephant'. Nairobi, 1948

banned in 1977 and then onwards there was only one way to shoot – with a camera. But the enforcement of such a law was another matter.

The poachers were still rampant and a step ahead of the warders. They took to using increasingly sophisticated methods such as automatic weapons and four-wheel drive vehicles to stalk and kill the animals. The only way to control them was for the Government to show equal resolve. In 1989, an all-out war resulted in the burning of great pyres of ivory.

The innocent had paid the price for man's selfishness, vanity and ego. If his mindset and culture could be changed, there was a fair chance that the savannah, prairie and rolling hills could belong, once again, to its rightful free-spirited creatures as nature had intended – and forever end to the killing fields.

Chapter 8

The Last Nail In Hitler's Coffin

**Only a fool would choose war instead of peace –
in peace, sons bury their fathers,
in war, fathers bury their sons.**

**Croesus, King of Lydia to
Cyrus, King of Persia**

Neville Chamberlain's visit to Hitler in Munich provided East
Africa and the rest of the world with a brief respite in which to
prepare itself for the oncoming hostilities. Although everyone
hoped for peace, the nations were steeling themselves for the
struggle. In early 1939, East Africa began voluntary registration of
men of all races for national service and this was followed by
considerable efforts to improve the territories' food supplies. The
'phoney war' of late 1939 and 1940 gave East Africa breathing
space in which to adjust to the new world struggle.

As the threat of war had been so long in the air, it came as
less of a shock to East Africa than in 1911. Then the country was
caught with its pants down. When the First World War was
declared on 4 August, the British could muster only 700 native
troops and only two machine guns, one of which was out of action.
The opposition, in contrast, was well prepared with a force which
consisted of 3,000 white men, 8,000 native troops, 70 machine
guns and 40 guns.[232]

This time around there were no qualms about dealing with the
enemy aliens even though they might be Europeans. Out of a total
population of 3,205 Germans in Tanganyika 1,858 German males
were quickly interned without a struggle. This easy success was
partly due to the efficiency with which this undertaking was
organised and partly, too, to the fact that expecting an early German
victory, the German leaders had issued instructions forbidding their

---

[232] Ref: p140 – Huxley, Elspeth – Nine Faces of Kenya. Collins Harvill. London
1990

264

followers to resist arrest. Nonetheless, the internment of the Germans was an important step since Nazi groups had been organised in centres as far as Dar es Salaam and Bukoba and they could have caused serious trouble had they been so inclined.

The next potential military threat came from the Italians in Ethiopia. The British Government was anxious to encourage Italian neutrality and it sent a telegram to East Africa on 30 August 1939 forbidding any military movements of a provocative nature in the North Frontier District of Kenya. So for some time it seemed, after the first few days of uncertainty, that East Africa's role was not to be a dramatic one.

The Governors Conference in November 1939 decided to lay stress on increased productivity so as to reduce East African dependence on imports in order to lighten the burden on merchant shipping of the western allies. This met with whole-hearted approval of the Secretary of State in June 1940. Meanwhile, the whites in East Africa were anxious to make a greater contribution to the allies' war effort. Various methods were adopted to raise public subscriptions and all met with generous response. The Tanganyika Government readily exhausted its reserve funds in order to contribute £200,000 to British coffers.[233] Income tax, which had been resisted during the 30s, was now accepted with enthusiasm in Tanganyika and Uganda, thus bringing the two territories into line with the taxation policy adopted in Kenya in 1937.

The likelihood that Italy would join the war on the side of the axis steadily increased and it was a matter of time before East Africa would be drawn into action. In February 1940, East African forces became part of the Middle East Command and they were assigned the task of harassing the Italians along the Kenya border. Meanwhile, the King's African Rifles were rapidly expanded and the defensive positions at Moyale, Marsabit and Wajir were strengthened against a possible Italian advance southward.

The ignominious British withdrawal from Dunkirk convinced Mussolini that Germany was the better side to join. Italy's declaration of war on 10 June 1940 was no surprise and East African soldiers were raiding over the border before midnight on the same

---

[233] Ref: pg 4 – *Tanganyika Territory: Proceeding of the Legislative Council*, fifteenth session, 1940-41, Pr 1. Government Printer, Dar es Salaam. 1941

day.[234] The Abyssinian armies of Mussolini numbered about 30,000 well-equipped men with powerful artillery and air support. Kenya faced them with six battalions of King's African Rifles and one mounted Indian Battery, numbering about 7,000 men.

The Italians began their first full-scale advance on 1 July and after a fortnight's fighting captured the outposts of Moyale and El Wak. By August 1940, they invaded and occupied British Somaliland. Much needed reinforcements to East Africa came from South Africa, Rhodesias, Nigeria and the Gold Coast, including units of the South African Air Force. In December 1940, the Allies, under the command of Lieutenant-General Cunningham, launched their counter-offensive with a lightning and successful raid on El Wak.

The British overall Commander, General Wavell, planned a three-pronged invasion of Abyssinia: from the east through British Somaliland; from the south from Kenya; and from the north through Sudan. In January 1941 an East African, a Nigerian and a South African brigade advanced at breakneck speed into British Somaliland and captured the capital, Kismayu, without a fight. Cunningham decided to press on with their advantage and invaded Italian Somaliland, and by the end of February, occupied the country and its capital, Mogadishu.[235]

The East African forces continued their whirlwind advance as they sped inland through the mountainous country towards the Abyssinian capital, Addis Ababa, which capitulated on 6 April 1941, just 40 days after the start of the advance from Kismayu. Brigadier Fowkes, who commanded the 22nd East African Brigade, was well to the fore and so determined to reach Addis Ababa first that he ignored all efforts by the Divisional Commander to stop him. The exasperated but equally determined Divisional Commander was forced to dispatch a plane with a message to stop any further advance on the capital. Captain Crosskill, who was accompanying Fowkes, wrote *"The pilot spotted the column without difficulty and then, flying so low that the drivers instinctively ducked their heads, dropped his message bag with ribbons fluttering almost on the*

---

[234] Ref: p153 – Huxley, Elspeth – Nine Faces of Kenya. Collins Harvill. London 1990

[235] Ref: p157 – Huxley, Elspeth – Nine Faces of Kenya. Collins Harvill. London 1990

bonnet of the Brigadier's car. This was force majeure *with a vengeance and he halted – ten miles from the capital"[236].*

The honours were divided fairly. General Wetherall was accompanied by Brigadier Fowkes, Brigadier Pinaar of the 1st South African Brigade and Brigadier Smallwood of the Nigerian Brigade when they went to the Duke of Aosta's residence for the signing of the armistice.

George Kinnear, a war correspondent with the EAST AFRICAN STANDARD wrote '*The proceedings were short and sharp and lamentably business-like. There were no flowery speeches. General Wetherall got out of his car, met General Mambrini, was saluted by the Italian guard of honour, and dived straight into the palace to get on with the signing.*

'*The Italian flag had been hauled down as soon as the British arrived, well before anyone was ready for it, and General Wetherall had it re-flown in order that it could be given full military honours. Once this had been done, down it came again and up went the Union Jack, to be saluted by the fascist guard.*

'*The Duke of Aosta, the Italian supremo, was still entrenched in the mountain stronghold of Amba Alagi. In May 1941, a mixed force under General Mayne, attacked this apparently impregnable fortress and on 16 May, 1941, brought the Duke to his knees. Some 5,000 Italians filed out while the pipers played "*The Flowers of the Forest*"*.[237]

The last battle of the campaign took place when a mixed force of British troops and Abyssinian patriots captured the fortress of Gondor in November 1941. The Italian threat to East Africa was finally at an end.

When Japan entered the war at the end of 1941, it at once changed the strategic significance of East Africa. Its defenders had to look eastward instead of northward. The African troops were regrouped, retrained and dispatched to South East Asia. After the fall of Singapore and the transfer of the main British Far Eastern naval base to Ceylon, the importance of Mombasa as a reserve base for naval patrols operating in the Indian Ocean increased. The

---

[236] Ref: p157 & p162 – Crosskill, Captain W.E. – *The Two Thousand Mile War.* Robert Hale, London 1980

[237] Ref: p162 – Huxley, Elspeth – Nine Faces of Kenya.

possibility of a Japanese landing in East Africa could not be ruled out in 1942, the year of their triumph.

Madagascar was of particular concern to East Africa and an even greater threat to Allied shipping if it should fall into Japanese hands. The Vichy French who controlled the island could not be induced to resist the Japanese, so it was seized in 1942 by mainly African troops and the campaign provided a further opportunity for East African troops to demonstrate their qualities. In 1944, the East African troops, retrained in jungle warfare, fulfilled a new role when they took part in the campaign against the Japanese in Burma.[238] In a matter of four years, East Africa had been freed from all danger of attack and the East African troops had played a very important part in the defeat of both Italy and Japan.

The war came to Kenya when the Indian landiwallas, like their brethren all over the world, were clamouring for independence of their motherland and anti-British feelings were running high. The Indians in East Africa felt particularly peeved against the *bwanas* who had repeatedly meted out the short end of the stick ever since the arrival of the coolies more than four decades ago. This was in spite of the fact that Mahatma Gandhi had spoken out in support of the British. He declared in a speech to the All India Congress Committee on 15 September 1940 *'I do not want England to be defeated or humiliated'*. In a letter to President Roosevelt, dated 1 July 1942, he wrote *'I have therefore nothing but good wishes for your country and Great Britain'*. When the Japanese swept to the borders of India and threatened to invade, Gandhi stood firmly against them. *'If the Japanese come, how are we to resist them non-violently?'* he was asked. *'Neither food or shelter is to be given,'* Gandhi replied in the HARIJAN of 14 June, 1942 *'nor any dealings to be established with them. They should be made to feel that they are not wanted...'*[239]

Around this time, the popularity of Bengali born *Netaji*, literally *Herr Fuhrer*, Subash Chandra Bose, was at an all time high in East Africa. He was a charismatic leader who on his return from Europe, declared to a select group *'I have seen Communism in Russia, I have seen National Socialism in Germany. We shall have National Communism'*. His slogan, 'Give me blood and I promise

---

[238] Ref: p162 – Huxley, Elspeth – Nine Faces of Kenya.

[239] Ref: p134 – Fischer Louis – Gandhi. Penguin Books USA Inc., New York, USA

you freedom' had attracted a big, restive following. His views were an opportunistic blend of leftist and rightist radicalism but he was not a statesman of Pundit Nehru's calibre, nor a political ideologue of Mahatma Gandhi's acumen. He created the Indian National Army under both Nazi and Japanese command and led the nation to believe that he would be the saviour who would remove the shackles of colonialism. [240]

At various Hindu festivals and religious gatherings in the Arya Samaj and the Hindu Temple in Nakuru, local leaders would work up the crowds with anti-British speeches. Many of the participants wore Indian dresses made from *khadi* (homespun cotton cloth of India) and sported spiffy Gandhi caps. The speeches and political rhetoric was followed by cheering, much flag waving and the belting out of nationalistic songs like *Vande Mataram, Bakri Gandhi Di* (Gandhi's Goat) and *Bharat Desh Azad Hoga* (India will soon be independent).

When the war came to the landies in Nakuru, the railwaymen were registered and organised into the local version of *'Dad's Army'*. The men were given identity cards. Some of the clerks were issued tin hats and red arm bands with the initials *A.R.P* (Air Raid Precautions) and each one was assigned a particular duty. Posters of 'Count Ten Before You Speak' appeared in public places and railway coaches and everyone was urged to stay home after dark. Those who had to go out after dark had to carry a torch and if challenged by an official, 'Who goes there,' one had to reply loudly and clearly 'A friend'. Blackout was imposed on all houses. While most people used paper or cardboard to board up the windows, my father in his enthusiasm to achieve a perfect result, cut up and used the linoleum which was covering the bedroom floor. He seemed quite proud of his handiwork but my mother was not amused.

Ramji Das Pathak, a loco clerk, was charged with the job of sounding the siren signalling an air raid and warning the landiwallas to take cover. He was chosen for no other reason than the siren was located just outside the loco-shed next to his office. At one point a mock exercise was announced for a midday Friday. This caused a lot of excitement and everyone held their breath. The appointed hour came but the siren did not sound. It was a full two minutes later that the piercing sound filled the air and suddenly the ARP were running

---

[240] Ref: p191-2 – Bharati, Agehananda – *The Asians in East Africa.* Nelson Hall Company, Chicago

everywhere, giving orders to evacuate the houses. Women and children were marched off to the white perimeter wall of the English graveyard and made to sit among the tall grass. Women complained bitterly as the area was crawling with ants, caterpillars and centipedes, and many refused to sit on the ground. Some of the women would not leave their houses with 'other men'. Others insisted on taking their trunks of valuables with them. These were piled on the heads of the houseboys and the whole caravan moved at a snail's pace. Suddenly there was a loud boom and some of the women panicked yelling *"The Germans are here. Bachao, bachao* (Help, help)*"*. The noise was in fact nothing but the coupling of empty wagons in the shunting yard nearby. While the whole pantomime was still in progress the 'all clear' sounded, adding further to the confusion.

At a subsequent post mortem of this exercise, Mr Pathak denied that he had been tardy in carrying out his duty and claimed that the siren was to be blamed for the delay as there was 'water in the whistle'. It was generally agreed that the ARP exercise was a *shamazel,* but officially, it was declared a success.

War brought a flurry of activity to our small and sleepy town of Nakuru. The permanent agricultural 'show grounds', located in the shadow of Menengai Hill, lay idle most of the year and only came to life during agricultural shows when farmers from miles around came into town to buy and sell stock and enjoy themselves. This was Nakuru's answer to Nairobi's 'Race Week'. Sounds and smells of a different kind were now the order of the day. The mud display *jumbas* became officer's quarters and the open grounds, where the horses and riders once showed off their paces and women in pretty dresses, jaunty hats and colourful saris came to see and be seen, became a tented city with motorised traffic. Long dusty convoys of camouflaged high lorries, some dragging field guns, and packed with black soldiers, and open 'jeeps' with bronzed white soldiers in khaki clothing, became a common sight.

At the weekends the crowds would gather at the Railway Institute Cricket Ground to watch the anti-aircraft gunners swivelling and firing and putting their hardware through its paces. It was fascinating to watch the dive-bombers that practised every day above the aerodrome near the lake. Each time the silvery missile hurtled downwards it seemed that it was sure to hit the ground and be blown to smithereens. But miraculously, one would see it rise and breathe again. The only creatures unimpressed by these human shenanigans were the flamingos that took no notice at all.

The grounds of our tiny four-room school were dug up by the prisoners from the local *'hotel ya kingi'* (Kings' Hotel) to form trenches in case of an air raid. Weekly exercises were held and the sound of the school bell was our cue to line up in what was left of the playground. The novelty soon wore off, for the trenches were deep, narrow and claustrophobic. The choking dust clouds from the stamping of feet and the heat of the blazing tropical sun made the whole exercise a miserable experience. The danger of the unsupported walls collapsing was dismissed by the authorities. The inevitable happened, but mercifully during the night, and that put an end to these drills.

Our games at school and at home began to reflect the war games unfolding before us. Khaki clothes, homemade replica guns and hob-nailed boots became fashion accessories we could not live without. Chewing gum suddenly became very popular and children who could get it from NAAFI sold it to their peers at an enormous profit. School children looked forward to free propaganda films at the African football ground. The deadly contest between the British Mongoose and the German Serpent kept us riveted to the ground. The cheers at the triumph of the Mongoose were led by a handful of officials who sat on wooden folding chairs in the front row.

Although the involvement of the children was negligible, I was lucky to have been asked to play an active role in 1942. This was the year in which *SS Tilawa* was torpedoed by the Japanese a few days after she had left Bombay for Mombasa. A large number of Kenyan Indians were lost at sea and suddenly a distant war became a reality.

One morning, Mr Mulkh Raj, the most junior of the three teachers, came into the classroom and asked me to accompany him. No explanation was given. Somewhat perplexed, I stood up and duly followed him. We left the school and made a beeline for the shops. All along the way I was wondering what was going on but could not bring myself to ask. At long last we stopped at Manubhai Tailor. The teacher showed him a picture, selected a suitable material and asked him to measure me. It was only later that day that my father explained that I had been selected to represent the Indian community in their endeavour to raise funds for the war effort.

On the appointed day, I was summoned to the principal's office and asked to change into a natty uniform and a sailor's hat. After giving me instructions, the senior teacher, Mr Gopal Dass, and the

Principal, Mr Patel, led me out to the school yard where the whole school had gathered for the P.T. session. I was asked to salute the fellow students and they responded with a thunderous applause. I was then given a collection box – a replica of a warship. Mr Patel dropped the first coin, gave me a hug and sent me on my way.

Much to my surprise, I was the centre of attraction wherever I went. This encouraged me and gave me the confidence to approach people, visit the shops and ask 'money for war'. Gohil's Cycle Mart was my first port of call. Mr Gohill recognised me and called the neighbouring shopkeepers to come and see *'Dhupaji na dikra'* (Dhupa's son). Not everyone was magnanimous. As soon as I entered one Indian shop, the owner rushed at me, swearing, cursing and frothing at the mouth *" Harami, harami* (bastard). *Get out, get out".* What prompted this outburst remains a mystery. Perhaps he had an anti-British chip on his shoulder. The European owner of Speke's Bakery offered me a dainty little cake and asked his staff to gather around while he took a photograph.

One of my stops on Donald Avenue was the *European Shop*, the Harrods of Nakuru. It was known throughout East Africa for its variety and quality of merchandise and superlative service. I felt very honoured when the owner, Mr Ibrahim Karimbux, an elderly gentleman with a flowing white beard, and his son, Councillor Umardin, came out to greet me and added silver ballast to my ship. Seth Karimbux, the *Nawab of Nakuru*, had literally gone from rags to riches. He unexpectedly left home after a tiff with his father and arrived in Bombay with just three rupees in his pocket. There he met a group of Indians who were on their way to Africa, the land of opportunities. He decided to join them. He paid Rs 1 for his passage to Mombasa and landed at the old harbour in 1896 with two rupees still in his pocket. The hospitable Indians of Mombasa offered him free food and accommodation, a common practice at the time, but he had to make his own living. After intense reconnaissance, he decided to set up a sweetmeat business and invested his two rupees in utensils and ingredients and started selling *halwa* by the side of the road. The *halwa* spoilt in the intense tropical heat and he was left penniless. He decided to try again after a shopkeeper agreed to give him the ingredients on credit. This time he was successful and soon he managed to save a few rupees. He decided to move up-country where there were more opportunities and less competition from other Indians. On arrival in Nakuru he became an auctioneer and a travelling merchant, using donkeys and ox carts for transport. The arrival of the Uganda Railway gave him such a fillip that he never had to look back. With the help of his sons, they went from strength to strength until they became one of the richest families in East Africa.

Eventually, I arrived at the STAG'S HEAD HOTEL and walked into the lounge. The all-European clientele stopped eating and drinking and enthusiastically dipped into their pockets. Someone offered me a glass of lemonade which I gulped readily and raised a laugh as I wiped my lips with the back of my hand.

I had reached the end of the town and my ship weighed a ton. It was now time to go to the centre of the activities, near the post office, and hand over the collection. The street was closed to all traffic and the shop fronts and ornamental trees were hung with colourful bunting and flags. The Kenya Africa Rifles band in smart uniforms and tall red tasselled fez hats was belting out martial music. I was led to someone in a military uniform bedecked with a row of medals. He accepted the ship, and taking me by the arm, led me to a long wooden box. He handed me a long nail and a heavy hammer and asked me to drive the nail into 'Hitler's coffin'. With encouragement from the cheering crowd and a little help from the 'General', I accomplished the task with gusto.

.

Satya Sood age 9 years. Sailors week May 1942.

That was my small contribution to the war effort. On reflection, I sometimes wonder whether my visit to the Stag's Head, the *sanctum sanctorum* of the European settlers, had inadvertently earned me the distinction of being the first Indian to have been offered a drink at this most exclusive of all European establishments in Kenya.

Seventy thousand Italians were taken prisoner from the North African Campaign. Most had insisted on surrender with the devious aim of imposing an intolerable burden on the British. According to the rules of war, all prisoners had to be fed once a day. They were dumped into various camps in Kenya. The influx of servicemen and prisoners created a boom of unprecedented proportions. Vast quantities of foodstuffs were needed and the farmers of Kenya rose to the challenge. However, supplies of meat were woefully inadequate, so the government had to resort to the shooting of game. As a result, the Likipia Plains that were once teaming with animals were virtually denuded of mammalian life.

The arrival of Italian P.O.W.s changed the social equation and added an extra dimension to life in the landies. Suddenly, there were European men who looked like *bwanas* but behaved like *pagazis*. They were dressed in tatty clothes and were wandering aimlessly, knocking on doors and begging for food by rubbing their bellies and pointing to their mouths. They were very friendly and kept the Indian children amused by their antics. Many Indians saw them as victims rather than aggressors.

It did not take long for the landiwallas to get used to their being around and soon the kids and housewives were cheerfully greeting them with *buon giorno* and handing over the left-over *chapattis*. The P.O.W.s bartered away their watches, rings and other trinkets for food, especially sugar. When these were gone, they took over some of the duties of the houseboys by washing dishes, doing laundry or splitting wood for the three stone cooking stoves. The more enterprising Italians started selling hand puppets, wire figurines and jewellery boxes. These exquisite wooden boxes had sliding panels and hidden compartments within compartments and we named them 'puzzle boxes' and they became so popular that there was hardly a household that did not have one.

Some of these *Il prigioniero di Guerra* started moonlighting as construction workers. Others, it is said, started cannibalising British army vehicles, replacing their new engines with old, and making a good income from local *trasportwallas*. They endeared themselves to many Indians by helping at weddings by constructing marquees and decorating them with tasteful bunting and landscaping.

The officials not only turned a blind eye but sometimes encouraged the Italians to work and accept payment. Mr Kuldip Moman, a Post Master at Kigonji near Nyeri, came to know the wardens and their charges who came to collect their mail and parcels from their families in Italy. The warden would send one of his prisoners whenever Moman needed a haircut, to whom he paid just one shilling.

Some P.O.W.s became friends with the ever hospitable Indian families who invited them for lunch. They loved spiced dishes and the sight of *semian* (vermicelli) filled them with nostalgia. They were fascinated to see Indian women making pasta. This was done by the timeless manner of rolling dough against a board producing a continuous length of fine vermicelli that was then hung on strings tied to the legs of an upturned charpoy and allowed to dry in the sun.

The Italians popularised, if not introduced, *Terrazzo* to Kenya. These highly polished, multi-coloured floors with marble chips became all the rage and a 'must have' item in all the fashionable homes and buildings. The houseboys were thankful for they were spared the painful job of rubbing red polish into concrete floors and shining them using fluffy shoes on their feet.

A lasting contribution of the Italians to Kenya was their backbreaking work on the highway from Nairobi to Naivasha. This tarmac road is said to follow down the wall of the Rift Valley along an ancient elephant trail. When the job was done, they built a small chapel at the foot of the escarpment and dedicated it to St. Mary of the Angels. The first voices of the congregation arose up to the top of the Rift Valley on Christmas Day 1943. There it stands to this day, as a symbol of good from evil, and no-one drives by without a second look at the little gem.

A bizarre episode was an attempt by three inmates at the Italian camp at Nanyuki to scale Mount Kenya. One day, Felice Benuzzi was gazing into the distance beyond the barbed wire fence when the mist suddenly lifted and the mountain appeared in all its glory – a mysterious maid beckoning him to her side.

Benuzzi was hypnotised and he knew he had to answer the call. He picked another camp mate, Giovanni Balleto, who was a medical doctor and an experienced rock climber, to be his partner in crime. The two got down to the business of planning the ascent and collecting equipment. They bartered their weekly ration of cigarettes for food and started hoarding it. They fashioned ice axes out of two stolen hammers and made crampons and spikes out of metal from an abandoned car. They needed a third man and chose Enzo Barsotti, who was not only in bad health but a complete novice to mountain climbing.

The three escaped after dark on 24 January 1943 and headed up the slopes along the course of the Nanyuki River. Enroute they had to shake off native trackers, toil through a mixed jungle and evade wild animals. At 8,000 feet they were confronted with thick bamboo, elephants and a progressive lack of oxygen. At 11,000 feet they entered a treeless wonderland of frost, ice and snow, and facing them was *Batian,* the tallest of Mount Kenya's twin peaks.

Here they lit a fire to signal to comrades in the camp below that they were well and still free. Barsotti, who had been suffering from fever, began to get weaker by the hour as the climbers made their way up the mountain. At 14,000 feet he became unconscious. He was revived but he had clearly come to the end of his line.

Unfortunately for the other two there was more disappointment in store. The route Benuzzi had selected was hopeless and they had rations for only a few more days. A sudden storm exposed all their weaknesses and put an end to the assault on *Batian*.

As a consolation, they scaled Point Lenana, the third highest peak at 16,355 feet. In actual fact, their escapade, which was completed within three weeks, was not a failure but a triumph and they proudly planted their homemade national flag on Mount Kenya. On their return to the camp, the Commandant and their fellow inmates remained unconvinced of their feat until a party of climbers found their Italian flag and reported their discovery to the EAST AFRICAN STANDARD. The prisoners became heroes and the Commandant reduced their statutory 28 day punishment in the cells to seven convivial ones.

One of the most important results of war for East Africa was the closer cooperation that occurred between the three territories. At first, both Uganda and Tanganyika were cautious and even suspicious of joint operations. Events, however, were moving fast so that by August 1940, the idea of setting up a joint economic and commercial unit was accepted. Each territory was to have one vote. The fear that Kenya would dominate the partners continued and a leader in the UGANDA HERALD on 13 October 1943 complained that the activities of the council amounted to nothing more than Kenya rule. The tide of public opinion in England was running in favour of larger and stronger colonial units and a statement made by the end of 1944 reinforced this view. At a meeting in Kampala in November 1944, the possibility of a federal system as regards certain services common to all the territories was freely accepted.

Food production during the war was of major concern to all the three territories of East Africa. The recruitment of so many able-bodied men into the military caused a general shortage of labour. The problem was compounded by the drought of 1943 and the visitation of the locust the same year. This devastated the maize crop, necessitating the introduction of famine measures. Thus a heavy burden was imposed on European farmers' wives and they fulfilled the tasks in noble fashion.

The war caused considerable difficulty in the exporting of cotton and sisal, the main crops of Uganda and Tanganyika respectively. Government intervention made sure that the prices did not fall too low and Japanese military successes helped to revive sisal sales by depriving the western allies of alternative resources. The fall of Malaya made rubber in Uganda and Tanganyika a vital commodity and gave an added boost to their economy.

A black market developed due to a shortage of some essential foodstuffs and this situation was made worse by the hoarding of such materials by the *dukawallas*. Although this caused some hardship, it did not seriously affect people's savings as the variety of goods for sale was too small. The Government therefore decided to authorise *talashi* (searches) of individual houses and confiscation of hoarded materials. This caused universal alarm for it would mean strange men coming into the house and looking where they pleased. The guilty parties, as usual, did most of the complaining.

A wife of one of the *babus* had filled her clothes trunks with rice and spread lentils on the flat roof of the outside toilet, happy at the thought that no one would look that high. But an ill-timed gust of wind let the cat out of the bag, for the search party was greeted with a hail of rice and lentils. As the confiscated materials were carried away, the incensed housewife could do little but yell insults, invoke the gods and ask for a victory for Hitler. She was not the only one harbouring such sentiments.

The end of the war was greeted by many of the landiwallas and others with unbridled joy. In Nakuru, a large crowd of Europeans, Africans and a smattering of Indians started to gather at the aerodrome that afternoon and grew manifold as the celebrations continued well into the night.

Wagons, cars, tractors and stalls of every kind were parked in a huge circle making the airfield into a giant corral. A band of smartly dressed *askaris* with an English conductor played 'British' music and the stilt-walkers from the African area of *Bondani* kept the crowd entertained. The Europeans, delirious with this success and fuelled with alcohol, went around hugging and kissing each other, and even shaking hands with others with gay abandon.

As evening fell, the mists from the *magadi* laden waters of the lake began to mingle with the areola of light from the gas lamps, turning the area into an amphitheatre of soft, strange, dancing shadows. The highlight of the celebrations was the sudden rumbling sound of aeroplanes in the darkening cupola of the sky above. As the planes appeared, they began to fill the heavens with hundreds of miniature parachutes, each with a red flare dangling underneath it. The sight of these shiny flamingo coloured umbrellas oscillating and drifting aimlessly on the warm air currents transformed the lake basin into a canvas of surreal images and sent the largest throng ever to gather in Nakuru into ecstasy.

This was perhaps a miniscule attempt by a small community to mark a victory in the largest conflict in the history of the world. However, it was their way to honour the men and women, black, white and brown, who had answered the call, as well as those who had laid down their lives, to ensure the triumph of good over evil and a better world for others.

Although the war was over, its fall-out was still to come. Much of the Indian community in East Africa had remained ambivalent to war and did not celebrate the Allied success with any enthusiasm. Many of the railway clerks had spent their war-time evenings at Ravjibhai guards' house, huddled around the only wireless set in the landis, listening to and analysing every word of the crackling voice of the BBC and All India Radio. British successes were greeted with considerable scepticism and their reverses with much elation. These '*babus* of blinkered vision' had been duped by Hitler's phoney use of Swastika and the Aryan myth, and it is doubtful if any of these Hindus and non-Hindus were aware of the anti-Indian, pro-colonialist and pro-British statements in *Mein Kampf*[241]. Their ignorance was bliss. What would have been their fate if the Hun had prevailed?

---

[241] Ref: p195 – Bharati, Agehananda – *The Asian in East Africa*

The independence of India remained uppermost in their minds. Many continued to believe that Subash Chandra Bose, 'a true hero, an *avtara,* the greatest statesman' had survived the war and that he was waiting in the wings for an appropriate moment to reappear and lead the nation to *azadi.*

The Indians felt less intimidated by the Europeans. The housewives got used to the friendly Italians being around. They felt confident in giving them orders and expecting them to do menial jobs. For the first time, some Indian men had unfettered access to European women. The refugee camp in Kampala saw to that. The ladies roamed the area of Simoni Hill nearby in the evenings and the johns had a field day with their Polish paramours.

The war provided the first opportunity for the East African blacks to participate in large-scale hostilities in Africa and Asia. The *askaris* were able to compare themselves with the Europeans and troops of other countries. This made them realise that the *bwana* was just as vulnerable to hunger, physical exhaustion, pain and fear. He had the same emotions, the same vices and the same virtues. Why then, he asked, were blacks all *askaris* and Europeans all officers and the food rations different between white and black soldiers.

The Europeans also, had a change of attitude. They developed mutual respect for the blacks who had shared the same trenches and fought side by side with them. Their racist views became softer and the right of others to self-determination more acceptable.

The hiatus created by the African men going off to war was temporary as the Indian housewives filled these jobs by employing African teenagers. These *totos* became very popular as they were not only capable of doing the job but were 'easy to keep in line.'

Many of the returning *askaris* found it difficult to get their jobs back and they were forced to look elsewhere or return to their villages. Soon their wartime experiences became colourful memories. Their quiet existence, the reality and the restrictions of civilian life and the lack of opportunity began to cause disenchantment and restlessness. The seeds of African nationalism had been sown during the 40s and many of these frustrated ex-servicemen were to play a prominent part in the Mau Mau insurrection and the quest for independence in the 1950s.

Chapter 9

Independence and its Aftermath

"Are you sure you wouldn't like to change your mind?"[242] whispered the Duke of Edinburgh to Kenyatta, as the floodlit Kenya flag fluttered up the flag post at midnight on 11 December 1963. This was preceded by the lowering of the Union Jack followed by a two-minute period of complete darkness and quiet reflection.

A crowd of 250,000 citizens had enjoyed a boisterous evening of *kinanda* (music) and *ngoma* (dance) during the evening's festivities. Then suddenly darkness engulfed the stadium. Everyone held their breath and waited for that moment of ecstasy when the lights would come on, putting an end to 68 years of British rule and heralding the arrival of *Uhuru*.

The First Minister's thoughts during the dark sojourn perhaps recollected the sacrifices and hardships of many ordinary people who had given up everything to make this auspicious occasion a reality. While he had languished in prison for nine long years, sleeping on a hard floor and eating beans, there were those who had suffered even worse hardships. The freedom fighters had lived in the most inhospitable damp jungles of the Aberdare, sometimes all alone with no clothes and food except for the leaves of wild nettles. Even these they often could not boil for the lack of a pot to hold water. Dedan Kimathi, the Supreme Commander of the Mau Mau and his braves, had to face the might of the British ground forces, the police, hoards of loyalist trackers and the bombs from the Lincolns in the sky. Eventually he had to make the supreme sacrifice for the cause. His limp, lifeless body, hanging from the white man's gallows, would continue to fan the winds of change until they began to blow like a gale throughout Kenya.

The freedom fighters who had survived sat some distance away from the podium. But they had to be ushered away, as they became the focus of the media's attention and began to steal the limelight from the more august overdressed dignitaries occupying the dais.

---

[242] Ref: p8 – Thesiger, Wilfred – My Kenya Days. Harper Collins. London 1994

Missing from the celebrations was Harry Thuku, the stalwart of the African freedom movement. He, with his wife Tabitha, had chosen to stay at home and celebrate *Uhuru* in his own unique way. He did this by planting 15,000 coffee seedlings on a flat piece of land on his farm where he was once told he could not plant coffee – only beans.

***

I first saw Kenyatta at a bus stop near the Khoja Mosque on Government Road in Nairobi. My friend, Farouk Ali, touched me on the shoulder and whispered, "Kenyatta".

"Kenyatta where?" I asked in a loud voice. Just then Kenyatta looked at us and smiled. He was dark and bronze, with a small beard, wearing a brown leather jacket and clutching a sheaf of papers under his right arm. Little did we realise that we were looking at a great man who would one day become the father of our nation.

Within days of this encounter Kenya was engulfed in Mau Mau hostilities. The beginning of this moment dated from 1947, when the Kikuyu Central Association was proscribed and one section went underground to form a secret society named Mau Mau. The two syllables are of no particular meaning and of unknown origin. In July 1952, Chief Nderi was heckled at a meeting of 30,000 Kikuyu organised by the Kenya African Union (KAU) in Nyeri, where he denounced violence. He was assassinated. In August 1952, Senior Chief Waruhiu also spoke out against the Mau Mau at a KAU organised meeting at Kiambu. He too was murdered. Kenyatta, who was the president of KAU, in a speech to the same assembly, declared that his organisation had no link with Mau Mau and denounced the Mau Mau in a solemn curse derived from Kikuyu mythology.

Although a time of great turmoil lay ahead, it apparently made little impression on Sir Phillip Mitchell, the outgoing Governor. In a letter to Sir Evelyn Baring, the incoming Governor, he gave no hint of the gathering storm, but concentrated instead on the problem of how an incoming Governor should behave towards divorced Europeans in a colony of cheerful adulterers.[243]

---

[243] Ref: p171 – Best, Nicholas – Happy Valley: The Story of the English in Kenya. Secker and Warburg. London 1979

Sir Evelyn Baring, however, summed up the situation within days of his arrival. He declared a State of Emergency on 21 October 1952 following the murder of Margaret Wright on the veranda of her farmhouse ten miles out of Nairobi and the killing of the Senior Chief a few days later. Kenyatta and eighty-two alleged Mau Mau leaders were rudely awakened just after midnight and arrested. Kenyatta was flown to Lokitaung in the hot, forbidding district of Turkana. The Lancashire Fusiliers were flown in from Egypt and a cruiser, the HMS Kenya, steamed into Kilindini harbour. Kenya Police also received backup from three black battalions of the King's African Rifles that had been discreetly moved to Kenya from other parts of East Africa.

Asian sympathies by and large lay with the African although outwardly they did not always express their views. The authorities encouraged the formation of vigilante groups to police their immediate areas. One such group was formed at the Arya Samaj premises on Third Parklands Avenue. It consisted of a ragtag of half-a-dozen unwilling Indian individuals carrying *rungus* (African clubs) and an air gun who walked up and down the road for an hour or so before abandoning this charade for good. An Asian platoon was subsequently formed but this was merely an exercise in window dressing by the Colonial Government.

The extent to which the Asians actively supported the Mau Mau is not known. Mr G. L. Vidyarthi had championed the cause of the natives through his weekly journal, the COLONIAL TIMES since its launch in 1932. For his connection with the Mau Mau he was detained three times. He was a key member of the Management Committee of the Arya Girls School Nairobi in February, 1955 when police raided the school premises and confiscated a cache of firearms and gun powder. Following this raid, G. L. Mitchell, Assistant Commissioner of Police, warned the Asian community against links with "the terrorists" and urged them not to give insurgents refuge in the servants quarters of their houses.

**President, Mzee Jomo Kenyatta, greeting Dewan Chaman
Lal who defended Mzee in the Kapenguria trial. Included are
Mr Barkatullah Khan and Mr Atal Behari Vajpayee.**
Kenyatta's trial opened on 25 November 1952 at Kapenguria.
He and five others were charged with managing or assisting to

manage, the Mau Mau. The presiding judge was Mr R. S. Thaker, QC and the Crown council was Deputy Public Prosecutor Somerhough. Kenyatta was represented by a team of distinguished lawyers led by D. N. Pritt, QC from Britain, Diwan Chaman Lal from India, Chief W .O. Davies from Nigeria and Messrs. A. R. Kaila, Fritz D'Souza and Jaswant Singh from Nairobi.

While the trial was in progress, full-scale hostilities broke out. Mau Mau gangs continued to murder settlers, in remote farms and their victims also included Kikuyus who were uncooperative or who supported the Europeans. Mau Mau forces were well disciplined and well organised under ex-army commanders. General China Waruhiu Itote was in command in the Mount Kenya area while the Aberdares area was under the charismatic General Dedan Kimathi Wachiuri.

African support for the freedom fighters was not universal. The massacre at Lari, a mainly loyalist settlement near Uplands, on 26 March 1953, resulted in the murder of at least eighty-four people, many of whom were women and children. Even livestock was not spared. The killings resulted in a change of African opinion against the movement.

The settlers, the Kenyan Police and the Army showed no restraint in their response and Mau Mau killings were brutally avenged. The settlers began to shoot first and ask questions later. Some regiments began to keep score-boards and organise competitions with cash prizes for the company or platoon that could kill the most freedom fighters. The Public Works Department built a portable gallows which could be erected in the condemned man's home area to teach others a lesson.

Mau Mau atrocities were exaggerated and sensationalised by the press in Kenya and abroad. The fact remains that two Europeans were killed before a State of Emergency was proclaimed. By the end of 1955, thirty-two European civilians were killed and twenty-six wounded. Against this, 1,826 Africans, mostly loyalist Kikuyu, had been murdered by their own kind and a further 928 were wounded. Official Mau Mau losses are estimated at 10,000 killed and an unknown number wounded. 1,090 were hanged for Mau Mau offences and 16, 500 Kikuyus were held permanently in camps. Worst of all was Hola, a special category camp in the Coast Province. In March 1959, almost five years after they had been arrested, eleven Hola detainees were beaten to death and twenty-two badly injured by 'unsupervised African guards'. Until this atrocity was unmasked by the press, the Kenya Government tried to pretend that the men had died of drinking bad water on an extremely hot day.[244]

On 8 April 1953, Kenyatta was found guilty of managing a 'proscribed society', after a trial lasting five months, during which Mr Pritt succeeded in making the prosecution's case look ridiculous. It was felt in many quarters that the trial was a disgrace to British justice and the verdict would never have been allowed in an English court. Kenyatta was sentenced to the maximum seven years hard labour. The judge afterwards received an *ex gratia* payment of £20,000 from the Kenyan Government as compensation for putting his own life at risk.

Kenyatta was initially held in Kapenguria in a small house surrounded by metal fence. Makhan Singh, the father of the trade union movement in Kenya, was also held there in a separate house, but they were not allowed to meet. Dr Dilbagh Bowry, the medical officer, treated Kenyatta on several occasions for minor ailments. He recalls that Kenyatta was always accompanied by a prison officer and there were strict orders for the attendants to stay aloof and not engage in unnecessary conversation. He found Kenyatta to be 'reserved and uncommunicative'.

The prisoner was later moved to Maralal, the headquarters of Samburu district, where every morning he had to report to the District Commissioner. Here he worked as the cook's assistant. On one occasion he asked for better food but this request was denied. He was provided with a rickety single bed but he preferred to sleep on the floor.

Kenyatta was initially under the care of a clean shaven Sikh doctor named Bakshi who supplied the prisoner with beer and spirits. When the District Commissioner discovered this he threatened the doctor with dismissal and deportation to India. Dr Bakshi was replaced by Dr Dev Raj Bowry. The new physician found Kenyatta to be well behaved and easy to speak with. The two became quite friendly and often spent the evening in animated discussion.

Kenyatta had access to newspapers, Reader's Digest and books. He enjoyed reading the works of the Indian author, Munshi. One evening, during a tête-à-tête, Dr Bowry suggested that if Kenyatta had read Munshi's books before his arrest, he might have

---

[244] Ref: p184 – Best, Nicholas – Happy Valley: the Story of the English in Kenya. Secker and Warburg. London 1979

acted differently. Kenyatta replied that he and his friends had decided to fight even if they had to live only on beans, or even eat grass.[245] When the doctor argued that violence was bad under all circumstances, Kenyatta disagreed.

Kenyatta confided in Dr Bowry that he had never trusted Dr Bakshi, who he thought was two-faced, saying one thing to Kenyatta and another to the authorities. In fact, Kenyatta's intuition appears to have been correct, since Dr Bakshi told Dr Bowry that he was of the opinion that Kenyatta was guilty and should have been hung.

One night, when the two of them were alone, Dr Bowry asked Kenyatta if he wanted a drink. Since he was not officially allowed to offer alcohol to the prisoner, however, Kenyatta would have to serve himself. Kenyatta was very amused and in spite of beer and whisky in the fridge, he helped himself to a Coke. Dr Bowry then asked Kenyatta if he thought he would be the first President of Independent Kenya. Kenyatta replied that he did not know, for he was not sure that the British would release him after he had served his full sentence.

Kenyatta respected Dr Bowry's honestly, his forthright views and his loyalty to the British. One evening he surprised the doctor by offering him the post of the Head of Kenya Prison Services, if and when he became the President. Dr Bowry refused the offer as he felt unsure of his capabilities and because of his inability to drive a motorcar. Kenyatta was adamant and assured him that he was most suitable. He said that if the doctor was so loyal to the British, he was convinced that he would be equally loyal to Africans. In return for his acceptance, he promised the doctor that he would always have a chauffer driven government car and a supply of *unga gano* (Swahili for wheat flour). President Kenyatta kept his promise.

The Asians were on the horns of a dilemma for they did not know if they had anything to celebrate. They were denied power by the whites and there was a fat chance now that the blacks would be any better. 'So what does it matter, what you don't have, you don't miss', summed up their feelings. There were no spontaneous celebrations, no traditional thanksgiving prayers, no parties and no customary distribution of *ladoos.*

The Indians who showed some interest were snubbed. Ambu Patel, an independent book binder, and his wife, Lila, were admirers of Kenyatta and they had devoted much of their life to the

---

[245] Dr D. R. Bowry was interviewed in Nairobi in 1989

betterment of others. During the Mau Mau uprising, the couple was involved in obtaining food for the freedom fighters and had often hid them in their coal shed. They organised the 'Release Jomo' campaign during which Ambu travelled 4,500 miles throughout East Africa to obtain signatures for the petition. During the incarceration of *Mzee* they financially supported his daughter, Margaret, for eight years and taught her the craft of book binding. This had counted for nothing, for Ambu was physically kicked out of the bus carrying the Freedom Fighters to the celebrations at the stadium.[246]

The end of the emergency in January 1960, was an ill wind for the whites and they had split into two opposing groups. Sir Michael Blundell led the New Kenya Group, a multi-racial party seeking compromise; the other group was headed by the Duke of Portland, who resigned his post as the Speaker of the Legislative Council to devote himself to the white settlers' cause. The election of the Conservatives under Harold McMillan led to much merry-making and raising of glasses at the Muthaiga Country Club. His decision to appoint Ian McLeod (whose brother was a settler in Kenya) as the Colonial Secretary was applauded as an excellent choice. At least, that was what they thought.

Their hopes were dashed by the outcome of the Lancaster House Conference in January 1960. The blacks were promised a majority of the seats in the Legislative Council and the Kenya Highlands were deemed to be sacrosanct no more. The furious settlers lost their heads and Blundell, on his return from England, was met at the airport with ugly demonstrations, verbal abuse and egg throwing.

The situation in other parts of Africa was also in a state of ferment and it naturally influenced events in Kenya. The independence of Congo in June 1960, followed by brutality against the Belgians, convinced the Westminster Government that for a smooth transference of power and property some cast-iron assurances to the white community were essential. Then came the first ever hanging in Kenya of a white man named Peter Poole, who was executed for the cold-blooded murder of an African and it made the white community even more jittery. Meanwhile, there was the ever-increasing clamour for the release of Kenyatta, the much-reviled arch enemy of the settlers. When Kenyatta was named as the

---

[246] Ref: p153 – Bharati, Agehananda – *The Asians in East Africa.*Nelson Hall Company, Chicago

288

President of the newly formed Kenya African National Union, even the Governor, Sir Patrick Dennison, refused to register the party unless Kenyatta's name was deleted from the list of members. But the Governor's finger was not on the national pulse, otherwise he would have known that it would take a cataclysm to keep Kenyatta out of the limelight.

The release of Kenyatta on 14 August 1961 so incensed the settlers that the *Kaburus* (Boers) of 'Sixty-four', the original number for a patch of land which was later re-named Eldoret, started a trek to South Africa. Their forefathers had come from there to the Uasin Gishu plateau in their ox-drawn wagons to set up homesteads almost 50 years prior and now it was time to retrace their footsteps to preserve their brand of life. The approach of *Uhuru* had caused many a man to choke on his whiskey sour and the gin soaked matron to observe that 'things ain't what they used to be'. The trickle of emigrants now became a flood, until 700 Europeans were leaving the country every month.

The flight of capital and farming expertise would inevitably spell disaster for Kenya and no one realised this better than *Mzee* himself. To persuade them to stay Kenyatta addressed a meeting of 400 hostile farmers in Nakuru, the unofficial capital of the white highlands. He offered a hand of friendship, promised moderation and urged them to be part of the new Kenya. He invited them to participate in nation building and join the spirit of *harambee*. He was very persuasive and the settlers were so impressed by his forthright manner and sincerity that they gave him a standing ovation. The floodwaters of emigration soon began to recede.

Once the fat lady had ceased to sing and the nation had started to recover from a collective hangover, reality and responsibility began to look the people in the face. The spotlight had shifted from Governor Malcolm MacDonald to *Mzee* Kenyatta. The new helmsman would now be expected to guide his ship through the muddy waters of local and international politics and intrigue. He had accepted thousands of accolades but would he take the blame if he steered into a sand bank? Was he capable of running the country fairly, efficiently and democratically? The wait to find out would not be long.

During the TRANSITION YEARS, from 1963 to 1968, the Government was faced with three main problems.

The ethnic Somali wanted their grazing lands in North Eastern Kenya annexed to Somalia. When their efforts were thwarted, bands of Somali bandits named *SHIFTA*,[247] who were aided and abetted by the Somali Government, took up arms and started raids across the border. Kenyatta's response was decisive and he proclaimed a state of emergency. He declared, *"We will covet no inch of our neighbour's territory. We will yield no inch of ours."* While these attempts at secession were met with force for three years, a door was left open for a peaceful settlement. Negotiations were eventually conducted under President Kaunda's mediation and in October 1967, they culminated in an agreement between *Mzee* and Mohammed Ibrahim Egal.

On 12 January 1964 during the Somali Crisis, the Government was severely shaken by a mutiny in the Nairobi-based battalion of the Kenya Rifles. The reasons for this uprising were the continued presence of white officers, slow promotion of indigenous Kenyans to officer ranks and unfulfilled expectations within the ranks. Without hesitation, the Prime Minister appealed to Britain for help and the uprising was quickly quelled with a loss of only a few lives. Kenyatta improved civil-military relations by improving conditions in the barracks and quick promotions. He also infiltrated all services with intelligence personnel and members of the KANU Youth League to increase partisan loyalty.

Another major crisis was the difference between Kenyatta and his left wing Vice-President, Oginga Odinga. Odinga's claim that *'Communism is like food to me'*[248] led Kenyatta in 1965 to denounce 'communist imperialism' and he reshuffled his cabinet to reduce Odinga's influence. The struggle that followed led to Odinga forming an opposition party, the Kenya People's Union (KPU). By 1968, the KPU was driven from the political scene and Kenya became a *de facto* one-party state.

***

In 1964, I went home to Kenya, after an absence of ten years in England where I had read medicine and then embarked on a period of specialisation. I was quite nervous as this was my first flight ever, and by sheer coincidence, this turned out to be the inaugural flight of the VC10 to Africa. I was allowed 22 kg of luggage and I had made

---

[247] Ref: Widely used Amharic term for bandits

[248] Ref: p 35 – Miller, Norman N. – Kenya: *The Quest for Prosperity.* Gower Pub. Company Ltd., 1984

sure that I was carrying the exact weight – not an ounce more and not an ounce less. In fact, I had managed to upset a relative by declining his request to carry a parcel for someone in Kenya, as I was afraid I might not be allowed to board if I had excess luggage! I had also made sure that I arrived at Heathrow in good time in order to have dinner as I had no idea that food would be provided on the plane. Imagine my surprise when I was offered champagne followed by a sumptuous dinner.

As the aircraft approached Kenya, I was overcome with nostalgia and I began to think of the things I had missed. My senses were inundated with a melange of bouquets and the taste buds became aroused at the thought of foods like *mhogo* (cassava), yams, *motoke* (plantain) and roasted corn-on-the-cob laced with lemon and chillies. I began to taste the mangoes of Malindi, *miwa* (sugar cane) of Miwani and passion fruit from the vine in our own back yard. Once again I would breakfast on a sizzling *paratha* straight from the griddle and wash it down with lashings of sweet masala tea. My mouth began to water.

The plane touched down at Embakasi (or was it Kenyatta?) Airport on a beautiful June morning. As it taxied to the tarmac opposite the terminal buildings, we noticed that there were flags and bunting everywhere and that hundreds of people were lined up all over the viewing area. *"What a welcome,"* exclaimed a fellow passenger. But why? We had no idea.

Once the aeroplane door was flung open, I found myself at the top of the steel steps, squinting into the bright, warm morning sun and felt the cool fresh highland air through my hair and against my face. This was the elixir I had once known. What a change from the damp smoke, smog and acrid *pea-soupers* of London and Birmingham. I took a deep breath, instinctively to overfill my lungs, as if to compensate my body, and with a song in my heart and a smile on my face, I bounded down the steps of the B.O.A.C. ladder and onto the soil of new Kenya.

Once inside the terminal we learnt that Emperor Haile Selasi had arrived on a state visit a few minutes before us, hence the carnival-like atmosphere and boisterous welcome of which we, too, were the beneficiaries. The country was still in the first flushes of freedom. The announcer spoke immaculate English with a Kenya lilt and she repeated all messages in Swahili, the new lingua franca. Smartly dressed African officers had replaced the Europeans and Asians. Interrogation by an African Passport Officer was a new experience. The officials were still a little tentative but polite and efficient. The day of the underdog had arrived.

The portly customs officer, in an all-white over-starched stiff uniform, asked the usual questions in English, and then reverting to Swahili and waving his thick sausage-like finger, asked me to *'fungua sanduku'*. I opened my neatly packed case and showed him the presents I had brought for my parents and a teddy bear for a niece. He was still examining the toy when he declared *"I have to charge you duty for these"*.

"That is O.K.", I replied and jovially remarked, *"Not for the toy I hope, the child might curse you"*.

He dropped the toy and immediately stepped backwards as if he had been stung. Flapping his hand he whispered, *"Kwenda, kwenda"* (go, go). As I picked up my bag and walked away, I chastised myself for making such a flippant remark that had so obviously upset his superstitious nature.

A strange sight greeted me downtown for scattered hither and thither were the shells of partially built high-rise buildings. These spiritless cadavers seemed to point to some sudden calamity that had befallen the city resulting in instantaneous abandonment of all work. In fact, they were a testimony to post-independence jitters. Investors, foreign and local, had pulled the plug and were marking time until it was clear which way the political winds were blowing. This had resulted in the demise of many Asian contractors adding to the instability and unemployment which was already rampant.

Around these eerie monuments of jim jam capitalism, the daily hustle and bustle went on regardless. The magnetism and bright lights of the city had caused an exodus from the country. There were black faces everywhere and the once sleepy town was now a throbbing metropolis with most of the blacks living in slums. The pace of life was much faster and everyone seemed to be scurrying around as if something urgent was in the offing. The Africans were generally much better dressed and many were wearing shoes. Sunglasses were the accessory of choice. Every other black seemed to be clutching a small transistor radio to their ear or carrying a large one on the shoulder. This Japanese made British invention was the new status symbol. An Indian friend of mine, a dealer in radio and cameras told me, *"Beg, borrow or mostly steal, every kala has to have a radio"*, adding, *"I don't care, it is good for biashara"*.

Some of the streets had assumed new African names. The Sixth Street of pioneer days, known to me as Delamare Avenue, was now

Kenyatta Avenue. This had once seen more game than the present game reserves.

Not all the game, in olden days, however, was of the four-footed variety. The rowdy, out of town farmers, deprived of the company of fellow whites for months at a time would ride into town for the 'Race Week,' determined to make up for all the time lost in the boondocks. They were a law unto themselves and with a large quantity of alcohol running through their veins and the authorities looking the other way, they behaved as boorishly as they pleased. They rode through the streets, shooting at the street lamps, fighting with each other and wrecking the hotels. When they wanted the company of a fair maiden, they buried their heads in the laps of 'Yokohama mammas' in the 'Japanese Legation' at the station end of Victoria Street (now Moi Avenue). The less affluent *bwanas* had no choice but to seek solace in the even seedier brothel in the Indian Bazaar at the other end of the street. In the morning it was time for horse-trading and the washed, shaven, well-dressed farmers turned up for wheeling and dealing, none the worse for the previous nights' escapades – a testimony to the powers of recovery of their livers!

The Government Road had somehow managed to survive the nationalistic broom of name changes. It was difficult to imagine that this lovely avenue with swaying palms, smart shops and fashion houses offering fine silks and the latest in *haute couture* was at one time a mere dirt track which served as Nairobi's answer to the Roman Circus of Mexentius. Here, the whites held the famous drag races, using rickshaws as their chariots. There may have been a lack of style but there was no shortage of enthusiasm. I looked for 'Jack Frost' which most Indians mispronounced as 'Jack Forest'. This was a minute kiosk, a window in the wall really, attached to a 'Europeans only' gourmet restaurant that served the most mouth-watering ice creams and lollipops. Mercifully, it did not bar non-whites and the rotund, red-faced owner with a handlebar moustache would often appear at the door and greet us with a cheerful 'Hello boys'. This had sadly vanished.

A familiar sight to everyone in Nairobi was the expressionless face of the 'traffic *askari*' at the station end of the road, for this used to be the hub of the town. Dressed in white with matching elbow length gloves, this imposing figure was the master of all he surveyed and from his high perch he directed the traffic of bicycles, rickshaws, handcarts, tongas and tiny cars. Motor traffic had, however, taken over and this institution too had been blown away by the eddies of modern traffic.

Some name changes were more popular than others. Harding Street, so called after Her Majesty's Agent and Council General in Zanzibar in 1894, was renamed Dedan Kimathi Street as a posthumous honour for the fallen Mau Mau General. At its junction with the renamed Kenyatta Avenue stood NEW STANLEY HOTEL, the most fashionable address in town.

It was from a vantage point on this street in 1952 that I caught a glimpse of Clark Gable, Ava Gardner and Grace Kelly coming out of the hotel during the filming of the movie MOGAMBO. I had skipped school to go downtown to see them. There was no choice but to stand on the farther side of the street to which all the coloured *wanainchi* (country men) had been pushed. This was the norm in those days and people were conditioned to accept such treatment without question.

The presence of such megastars in Kenya was an event of major proportions and is best described by one of them. *"The whole damn trip"*, according to Ava Gardner, *"was what the publicists like to call the greatest safari of modern times, and I wasn't about to argue. Not only did it take eight genuine white hunters to get us in gear, but also once we settled our encampment were 300 tents strong. And if you think those were just for sleeping, think again. My God, we had tents for every little thing you could think of: dining tents, wardrobe tents with electric irons, a rec room tent with darts for the Brits and table tennis for the Yanks, even a hospital tent complete with X-ray machine, and a jail tent in case anybody got a tiny bit too rowdy.*

"I really shouldn't joke about security, because there were genuine worries for our safety in Africa. The movie company had its own 30-man police force, and when we first got to what was then British East Africa we were under the protection of both the Lancashire Fusiliers and the Queen's African Rifles. The Mau Mau uprising was just getting started, and everyone in the cast was issued a weapon. Clark, an experienced hunter got a high-powered hunting rifle, while they gave me a presumably more ladylike .38 police special revolver.

"That was just like Metro, thinking of everything. They brought in three copies of everyone's costumes just in case and built a 1,800-yard airstrip in the middle of the jungle in a whirlwind five days. Every day, supplies and mail were flown in from Nairobi on sturdy

old DC3s, and exposed film stock, carefully packed in dry ice, would be flown out. The film's expense account even had a notation of 5,000 African francs (fourteen dollars and change in those days) written off as 'gratuities to witch doctors for favorable omens". [249]

For the film stars, the days in the African bush were a mixed blessing for they would bring adulation, romance, love, criticism, tragedy and success all in a period of a few months. *"It was great working with Clark again – he will always be my Sir Galahad",* wrote Ava Gardner. *"But as far as romance went, Clark's eyes were quite definitely on Gracie, and hers, for that matter, were on him. They were both single at the time, and it's very normal for any woman to be in love with Clark. But Gracie was a good Catholic girl, and she was having a hard time feeling the way she did about Clark. Not to mention that being in Africa, with exotic flora and fauna all over the place, and Clark, strong and smiling and completely at home, made her love him more".* [250]

In November 1952, I was a part of a very large crowd that was lining Delamare Avenue for the Annual Remembrance Day Parade. All eyes were on one of the hotel balconies where all three of the Hollywood stars were seated. When the National Anthem was played, the whole population stood up but not the distinguished guests, for they sat glued to their seats. What a let-down.

Nestling between the two wings of the NEW STANLEY was the famous *THORN TREE,* a café named after a giant acacia. This arose from the middle of the floor and spread its benevolent flat feathery branches over the courtyard, filtering the harsh rays of the tropical sun into a soft, warm glow. This had always been a meeting point for the 'in' crowd. A place where the rich, the young and the beautiful, came to see and be seen. The only change that had occurred was that the clientele was now drawn from all races.

Instinctively, I hesitated for a moment before making my way to a table at the far side of the restaurant. I could not help but reflect upon the days when only a chosen few could enjoy the ambience of the most fashionable watering hole in all of Africa. The non-whites felt so intimidated that they often crossed over and walked on the other side of the street. The one-time clientele of white women, with bronze skin and flowing long frocks, had given way to a more casual

[249] Ref: p179 – Gardner, Ava – *Ava My Story.* Bateman Press, London 1990

[250] Ref: p179 – Gardner, Ava – *Ava My Story.* Bateman Press, London 1990

set with cut-off jeans or shorts and flimsy loose T-shirts. Tall European men in well pressed light suits with tall glasses of beer, too, had gone, and instead, unshaven faces with ill-fitting clothes and heavy shoes had taken over. Their manners too, left much to be desired. The style and glamour now came from Indian women elegantly dressed in colourful chiffon *saris*, tiny *chollies* and dark glasses resting in their hair.

The tall, bored black waiters covered with long *kanzus* and red fez hats stood like granite gods, as if surveying the scene with disdain. They never hurried, never smiled and showed no affect. They served the customers when and in the order they pleased – a cursory nod instead of 'thank you' was all most could muster. A young, female doctor oozing confidence, soon joined me. *"Two orange juice tafadali"*, she ordered.

"Tafadali, what is that?" I asked.

"Please", she replied, adding, *"it confers dignity, costs nothing and gets results"*.

The *RENDEZVOUS*, mostly mispronounced RAN DES VUS, almost kitty corner to the THORN TREE, was the haunt of the Asian community. On Saturday mornings, the place was overrun with young men sipping the latest fads in coffee, munching *bhajia* and generally putting on the style. Of course, they were also checking out the *chuklies* ('birds'). Although the clientele lacked a few social graces and table manners, they behaved much like their peers in western countries except that there was no open affection between the sexes.

Eating out in the evenings, night-clubbing and dinner dances at hotels were still largely the domain of the others. The Asians who ventured into such waters did so more out of curiosity and adventure. A young accountant, a relation of mine, who had dinner at a 'posh restaurant' at the INTER-CONTINENTAL HOTEL, talked incessantly about the money he had spent but never once mentioned the cuisine. The nightclubs were garish and seedy. Most had a sparse crowd of a dozen or so well-oiled white men shuffling around the floor and trying to romance bored and half asleep mulatto girls. The all-black bands were surprisingly good but totally wasted on the inebriated revellers. As one of the musicians put it, *"All they come here is for tembo and tomba* (drink and sex)".

Western ways were beginning to permeate into Asian behaviour and their adoption by the youth and the *nouveau riche* was beginning to cause problems among many families. The

296

traditional older generation was losing its grip over the once nuclear family and its inability to enforce its values on the progeny caused much unhappiness.

The young had disposable income and could do much as they pleased. Western-type house parties were in vogue, and here, whiskey (everyone swore by Johnny Walker Black Label) and beer flowed liberally. Many women camouflaged their alcohol in Coca-Cola, but they fooled no-one. Curiously, smoking by women seemed to carry more stigma than drink and they often slipped out into the dark to have a few quick drags. As is often the case, as alcohol began to take hold, many inhibitions were cast to the winds and tongues loosened. The conversation veered from small talk to weightier matters of sex and sexual escapades. Promiscuity and adultery was discussed freely amidst great mirth and laughter. It was embarrassing to hear women openly discussing spousal inadequacies and other secrets of the *boudoir*. Wife swapping was inferred but I saw no evidence of it.

The familiar landmarks were all there. The pink stone beldame, the Railway headquarters, looked as elegant as the day it was completed in July 1929 at a cost of £115,000. The addition of a third storey to the original design of a double-storey building ensured a much-improved architecture and provided for future needs. The McMillan Library, a structure with the most beautiful façade in all Kenya, was still a welcoming sight for those hungry for knowledge and literary bent. The movie moguls, too, were impressed by its charm. The library was built by Sir Northrup McMillan's wife to commemorate this wealthy American pioneer who had come to Kenya to hunt but had fallen in love with the tropical paradise and stayed on to develop the land. His enormous frame of 25 stone earned him the title of the largest *Mzungu* in the world. He had endeared himself to Kenyans by building two nursing homes at his own expense and his war effort led to a knighthood.

Downtown, the divinely beautiful Central Mosque continued to lend its charm to the heart of Nairobi. Farther out, the rustic blue stone Khoja Mosque and the cathedral beckoned their respective congregations. After the completion of the Anglican cathedral after the First World War, the white congregation demanded that the English speaking service be held before the Swahili one on the grounds that the pews would then not be soiled by their black co-religionists. The bishops resisted these demands for a segregated church synod with the result that it was the first multi-racial governing body in the land.

As is so often the case, the *Nairobiwallas* took these gems for granted. All the talk now was of the newest jewel in the crown – the cigar shaped HILTON HOTEL. It occupied the hub of the city, the site of the one time Harding Street Bus Terminal, which was nothing but an open wound in the choicest of locations. The large open field was a dust bowl during most of the year which became a thick chocolaty quagmire when it rained. Here, all the city and country buses congregated – huge monsters with giant wheels belching dark acrid smoke from their exhausts. Each arrival and departure sent up clouds of red dust as the buses lurched, listed and pitched dangerously as they ploughed through potholes the size of swimming pools. The broom of modernisation had swept away all that. The old order had changed and the mandarins were now dreaming of a city to rival the best in the world. A few people tried to raise the spectre of Malthus' theory but no-one was listening.

***

The MIDDLE YEARS of Kenyatta's Presidency, between 1969 and 1974, were characterised by recession, major drought, oil price uncertainties, land problems, ethnicity and student issues. The year 1969 was *annus mirabilis,* a year of murder and bloodshed. On 5 July, Tom Mboya was gunned down in broad daylight as he stepped out of Chani's Pharmacy on Government Road in the very heart of Nairobi. Mboya, an ardent supporter of Kenyatta, was the Minister of Economic Planning and Secretary of KANU. He was a Jaluo by birth and had become a truly national leader with support across ethnic lines. His ability, pleasant manner, good communication skills and film star looks endeared him to people at home and abroad. The news of his murder spread like a brush fire and within hours rioting broke out in parts of Nairobi and Kisumu.

Tom Mboya.
Courtesy of the *'Daily Nation'*.

Four days later, Kenyatta's car was stoned outside Nairobi Cathedral where he attended the requiem mass for Mboya. There were shouts of *dume* (bull), the symbol of KPU, the opposition party. The police tore into the crowd with tear gas and batons, causing two deaths and 60 hospital admissions. Three hundred people were arrested.[251]

A Kikuyu named Njenga Njoroge was arrested sixteen days after the assassination and charged with Mboya's murder. He was

---

[251] Ref: p45 – Miller, Norman N. – Kenya: The Quest for prosperity. Gower Pub. Company Ltd. 1984

tried, found guilty and hanged without any independent observers or members of the press being present.[252] The public was unconvinced and suspected a cover-up and complicity at the highest level of the Government.

In November, Kenyatta went to Kisumu, ostensibly to open a new hospital, but it is widely believed that this was a step to placate the Jaluo. Repeated heckling from KPU Youth in the presence of Odinga got under the President's skin and he reacted by delivering 'an angry, curse-laden attack on Odinga', and threatened 'to crush Jaluo [the Luo] into the floor'. As the presidential convoy was leaving, Kenyatta's car was stoned and his personal bodyguards reacted by shooting indiscriminately, killing eleven and injuring 78. The unofficial count was higher.[253]

The dominance of the Kikuyu over other ethnic groups became a major bone of contention. In 1972, the Kikuyu, who then comprised 20 percent of the total population, held 40 percent of senior government positions. The Luo, who were eighteen percent of the population, held only 8.6 percent of senior positions. Kenyatta's response was to make some token appointments of non-Kikuyu individuals to government jobs and to instruct the telephonists and secretaries at the University of Nairobi not to answer the telephones in the Kikuyu language. He also started to make more speeches to impress upon the people that Kenya was a fair and unified country.

The *Muhindi question* was another thorn in Kenyatta's flesh. During the six decades of their presence on the mainland of East Africa, Indians had become a very important cog in the national wheel. This enviable position was the result of their vision, enterprise, tenacity, frugality, self-sacrifice and sheer hard slog. Their financial stability became a source of jealousy for both the Europeans and the Africans. Their ambivalence towards independence stemmed from the fact that they had failed to achieve any political clout and the change of power in Kenya was viewed sceptically as 'the same old horse, just a different rider'. The Indians had learnt to live under the British Raj, and indeed, they had thrived. But the 'black *bwana*' was an unknown entity.

A major restriction on Indian businesses was the exclusion of Asians who did not hold Kenya citizenship from trade licence

---

[252] Ref: pp279-289 – Goldsworthy, David – *Tom Mboya: The Man Kenya Wanted to Forget.* Heinemann, Nairobi and London, 1982

[253] Ref: p46 – Miller, Norman N. – Kenya: The Quest for prosperity.

renewals. Greater restrictions were not feasible because the Constitution protected all minorities. Furthermore, Kenyatta's capitalistic philosophy also protected the Asian citizen of Kenya from even greater hardships. However, under political pressure, the government made it clear that even the *wanainchi* could lose his Kenya passport for being 'disloyal'. This ambiguous and effectively undefined term silenced the Asian political expression.

The gut feeling of the majority of Asians was that the game was over and sooner than later the country would go to the dogs. What could they do? Where would they go? What would happen to the children? These were the burning questions on their lips.

The businessmen, with their acumen, and given a reasonably level playing field, thought they would be all right. The Africans, they argued, were sure to have increasing buying power and they were hungry for consumer goods. The Africans were regarded as poor managers of money and great spendthrifts, and accordingly, would fuel the economy for quite some time.

Physicians, lawyers and others whose skills were in great demand had little to worry about even if they had foreign passports. Tradesmen and businessmen who were not Kenyan citizens, however, were quite vulnerable and were excluded from trade licence renewals. This group became fair game for the uncouth officials to prey upon. A Sikh architect in Nairobi, a class fellow of mine, had opted for a British passport and he was unable to renew his business licence – until he discovered the 'right way'. That entailed a visit to the proper official, armed with a briefcase full of currency notes. He approached the office with great trepidation and when he entered the waiting room he was surprised to see half-a-dozen others waiting to see the same official. Each one was carrying a brief case. When he was called in the officer took the case, examined its contents, handed it over to another person, and the rest was plain sailing. As my friend got up to leave he was told that there was no need to come in person and to 'just send the office boy next time with the necessary papers'. This system turned out to be foolproof.

The group of Asians in the greatest peril were clerks, railway and government workers and the semi-skilled. They were easily replaceable and would be the first to go in the Government's attempt to 'Africanise' and 'Kenyanise' the country.

While the situation in Kenya was in turmoil, Tanzania, its neighbour to the south, was having problems of its own. In 1964, I took a train journey from Nairobi to Dar es Salaam. The once pristine railway station was dirty and the orderliness of yesteryear had disappeared. Thick matted strands of cobwebs hung everywhere.

The train compartment was covered in a thick layer of fine red dust. There was a deafening clatter in the toilet because someone had made off with the seat leaving a dangerous hole in the floor. The water filter remained but there were no paper cups. The coach attendant, when questioned about the sad state of the coach, could only shrug his shoulders and give the now familiar answer *'Sijui'* (Don't know). The Sikh ticket inspector bemoaned that the railway was *'going to the dogs'* and added, *"What is the use of complaining, no one listens"*. He was biding time until he could retire and leave the country for the UK at the first possible opportunity.

The morning at Moshi was bright and beautiful and showed Kilimanjaro in all its glory. The gun-totting police officers who examined the passports were cocky and abrupt. They took away a fellow passenger, a beautiful half-caste girl, because her 'passport was not in order'. She claimed on her return that all the officers did was drive her around the town in an open Jeep, showing her off to their friends and acquaintances. The passport was never scrutinised. She was delivered to the train a few minutes before its departure to Dar.

Mt Kilimanjaro – Painting by Paul Nijiru.

Dar es Salaam, meaning Heaven of Peace, was the creation of Seyyid Majid. Majid, an epileptic, was a peace-loving man happy in the pleasures of his harem. After the death of his father, Seyyid Said, the Sultan of Oman, in 1856, Zanzibar and Oman, although nominally one, were in fact ruled separately by two of the Sultan's sons, Majid in Zanzibar and Thuwaini in Oman. Majid, with the help of the British, thwarted his brother's claim of sovereignty over both halves of the domain. Lord Canning, the Governor General of India, to whom grievances were submitted, legally separated Oman from Zanizibar and recognised each as an independent state. Thus the ending of the old Oman Empire inadvertently increased British influence in eastern Africa. After independence, it remained the seat of the Government of Tanganyika and the home of its first President, *Mwalimu* Julius Nyerere.

Nyerere was a sincere, fair and idealistic leader. In December 1961, as the first Prime Minister of the newly independent Tanganyika, he threatened to resign if there should be unfair discrimination against non-Africans in the country's citizenship laws. He also acknowledged the country's debt to the British and its civil servants and encouraged Indians to stay in Tanganyika.

The Mwalimu was not afraid to speak up and speak out and was even willing to forego membership in the Commonwealth rather than sit side-by-side with the Republic of South Africa because of its evil institutional policy of Apartheid. In April 1963, he was responsible for the Tanganyika National Assembly passing a motion condemning Southern Rhodesia's bid for independence under a white majority. He also showed courage when he welcomed the headquarters of the African Liberation Committee.

The President's idealism received a sharp jolt in January 1964, when a mutiny broke out in the Tanganyika Army. For two to three days the helmsman could not be found and the ship of state drifted aimlessly. It was a popular belief that the President had gone into hiding in the all-white Yacht Club of Dar. Law and order was restored with the aid of British marines – a mirror image of happenings in neighbouring Kenya. Thus, the man who wanted his country to be non-aligned and at liberty to seek friendship where and with whom he wished found himself eating humble pie. But in a characteristic fashion, he rode out the storm by summoning a meeting in Dar es Salaam of the Organisation for African Unity and vindicated himself while striking a blow for African co-operation by persuading Nigeria to send a military force to replace the British forces.

On arrival, I found Dar to be a calm, peaceful and sleepy town. The natives were welcoming, friendly and busy in day-to-day activities, trying to earn an honest living. There was no crime to speak of and everyone felt safe. The only sign of the recent mutiny was the presence of topless, tall, ugly stumps of coconut palms that dotted the affluent Upanga area of town. This was blamed on the hooligans who, in their haste to steal the fruit, chose to behead the palms. The politicians were busy promoting the newly formed state of Tanzania after Tanganyika's union with Zanzibar and the President had joined the debate as to the right pronunciation of the name.

Whilst the changes in Tanganyika were essentially peaceful, Zanzibar had to go through a bloody revolution. One of the main reasons for this was the fact that although the population was black, mostly as a result of a mixture of blood between the Arabs and their black slaves from the mainland, the power and control lay in the hands of the Arab ruling class and Indian businessmen. There was much bad blood between the African dominated Afro-Shirazi Party and the Arab led Zanzibar Nationalist Party. Eventually the latter won the elections of July 1963 with the support of the much smaller Zanzibar and Pemba People's Party. Simultaneously with the independence celebrations of 10 December, the Sultan's authority over the Kenya coast ceased and the region was transferred to Kenya.

On 12 January 1964, the country was greeted by a shock revolt against the Government. Within 24 hours, the Sultan had fled and a new Government had been announced under the Presidency of Abeid Amani Karume, the leader of the Afro-Shirazi Party. Five thousand Arabs and Indians were put to the sword. The leader of the revolt was John Okello, a Ugandan African who had been trained in Cuba. Karume and his ministers feared Okello's power, however, and got rid of their dangerous ally. In March, Okello was refused re-admission to the island after a visit to the mainland. At the end of April, Karume agreed to unite Zanzibar with Tanganyika under the presidency of Julius Nyerere.

The Asians of Dar es Salaam seemed to be quite happy. Their businesses were thriving, their jobs were secure, there was religious freedom and they could move about unmolested. They appeared to be far less nervous than their counterparts in Kenya. The Ismaili community was investing heavily in the country and had every intention of staying put. Young Asian professionals had returned after training in the United Kingdom and elsewhere and had set up law offices and pharmacies. The first fully trained obstetrician and gynaecologist with a British degree was now in charge of the two main hospitals. On occasion, however, there was some bullying of shopkeepers by Government ministers who wanted the Asians to close their businesses and attend various political rallies and listen to their harangue.

For a time, relations with Britain and the United States were strained and East Germany and China were beginning to exert more influence. The Indians viewed the Communist role with great suspicion and were convinced that Nyerere was heading in the wrong direction and would live to regret forging relationships with these countries in the not too distant future. In August 1964, two Chinese ships visited Dar on a goodwill visit. The ships were loaded with consumer goods and so much merchandise was sold to locals at give-away prices that the local economy was upset for many months. The goodwill was thus double-edged and soured the new found relationship.

In 1969, I made my second visit to post-independence Kenya. This for me was a year of decision. I was now a specialist and I had to decide whether to settle in Kenya, the country of my birth, or to go on a self-imposed exile somewhere in the west.

I was taken aback when the airline informed me that I needed a visa. *"But how can that be"* I protested. *"I am a Kenya citizen by birth and my mother was born in Kenya in 1907"*. Imagine my surprise when I discovered that a white person from the United Kingdom did not need a visa. I confirmed this with the Kenya Embassy in London and sent my passport to London along with the appropriate fee of six shillings.

I arrived at Nairobi Airport in the early hours of the morning and was flabbergasted when I was informed that I would not be allowed to set foot in Kenya as my passport had the wrong stamp. My protest that I was a *wanainchi* returning to my mother country and my appeals for compassion fell on deaf ears. *"No, you are a* persona non grata*"* I was told, *"and you will be deported to England on the evening flight"*.

While I waited in the airport lounge the same officer and a couple of his colleagues came and sat next to me. They wanted to know all about England, especially the 'white girls'. They were curious to know why the Asians returning from the United Kingdom did not use hair oil like the 'smart Indians in Kenya'. During this *tête-a-tête* I managed to persuade the officers to send me to Dar es Salaam.

So once again I was on my way to Tanzania, albeit reluctantly. The flight path of the small shuddering plane took us over the aquamarine of the Indian Ocean, and soon we were over Zanzibar, a beautiful emerald and brown island surrounded by a white halo of the breaking waves. One could hardly believe that this jewel of nature was once the centre of the despicable trade in human cargo. The Anglican Cathedral now stood over the site of the old slave market, perhaps built here to atone for the sins of the past. The high altar had replaced the whipping post where the chained blacks were displayed like cattle. Here they had been whipped and bullied. Those who had cried were disposed of and the tough ones who had survived were sold to the Arab masters.

Gouged out of the green vegetation I could see a large stadium. It was *déjà vu* for I had seen the same camera images on television in England just a few days earlier. *"Mau Tse Tung Stadium"* I said to the passenger next to me. He leaned over my shoulder to take a good look and easing back into his seat asked, *"How do you know that?"*

"Panorama", I replied. *"I saw the same shots on Panorama on the BBC only a few days ago"*.

He rolled his eyes, took a deep breath and said softly, *"You know more about us in England than we know living here"*.

At the airport, I asked a clerk behind a weather-beaten desk and an equally ancient black phone if I could make a call. He looked up the number of Dr. Dhupa in the directory, dialled the number and passed the handset saying, *"Here bwana"*. I offered to pay but he just shook his head and with a polite *'asante'* showed me the door.

Physically the town had changed little, if at all, except for the spanking new *TWIGA HOTEL*. Here I attended a meeting of the Rotary Club as a guest and immediately noticed that there were no black members. This was because, I was informed, they would not pay their dues and lost their membership by default.

On arrival in Dar I noticed that the town was covered in a stench which was particularly offensive when there were no sea breezes. The more affluent areas were even worse off. A quick *coup d'oeil* revealed that this was due to a recent practice by the wealthier households to rear chickens and ducks in their own backyards. The practice caught on until whole areas resembled large chicken coops. The authorities were slow in recognising this as aesthetically unacceptable and an obvious danger to health. Eventually the Municipality took action and the problem disappeared almost overnight.

My perception was that the Indian resolve to stay in Tanzania seemed to be softening. They appeared quite nervous and were much more inquisitive of life in the United Kingdom. The Ismaili community, too, was becoming disenchanted. The feelings of doubt, despair and foreboding were in part fuelled by inconsistency in the statements made by various government ministers and a spate of deportations of Asians. These expulsions were arbitrary and at the whim of the authorities. There was a distinct lack of communication and liaison between government departments.

One late morning I was in the office of the Chief Immigration Officer, who being a friend of my brother had offered to help me to obtain a visa to Kenya. That morning the whole Asian community was abuzz with the news that two prominent Asian brothers were being deported at midday. The officer told us that there was no chance of a reprieve. Just then, the telephone rang and at the end of the conversation the officer, who appeared very relieved, turned to my brother and said, *"Kwisha Undoka"* ("They have taken off"). In fact, he was misinformed, for the flight had been delayed pending yet another review of the case.

Early that year Tanzania had welcomed the first black locally born and bred obstetrician and gynaecologist who was trained in the UK. By a strange coincidence, Tito Mzrai turned out to be a friend who was my fellow Registrar at Freedom Fields Hospital in Plymouth in 1967. He very kindly invited me to dinner and we had a pleasant time bending the elbow late into the night.

It was two agonisingly long weeks before I obtained a visa to get back into Kenya. The first flush of *Uhuru* was definitely over and a definite pattern of African attitude and behaviour towards the Asians was beginning to emerge. Their situation was fragile and some of the signs did not bode well.

The Asians in all three East African countries, who had so far remained ambivalent, were becoming increasingly unhappy at the direction in which these countries were heading. They were relatively small in numbers and likely to suffer the fate that often befalls minorities. Their community of 300,000 was surrounded by an ever-increasing sea of blacks who did not like them. Any talk of rights in a multi-cultural society was just that and they were afraid to build their future on an abyss of uncertainties. They felt they were living under duress and that their survival in East Africa was in considerable doubt.

Mwalimu Nyerere had proclaimed that there would be no private capital and this was followed by nationalisation of banks and other institutions owned by Asians. Further, all the three countries had legalised strictures soon after independence which implicitly discriminated against Asians. These involved questions of citizenship, employment in government services and compulsory national service. In spite of the urgings by leaders such as Makhan Singh and the Aga Khan for Asians to throw in their lot with the Africans, the vast majority of them remained unconvinced. The 'sceptics', on the one end of the spectrum, had begun to vote with their feet, while the 'martyrs' wanted to stay – 'come what may'. They loved the climate, the servants and the good life and nothing else mattered.

The Africans were resentful as they felt that the Asians had usurped what was legitimately theirs and regarded them as ruthless exploiters. Their leaders often resorted to xenophobic political rhetoric to get African votes and both Nyerere and Kenyatta had called the Asians bloodsuckers and leeches. They dismissed the Asian support, moral and monetary over many decades, as nothing more than a bribe to gain a better place in society. The Asian aloofness and reluctance to engage in social intercourse with the Africans also rankled the natives.

The Asians were no doubt full of their own prejudices. The pioneers and the older generation were ignorant and illiterate, a product of the Indian caste system, and victims of the old ideas from their homeland. The subsequent generations often reflected the bias of their parents and were influenced by the system of apartheid promulgated by the Europeans. The system of education was designed to exclude all African history, culture and heritage and this further encouraged ignorance and prejudice. The African was at the bottom of the totem pole and it suited every Asian to keep him there. The Asians believed that the Africans were *'junglys'* (savages) and therefore inferior. The Africans were referred to by such derogatory terms as *'Kalas'*, or *'Kalea'* ('blacks'), or as *'boyees'*, a distortion of 'boys'. When the Africans became aware of this, the Asians began to call them *'Undheras'* ('darkies'), or *'Krishan'*, after the cyanotic Hindu god Krishna.

Fortunately, as a result of education, increasing contact in schools, workplaces and sports fields, and the general relaxation of attitudes worldwide, such bigotry and prejudice began to decrease. It did not, however, disappear. Marriage with Africans, for example, remained out of the question. One hypothesis advanced to explain the lack of such relationships is that Asians tend to be very colour conscious and are not attracted to the African physiognomy. But is this theory correct? If so, it does not explain why the railway work camps had a large number of followers, female and male, consorting openly with the coolies. There are also numerous examples in that period of men who had African wives and many more who kept concubines, albeit usually in rural and remote areas. Even in the towns and cities, men had mistresses and were patrons of bordellos. It was certainly not uncommon for young Asian men to have their first sexual experience with a Bantu or Swahili prostitute.

The change of the African attitude towards the Asians was epitomised at Kenyatta Airport. The customs officers targeted the Asians, scattering the contents of their suitcases and demanding duties on anything that took their fancy. Departing passengers were kept waiting, were searched, and often their parcels were ripped open. Security officers demanded *'wapi chai'* ('tea money') as they frisked passengers and passport clerks tried to find faults with the documents when there were none. The trick to avoid all this grief was to cross the palm of the porter who no doubt shared the ill-gotten gain with the bigger sharks.

During the middle years of Kenyatta's stewardship the progressive deterioration of the infrastructure of Nairobi was sad to behold. The road surfaces were allowed to crack, crumble and develop potholes of such a size that a jeep could not negotiate them. On one occasion when a Gujarati contractor's car got stuck in one such crater on Desai Road (now Digo Road), he used a truck to haul the car out and filled the hole with leftover gravel. That night he was visited by an *askari* who accused him of dumping rubbish in the pothole. The policeman would not budge until his demand of ten shillings was met. Champa Road (now Rungu Irika Road), a 40-foot wide tarmac route which ran in front of my father's house in what was popularly known as the *Sikh Colony,* was commandeered by African mechanics and turned into a workshop for lorries, and woe betide the man who objected to their presence. Downtown Kenyatta

Avenue, once a magnificent dual-carriageway with wide, flower-covered boulevards, had become a neglected eyesore. The metal barriers that once protected the flower beds lay in a twisted heap and the cenotaph had fallen prey to vandals, the stones laying half buried where they had fallen.

Minor crimes were becoming an accepted way of life. Mischievous *totos,* Kenya's own version of artful dodgers, were all over the city. They insisted on finding a parking space for the motorist at the Central Post Office and would 'guard' the vehicle while the owner emptied his post box. Those who forgot to tip were sure to be rewarded with a flat tyre and scratched paintwork on their next visit. Pickpockets and bag snatchers had spread through the city like the plague and every tourist and anyone with a bulging pocket was fair game. Jewellery snatching and muggings became so common that the City Park, once a heavenly oasis where people of all races went to chill out in the evenings and weekends, became a 'ghost park'. The Asians started frequenting a safer open area in the vicinity of the Cathedral which locals soon dubbed *Cutchi Park* or *Chevra Park.* When the criminals started attacking in broad daylight, however, this too was abandoned.

The more affluent Asians started fleeing to the suburbs, buying houses in the once exclusive 'European areas'. Many built their own edifices to reflect their status and wealth. This, however, provided only a short respite for they became the targets of armed gangs that began to terrorise the outskirts. The owners responded by erecting metal stockades with powerful security lights and employing African *machungis* (night watchmen) – thus becoming prisoners in their own homes. Ironically, all of the security only helped to highlight the targets. The weakest link was the *askaris* who handed over the keys of the donjon at the first signs of danger and often joined burglars to bite the hand that fed them. Their predilection for hard currency meant that most Asians had a stash of ready cash to hand over to avoid being cut up. The police were of no help as they were often the culprits themselves. On one occasion, an Indian family arrived at the Masari Road Police Station to report an armed robbery, only to be greeted by the burglar sitting behind the desk twiddling his firearm. On another occasion, it was said that an Indian was drinking Scotch when the burglars burst in. As they were leaving one of the men picked up the half full bottle. Unphased by the events the Indian said, *"That is mine, leave it alone."* The robber put the bottle down.

The thieves were not always so obliging. Two senior doctors, a cardiologist and his pathologist wife, were hacked to death even when no resistance was offered. Mrs Vimal Dosaj, a septuagenarian, was strangled by her female servant, all for the sake of a few shillings. Foreign and Asian motorists were commonly beaten up if they were involved in an accident with an African, regardless of who was at fault. All the police could do was advise these motorists not to stop but drive to the nearest police station to report the incident.

The average black man on the street seemed to abhor crime and was not averse to administering instant justice to someone caught committing an offence. The black passers-by would set upon a bag snatcher or a pickpocket, mercilessly kicking and punching him until he was half dead. This kind of behaviour was perhaps a reflection of the pre-colonial days when there were no prisons and tribal law prevailed. A thief in those days was beaten, tortured or even killed and his farm animals destroyed according to the severity of his misdeed. A woman might be subjected to similar abuse which included beatings and thrashing with stinging nettles if she annoyed her husband. Children were no exception. Even livestock was punished with stinging nettles pushed up their orifices if they strayed onto a plantation.

Inefficiency, real or contrived, became the hallmark of government departments and escalated with the passage of time. The counter-clerks seemed to be quite oblivious to lengthening queues outside every office and the black *bwana* extended his siesta for as long as he liked. Files disappeared with regular monotony and every transaction took many visits to the same office. *'Sijui'* ('don't know')and *'Kuja Kesho'* ('come tomorrow') were stock answers to every enquiry.

This kind of behaviour was often a ploy to extract money from the unsuspecting punter. The jingle of coins and rustle of currency notes was a sure way to kick-start stalled government machinery. Every transaction had its price, from a few shillings pressed into the palm of the péon to a bag full of banknotes for a business licence or a government contract. Busy people often avoided such hassle by employing an agent to do the 'dirty work'. I met a beautifully dressed Indian man in Nairobi who, it was said, could open any door and get anything done at the right price. *"The magic is in the suitcase"* he said with a wink and a smile.

311

Most Indians, businessmen and professionals alike, who had substantial funds, regularly sent money abroad to safeguard against 'a rainy day' which they were sure would come sooner or later. These funds were transferred through middlemen at a hefty fee. Indians were not alone in this unpatriotic plunder of the nation, for Europeans and Africans were equally involved in 'safeguarding' their assets. A story circulating in East African circles was that Idi Amin once boasted in a bar in Kampala that he would be okay if things went sour in Uganda as he had 5,000 pounds saved in a bank abroad. The listeners nearly killed themselves laughing at his naivety, for this paltry sum was chicken-feed compared to the hundreds of thousands they had themselves stashed away in foreign banks.

The middlemen were usually Asian businessmen and bankers, African and European travellers and staff of African and European embassies. On one occasion, I accompanied a friend to a bank owned by a Gujarati gentleman. Here the customers had a choice of two accounts. 'Number One' was an ordinary legitimate account, whilst a 'Number Two' account was managed by the owner in person from his office at the back. Here cash changed hands and the banker made appropriate entries in a 'pass book' in his own handwriting in Gujarati. The transaction was carried out in a remarkably casual manner and the customer had no cause for concern as the money would always appear in his account in the UK minus the bank's cut of 25 percent.

One inevitable change in the wake of Uhuru was the opening of the hitherto segregated schools to all races and the adoption of Swahili as the lingua franca. However, the simultaneous abolition of 'vernacular classes' did not sit well with Asians as they feared that inability of children to read and write their own language would lead to a loss of culture and identity. They were also afraid, not without cause, that educational standards would fall and the buildings would go to wrack and ruin. Affluent families withdrew their children from state schools and enrolled them into private, often Mission, schools. This proved to be a mixed blessing, for while the academic attainment was excellent, language skills suffered. Within a generation, young Asians became very westernised, hard-pressed even to speak pidgin Punjabi and Gujarati.

During a subsequent visit to Kenya in 1979, I was a guest at a party hosted by a charming friend, the late Mrs Surinder Narayan. There I had a chance encounter with Mr Krishan Gautama, a portly lawyer whom I had known since my childhood days in Nakuru in the early 1940s. He was a member of the Kenya Parliament representing Parklands area of Nairobi. It was disheartening, however, to discover that he was the only Asian MP representing a population that was about 70,000 in number. In 1959, the Asians were allocated fifteen out of 91 seats, representing a population of approximately 177,000. At independence, four years later, they held a paltry two nominated seats in what became the Kenyan Parliament.[254]

One of the incumbents was Pio Gama Pinto, a Kenyan-born Goan, who was a staunch Socialist and a vociferous supporter of the Mau Mau. He had helped Dr A. C. L. de Souza found *GOAN VOICE* in 1948 and later moved to become the editor of the *DAILY CHRONICLE* when it was launched in the 1950s. The other representative was Fitz D'Souza, also a Goan, who had distinguished himself as a member of the Indian-Christian Union. After Pinto's assassination in 1965 and the expiry of D'Souza's term, there was a hiatus of many years before Gautama revived the Asian spirits by getting elected in 1979. He, too, was gone in the next election.

This surprise meeting with the MP turned out to be quite an eye-opener. The conversation during the evening veered on to politics and the adverse conditions prevailing in Kenya at the time. There were daily cuts in electric and water supplies, and meat, milk and eggs were difficult to obtain. *Posho* (white maize flour) was in such shortage that long queues formed wherever there was some to be had – all this in a country that was once self-sufficient. The MP tried to ignore the conversation but as the discussion continued he became quite agitated and demanded, *"Such talk must stop, otherwise I will have to leave"*. He confessed later that if someone reported to the authorities that he had taken part in such a discussion he would be in 'trouble'!

The middle years of Kenyatta's presidency would witness the exodus of Asians. Not long after independence, many could feel the noose tightening around their necks. In 1964, the Government declared its unease at the slow pace of Africanisation of the economy. The main target was the large Asian community which was estimated at about 177,000 in 1962. A large but unknown

---

[254] Ref: p97 – Gregory, Robert G – Quest for Equality. Asian Politics in East Africa 1900-1967 Oruental Longman Ltd., New Delhi, 1993

number had opted to remain 'Citizens of United Kingdom and Colonies.' In 1967, the Government announced that the vast majority of Asians were to be expelled.

Public opinion in Britain, as to whether these Asians had a right to enter the UK, was divided. Ian McLeod,[255] in 1968, argued that these Asians had been promised free entry into the UK and all those expelled by Kenya had a right of entry. Enoch Powell and his allies argued that the intention of the Commonwealth Immigration Act of 1962 was to restrict the right of entry to those born in the UK and to those holding a passport issued in the UK. In Britain, there was mounting opposition to immigration as the public was afraid of being swamped by the newcomers. Labour politicians, too, had such concerns. When Roy Jenkins left the Home Office in 1967, he had discussed with the Leader of the House of Commons, Richard Crossman, the possibility of finding time in the parliamentary programme for a bill to restrict the immigration of Kenya Asians. Confidential talks had taken place with the Kenyan and Indian Governments to persuade the former to at least relax its rate of expulsions and the latter to offer succour to as many Asians from East Africa as possible. Kenyatta, however, remained adamant and although Mrs Indira Gandhi, the Indian Prime Minister, was willing to offer private professions of assistance, she was unwilling to make public statements since to do so might encourage more expulsions.[256]

On Saturday, 20 April 1968, Powell delivered his infamous speech to the Conservatives of West Midlands. He spoke of the concerns of a constituent who thought that ' in this country in fifteen or twenty years' time the black man will have the whip hand over the white man'.[257] Powell urged the stopping of the inflow and promoting of repatriation. He then dropped a bombshell saying, *"As I look ahead, I am filled with foreboding. Like the Roman, I seem to see the River Tiber foaming with much blood."*[258]

In 1968, the British Parliament passed strongly restrictive legislation against Asian immigration barring entry into the UK to those individuals who held British passports. On the other hand, in

---

[255] Ref: p239 – Cosgrave, Patrick – *Enoch Powell.* The Bodley Head Ltd. 31 Bedford Square, London, 1989

[256] Ref: p244 – Cosgrave, Patrick – *Enoch Powell.* London 1989

[257] Ref: p246 – Cosgrave, Patrick – *Enoch Powell.* London 1989

[258] Ref: p250 – Cosgrave, Patrick – *Enoch Powell.* London 1989

January 1969, the Trade Licences Act came into effect in Kenya. Non-citizen (i.e. Asian) traders had their licences revoked as part of the Government policy of promoting citizen (i.e. African) businesses, particularly in small towns and villages.

There were many reasons for African resentment towards Asians. The Africans were jealous of their place in society and economic superiority, but the Asians did not feel that they needed to apologise for this. With a few exceptions, their success was built upon decades of experience, self-denial, frugality and entrepreneurship. Above all, it was the result of what they called *khoon-pasina* (blood and sweat). The Africans disapproved of Asian social aloofness which they equated with snobbishness and elitism. They found Asian women attractive and desirable but totally unattainable. This was perhaps a symptom of Asian cultural values, which imposed strictures on female behaviour and separation of the sexes. These restrictions were equally galling for Asian men for, like others, they could see but not touch. Dating was, and still is, frowned upon in most circles and most marriages are a result of introductions arranged by parents.

The Africans, with some justification, disapproved and distrusted those who had opted for foreign passports – and a large number of *Muhindi* had done just that. Many who chose to become Kenyan citizens did so with an ulterior motive of safeguarding their jobs or business interests and to be the beneficiaries of bursaries, scholarships and other such perks. Their loyalty was questionable.

The British had also eyed the Asian economic strength with some trepidation but were unconcerned with social compartmentalisation, being the architects of separation themselves. Social contact after independence was facilitated by common schools, westernisation of the younger generations and the use of English as a common language. Such contact occurred at workplaces, clubs, pubs and public functions, but rarely extended to people's homes. The congregation of races, it would seem, was driven by necessity rather than mutual affection or a desire to know others better. I visited Kenya on numerous occasions and attended many parties in Asian homes, but I never once saw an African or European guest.

Even at public dinners and social gatherings, a racial divide was very apparent. Asians complained that Africans drank too much and pointed to their custom of not allowing the waiters to remove empty beer bottles from their tables. This, I was told, was to impress others! Some of these meetings were good as an exercise in social engineering but lacked warmth and affection. At a medical sundowner, I was talking to a jovial African internist when I happened to mention that I was a Canadian, born and raised in Kenya. He immediately turned on his heels and walked away in mid conversation saying, *"So you left us"*.

The Asians were in a dilemma. It was not a question of when to go but where to go. The choice lay between the Indian sub-continent and Britain. Time had not only loosened their ties with their ancestral homelands but many of those born in Kenya (62 per cent of the total Asian population by 1962) had never been to India or Pakistan.[259] The experience of those who had returned to *Matri Bhumi* (the Motherland) was often disappointing. Jobs were scarce, business opportunities limited and competition fierce. Many of the retirees who had carted away modern electric appliances to India and invested their earnings in new *hawelis* (houses) were frustrated because of the lack of amenities. Their cookers and refrigerators stood idle for the lack of power and were only useful as storage units. They were ill-prepared for the dirt and disease, the lack of medical care and the belt tightening that was often necessary. Many were subjected to harassment by relatives, neighbours and the local 'mafia'.

Mr Inder Singh, a retired railway guard, had hardly settled down in his new house in Chandigarh when the local thug began to shatter his windows and threatened to cause more trouble unless he was paid protection money. When Singh refused, the 'Tax man' came along for an 'investigation'. The last straw was the discovery one morning of a 'refugee family' that had set up a tent on his front lawn. The exasperated old gentleman sold his assets and returned to his sons in Kenya.

The United Kingdom, on the other hand, was Shangri-la. The reports from early immigrants and students were very encouraging. Education, a major concern of many ordinary families, was free and there was a golden chance for their children to become professionals. Social security and the National Health Service were very enticing. Job opportunities were plentiful and with their work ethic and knowledge of English, they stood a good chance of employment. The small businessman saw great potential in small

---

[259] Ref: p12 – Gregory, Robert G. – *Quest for Equality. Asian Politics in East Africa 1900-1967.* Orient Longman Ltd., New Delhi 1993

dukas and corner shops. Over and above all these considerations was the real possibility of a peaceful and secure life in a decent and tolerant society. The cry soon rang out: *"Blighty, here we come."* In one year alone (March 1968 to 1969), 18,000 Asians left Kenya and this momentum continued until their number of 192,000 in 1967-8 fell to 78,000 in 1979.

The middle years of Kenyatta's Presidency were also blighted by poor relations between civilian authorities and the military. Matters came to a head in March 1971 and a *coup d'etat* by Jaluo, Kamba and Kalenjin military personnel was crushed by the Kenya Government. Thirteen men were tried, convicted and jailed. The trial tainted several high officials, including Kenya's Chief Justice and the army Chief of Staff. Neither was prosecuted, although both resigned.

Kenyatta sensed that there was a distinct possibility Kenya may drift into a situation in which a military government could replace a civilian administration. He therefore took steps to keep the army small, increase the 'intelligence system' within the ranks and make pay and benefits more attractive. The British advisory role was maintained but the presence of British forces was never publicised. Soldiers from the United Kingdom were kept out of the capital but widely believed to be available to the civilian government if called upon.[260]

The period between 1974 and 1978 has been described as MONARCHY for these were the years of nepotism, favouritism, corruption and political murder. Kenyatta's health, age and succession were topics of constant concern.

The President's wife, Mama Ngina, who he had met in prison and married soon after his release, began to grab whatever she could. She acquired uncultivated land, working farms, hotels and businesses. She was actively engaged in the illegal export of ivory and wildlife trophies. Members of her family and those hanging onto the Presidential apron strings, too, were amassing wealth hand-over-fist. Meanwhile, the lot of the common man went from bad to worse. The oil-based recession and drought of 1973-1974 made the situation desperate.

---

[260] Ref: p157 – Miller, Norman N. – Kenya: *The Quest for Prosperity.* Gower Pub. Company Ltd., 1984

Mama Ngina Kenyatta. Courtesy of the _'Daily Nation'_.

The murder of Mr J.M. Kariuki plunged the country into its darkest period. Kariuki was a former Mau Mau detainee who had supported Kenyatta and at one time served as the President's secretary. His flamboyant lifestyle, his public criticism of the President and his concern for the poor, made him a darling of the masses but did not sit well with the authorities. He was arrested in a Nairobi hotel in March 1975 by senior police officers and murdered by unidentified assassins. This resulted in student riots, a parliamentary revolt and a split among the Kikuyu. The finger was pointed at the Government.

To diffuse the situation, Kenyatta hurriedly set up a blue-ribbon commission. Its reports, in June 1975, accused the Kenya Police of a massive cover-up and blamed the commander of the paramilitary Government Service Unit (GSU) as 'the person who took an active part in the murder himself or was an accomplice of the actual murder or murderers'.[261]

J M Kariuki. Member of Parliament. Courtesy of the *'Daily Nation'*.

An acrimonious debate followed in Parliament. Kenyatta reacted by dismissing critics who held government posts. The Deputy Speaker, Martin Shikuku, and MPs Mark Mwithaga and John Serony, were arrested. In a vicious speech, on the annual Kenyatta Day, reminiscent of the one he made after Tom Mboya's murder, Kenyatta declared, *"The hawk is in the sky. It is ready to descend on the chickens who stray from the path."*[262] Kenyatta managed to contain dissent by his charisma and the threat of force but his Government was tainted forever.

---

[261] Ref: p52 – Miller, Norman N. – Kenya: *The Quest for Prosperity.* London 1984

[262] Ref: p53 – Miller, Norman N. – Kenya: *The Quest for Prosperity.* London 1984

In 1975, the SUNDAY TIMES of London published a series of articles entitled **"Kenya on the brink".** This was an exposé of the Kariuki murder and its subsequent cover-up. It also gave details of the wealth accumulated by Mama Ngina and her blatant profiteering at the expense of Kenya's wildlife and rainforests, which were burnt down to make charcoal for sale to Arab Gulf States. It was also suggested that the Government was involved in corrupt practices of accepting bribes from European businessmen. These revelations were perhaps most damaging to Kenyatta's reputation. But the gods were on his side.

An important happening that helped to divert attention and stabilise the regime in Kenya occurred thousands of miles away in Brazil. This was a severe frost that had damaged the coffee crop and the resultant shortage sent prices soaring in 1976-7. Not only were enormous profits made on the sale of Kenyan coffee, but Kenyans also profited from the smuggling of Ugandan coffee which was illegally shipped through Kenya. The boom filled the pockets of the nation and curtailed open political dissent.

Presidential succession was another matter of national concern. The Vice-President, according to law, automatically assumed presidential powers in three months should the office fall vacant. Some Kikuyu-led politicians feared this gave the incumbent an opportunity and the power to promote his own nominee. Their attempts to block this possibility were thwarted by a coalition of Daniel Arap Moi, the Vice President, and Charles Njonjo, the Attorney General, with eventual support of Kenyatta and his cabinet.

Mzee Kenyatta moved to his heavenly abode on 23 August 1978. There was genuine nationwide grief at his passing and his body was laid to rest with great pomp, ceremony and the respect that he had earned. Tributes and messages of sympathy poured in from all over the world. It was now time to reflect and assess the man and an important era that had just come to a close.

Kenyatta was an autocratic, ruthless leader who knew what was best for his nation. He and his Government were implicated in the murders of Mboya and Kariuki and the cover-ups that followed. He was brutal in his stifling of opposition parties and student dissenters and was not averse to using force when it suited his purpose. Under his regime, his wife and relations were allowed to wield undue influence and amass vast amounts of wealth at the expense of fellow countrymen, natural resources and wildlife. But the man must be judged in the context of what the situation was like at home and what was happening in the African countries around him.

President Jomo Kenyatta, circa 1900 – 1978.

Kenyatta had the ability, foresight and courage to lead a bold challenge against the might of the British with scant regard for his own safety and suffering. Under difficult circumstances he continued to allow freedom of speech and freedom of the press. He permitted religious freedom and let ordinary people grow and flourish. The stability of his regime ensured foreign confidence and the inward flow of investment. The establishment of the headquarters of many world agencies in Nairobi was a credit to his leadership. In spite of the fact that an overwhelming majority of Asian community in Kenya supported the African stand for freedom and democracy,[263] they did not reap any of the fruits of *UHURU*.

Kenyatta's policy of Kenyanisation and Africanisation became the main cause of Asian exodus to other countries. Pragmatism was on balance the essence of this era.

When it was time to go, *Mzee* – the honoured elder, the Father of the nation – left behind the rarest of all gifts: PEACE.

---

[263] Ref: p112 – Mboya, Tom J. – Freedom and After. London 1963

CHRONOLOGY

AD

95-110	*The Periplus of the Erythraen Sea* written by an anonymous Greek.
650-800	Arabs and Persians colonise East African coastal towns.
1327-1330	Ibn Batutta arrives off the coast of Zinj (East Africa) and visits Mogadishu, Mombasa and Kilwa.
1414	Chinese fleet arrives off coast of Zinj.
1415	King of Malindi presents a giraffe (K'i-lin) to Emperor of China.
1498-7 April	Vasco da Gama anchors off Mombasa.
1499-7 January	Vasco da Gama reaches Malindi on his return from India.
1505	Francisco d'Almeida sacks Mombasa – start of Portuguese rule.
1587	Zimba, a tribe of cannibals, invade Mombasa and devour its citizens.
1593-96	Portuguese build Fort Jesus in Mombasa.
1631	Yusuf bin Hassan appointed Sultan of Mombasa.
1635	Fort Jesus recaptured by the Portuguese.
1651	Omani Arabs capture Muscat.
1696 March	Siege of Fort Jesus by Arab fleet.
1698-12 Dec	Omani Arabs capture Fort Jesus.
1729-26 Nov	Portuguese finally evacuate Fort Jesus – end of rule in East Africa north of Cape Delgado.
1823	HMS Barracuda arrives in Mombasa.
1832-40	Seyyid Said ibn Sultan moves his headquarters from Oman to Zanzibar.
1833	Imperial Act for abolition of slavery in the Empire.
1837	American Consulate established in Zanzibar.
1840	Sultan Seyyid settles in Zanzibar and brings cloves to the island. Population of Indians about 400.
1841	British Consulate established in Zanzibar.
1848	Johann Rebmann sees Mount Kilimanjaro.
1849	Johann Ludwig Kraff sights Mount Kenya.
1856	Indian population in Zanzibar increases 16-fold in sixteen years to 6,400.
1862-28 July	John Hanning Speke reaches the source of the River Nile at Rippon Falls.

1888-3 Sept	Imperial British East Africa Company, founded by Sir William Mackinnon, receives a Royal Charter.
1889	IBEAC opens first inland station at Machakos.
1893	First coffee planted by John Patterson at Kibwezi.
1894	First Sanatan Dharam temple in Mombasa.
1897	Total abolition of slavery in Zanzibar.
1902	Sir Charles Eliot proposes Highlands exclusively for Europeans.
1904	Lord Delamare arrives at his 100,000 acre farm at Njoro.
	Forty-seven horses imported for racing.
	First Agricultural Show held in Jeevanjee Gardens, Nairobi.
1905	Zionists offered the Uasin Gishu plateau as 'an ante-chamber to the Holy Land'.
	Arya Samaj's first temple – President K.R. Bowry.
1906	Duke of Connaught opens Jeevanjee Gardens in Nairobi.
	Lowlands around Kibos sold to Indians for farming.
	Allidina Visram is elected the founding President of Indian Association of Nairobi.
1907	Total abolition of slavery on mainland.
	Legislative Council formed – all members being government officials except two representing the settlers.
	Formation of British East Africa Indian Association in Mombasa.
	Fakir Chand Mayor becomes the first Asian to be appointed as Assistant Station Master at Port Florence (Kisumu).
	Winston Churchill visits IBEA: publishes *My African Journey* a year later.
1908	Forty-seven Afrikaner families arrive to settle the Uasin Gishu plateau.
	Governor Sir James Sadler supports Indian demands for equal rights – settlers label him 'Flannel Foot'.
1909	Theodore Roosevelt arrives on a hunting safari.
1910	A.M. Jeevanjee appointed to the Legislative Council.
	Arya Samaj temple in Kisumu – President is F.C. Mayor.
	First European farmer arrives in the Nanyuki district with a dog and thirteen chickens.

1912	Introduction of poll tax.
1914	Formation of East African National Congress in Mombasa with A.M. Jeevanjee as President.
1915	Manilal A. Desai arrives in Kenya.
-17 August	Arya Samajists arrested during prayer meeting in Mombasa.
	Arya Samaj Nairobi closed by government.
	Harassment and killing of Indians.
1916	Allidina Visram dies.
	British Forces under General Jan Smuts invade German East Africa.
1918	General von Lettow-Vorbeck surrenders to a battalion of King's African Rifles.
1919	Review Committee releases all Indian prisoners and rescinds deportation orders.
1920	The British East Africa Protectorate becomes Kenya Colony.
	M.A. Desai founds *East African Chronicle* in Nairobi.
1921	Indian currency, *rupees* and *pice*, replaced by British based currency, initially *florins*, then *shillings* and *cents*.
	Winston Churchill succeeds Milner as Secretary of State for the Colonies.
1922	Harry Thuku arrested – followed by a riot – eighteen Africans killed.
-27 January	Churchill 'bombshell' – Government pledge to 'reserve Highlands exclusively for European settlers'.
1923	In response to Indian demands for a common roll, the Secretary of State for the Colonies issues a White Paper stating that 'the interests of the African natives must be paramount'.
	Sitaram Achariar founds *Mombasa Weekly Democrat* in Mombasa. Later arrested, found guilty and remanded for deportation prompting Indian *hartal*.
1924	Desai and Virji arrested.
1925	Railway extended to Eldoret and then to Kampala.
	F.C. Mayor elected President of East African Samajists.
1926	Tea plantations established in Kericho.
	M.A. Desai dies.

1927	Dr A.C.L. de Souza founds *Fair Play*.
	Isher Dass arrives in Kenya to serve as Jeevanjee's private secretary.
	Archariar guides Kenyatta in publishing.
1928	Prince of Wales visits East Africa. Presents a medal to F.C. Mayor in Kisumu.
	Start of World Depression.
1930-26 January - April	India celebrates Independence Day. Gandhi makes his 'Salt March'.
	A.B. Patel and Indians support Native paramountcy.
1931	F.C. Mayor asked by the railways to examine staffing arrangements on the entire railway network.
1933	G.L. Vidyarthi, son of a station master, Horra, founds *Colonial Times*.
1939	Voluntary registration of men of all races.
1940-10 June	Mussolini declares war on Allies.
1941-2 June	Death of F.C. Mayor
1941-27 Nov	Capture of the fortress of Gondor and end of East African campaign.
	East African forces dispatched to Burma.
1945-10 August	Surrender of Japan and end of Second World War.
1946	First National Park established in Nairobi.
1952-20 Oct	State of Emergency and arrest of Mau Mau leaders.
1953-April	Jomo Kenyatta found guilty and sentenced to seven years' imprisonment.
1956-21 Oct	Capture of Dedan Kimathi.
1960	End of Mau Mau Emergency.
	First Lancaster House Conference. British intention to introduce majority rule based on universal suffrage.
1961-14 August	Kenyatta freed from prison.
	'Million acre scheme' – land in 'White Highlands' bought by Government and redistributed to Africans.
1963-12 Dec	Kenya becomes an independent nation with Jomo Kenyatta as its first Prime Minister.
1964-12 Dec	Kenya becomes a Republic – Jomo Kenyatta its first President.
1967-July	Murder of Tom Mboya – Minister of Economic Planning – by a Kikiyu gunman.
	Disquiet among Asians.
1968	Asian exodus starts, following Africanisation policy.

1974-July	Swahili declared as the *lingua franca*.
1977-May	Hunting of wild animals banned by Kenya Government.
1978-22 August	Death of President Jomo Kenyatta.

SELECT BIBLIOGRAPHY

1. Bell, W.D.M. – *The Wanderings of an Elephant Hunter.* Neville Spearman. London 1923
2. Bharati, Agehananda – *The Asians in East Africa.* Nelson-Hall Company. Chicago 1972
3. Blixen, Karen – *Out of Africa.* Putnam. London 1937
4. Blundell, Michael – *So Rough a Wind.* Weidenfeld & Nicolson. London 1964
5. Boyes, John – *John Boyes, King of the Wa-Kikuyu.* Methuen. London 1911
6. Churchill, Winston – *My African Journey.* Hodder & Stoughton. London 1908
7. Cosgrave, Patrick – *Enoch Powell.* The Bodley Head Ltd. London 1989
8. Crosskill, Captain E.W. – *The Two Thousand Mile War.* Robert Hale. London 1980
9. Foran, W. Robert – *A Cuckoo in Kenya.* Hutchinson. London 1936
10. Foran, W. Robert – *The Kenya Police, 1887-1960.* Robert Hale. London 1962
11. Fox, James – *White Mischief.* Penguin Books. England 1984
12. Gardner, Ava – *Ava- My Story.* Bantam Press. London 1990
13. Ghai, D.P. and Ghai, Y.P. – *Portrait of a Minority:The Asians in East Africa.* Oxford University Press. London 1970
14. Goldsworthy, David – *Tom Mboya – The Man Kenya Wanted to Forget.* Heinemann. London
15. Gregory, Robert G. – *India and East Africa: A History of Race Relations Within the British Empire, 1890-1939.* Oxford:Clarendon Press 1971
16. Gregory, Robert G. – Quest for Equality, *Asian Politics in East Africa 1900-1967.* Orient Longman. New Dehli 1993
17. Guha Ramchandra – *A Corner of Foreign Field.* Picador
18. Heathcote, William – *Elephant.* Jonathan Cape. London
19. Hill, M.H. – *Permanent Way.* Hazell Watson and Viney Ltd. Aylesbury and London 1949
20. Hobley, C.W. – *Kenya: From Chartered Company to Crown Colony.* H.F.& G. Witherby. London 1929
21. Huxley, Elspeth – *White Man's Country* (2 Vols). Chatto & Windus. London 1935
22. Huxley, Elspeth – *Out in the Midday Sun.* Chatto & Windus. London 1985
23. Huxley, Elspeth – *Nine Faces of Kenya.* Collins Harvil. London 1990

24. Jackson, Frederick – *Early Days in East Africa*. Edward Arnold. London 1930

25. Kenyatta, Jomo – *Facing Mount Kenya*. Secker & Warburg. London 1938

26. Lorimer, Norma – *By the Waters of Africa*. Robert Scott. London 1917

27. Mangat, J.S. – *History of the Asians in East Africa, 1896-1965*. Clarendon Press. Oxford 1969

28. Mayor, Ram Karan – *An Autobiography*. London 1984

29. Mboya, Tom – *The Challenge of Nationhood*. Heinemann. New York 1970

30. Meinertzhagen, Richard – *Kenya Diary 1902-1906*. Eland Books. London 1983

31. Miller, Charles – *The Lunatic Express*. Macmillan. London 1971

32. Miller, Norman N. – *Kenya: The Quest for Prosperity*. Gower. London 1984

33. Mutibwa, Phares - *Uganda Since Independence – A Story of Unfulfilled Hopes*. Hurst & Company. London 1992

34. Odinga, Oginga – *Not yet Uhuru*: An Autobiography. Hill and Young. New York 1967

35. Parker, John – *King of Fools*. St. Martin's Press. New York 1938

36. Parrinder, Geoffrey – *World Religions*. Facts on File Publications. New York 1971

37. Reitz, Deneys – *Trekking On*. Travel Book Club. London 1933

38. Roosevelt, Theodore – *African Game Trails*. John Murray. London 1910

39. Salvadori, Cynthia – *We came in Dhows*. Paperchase Kenya Ltd. Nairobi 1996

40. Shastri, Anant – *History of Arya Samaj, Mombasa*. New India Press. New Dehli (Published in Hindi)

41. Singh, Gurcharan – *Studies in Punjab History and Culture*. Enkay Publishers Pvt. Ltd. New Dehli 1990

42. Singh, Khushwant – *A History of the Sikhs*. Oxford University Press. New York 1963

43. Speke, John Henning – *Journal of the Discovery of the Nile*. J.M. Dent & Sons. London 1906

44. Tennahill, Reay – *Sex in History*. Stein and Day. New York 1980

45. Trench, Charles Chenevix – *Men who Ruled Kenya. The Kenya Administration 1892-1963*. The Radcliffe Press. London 1993

46. Trzebinski, Errol – *The Kenya Pioneers*. Heinemann. London 1985

47. Fischer, Louis – Ghandi: His Life and Message for the World. Mentor.Penguin Books USA Inc. 1954

48 Thesiger, Wilfred – My Kenya Days. Harper Collins Publishers. London 1994
49 Mboya, Tom J. – Freedom and After. London 1963
50 Best, Nicholas. – Happy Valley: The Story of the English in Kenya. Secker and Warburg. London 1979

Index

Abdul Wahid, 258
Abyssinia, 217, 256, 266, 267
Achariar, Sitaram, 78, 82, 86, 249, 325
Africa Hotel, 136, 194
Aga Khan, 73, 195, 208, 254, 308
Ahmed Brothers, 253
Ainsworth, John, 61, 72, 73, 141, 156, 196
Ali Bey, 26
Ali, Farouk, 282
Amar, G.S., 202, 203
Amara, 94
American Bridge Company, 65
American Consulate, 323
Americani (Merikani), 62, 137, 250
Amery, 84, 86, 87
Amin, Idi, 228, 231, 232, 237, 238, 239, 240, 312
Andrews, Reverend Charles F., 81, 82, 152
aparica, 19
Arabs, 22, 24, 25, 26, 27, 31, 33, 35, 72, 78, 92, 136, 304, 323
Arain, Shafiq, 230, 231, 233, 236
Arya Samaj, 97, 132, 140, 147, 149, 150, 151, 152, 153, 183, 202, 209, 212, 213, 220, 226, 227, 230, 243, 261, 269, 283, 324, 325, 329
Asians, 40, 112, 120, 127, 192, 207, 210, 213, 229, 230, 231, 232, 233, 236, 237, 238, 239, 260, 283, 287, 291, 296, 300, 301, 304, 305, 306, 307, 308, 309, 310, 312, 313, 314, 315, 316, 317, 326
askari, 66, 148, 182, 279, 280, 293, 309, 310
Athi Plains, 59, 250
Ayurvedic medicine, 47
Azania, 20

babu, 51, 69, 97, 99, 101, 103, 106, 107, 115, 129, 138, 141, 144, 147, 153, 160, 184, 187, 192, 205, 210, 219, 222, 278, 279
Bache, 107
Badalas, 134
Bagamoyo, 32
Baganda, 237, 242
Bagge, Stephen, 141
Bajaj, 110
Baker, Sandbach 'siagi ya Queenie', 121
Bali, Yograj, 150
Bandar Abass, 28
Bantu, 22, 26, 214, 309
Banya, 35
Baring, Sir Evelyn, 282, 283
Barracuda, H.M.S., 28, 323
Bates, Marlene, 201
Batutta, ibn, 24, 93, 323
Belfield, Sir Henery, 76, 111, 114
Bell, W.D.M., 248
Besant, A., 83, 257
Bey:*See* Ali Bey
Bhatias, 134
Binaisa, Godfrey, Q.C., 232
Blixen, Karen, 114
Boers, 289
Bohras, 73
Bombay, 23, 30, 35, 62, 83, 121, 157, 197, 203, 224, 248, 271, 272
Bose, Subash Chandra-Netaji, 92, 217, 268, 280
Bowring, Sir Charles, 152
Bowry, Dr Dev Raj, 286, 287
Bowry, Dr Dilbagh, 286
Bowry, Kanshi Ram, 147
Bowry, Shiv Chand, 97
Bowry, Vishnu, 200
Bowry, Walaiti Ram, 147
Boyes, John, 328
brain fever bird (hawk cuckoo), 21
British East Africa Indian Association, 74, 324

Brock, Dr, 55
Bror Von Blixen-Finecke, 114,
    253
bubonic plague
    India 1897, 46
    Nairobi, 62, 224
Buongo (Miwani 1922), 159, 160,
    166, 167
Burjorji, Commissariat, 196
Burton, Sir Richard, 31, 35, 36
Cable, J.A., 90
Calcutta, 132
Cali, 94
Carter Land Commission, 72, 91,
    168
cassava, 291
Cavendish, Victor, Duke of
    Devonshire, 81
Cecil Hotel, 136, 194
Chani's Pharmacy, 298
China, 19, 22, 305, 323
China, General Waruhiu Itote, 285
Cholmondeley, Hugh (Lord
    Delamare), 157
Church Missionary Society, 38
Churchill, H.A., 34
Churchill, Winston, 74, 79, 80, 81,
    142, 246, 251, 324
Clerk, Anil, 231
Club
    Mombasa, 138, 194, 196, 199
    Muthiaga, 253, 254
    Railway, 191, 194
coffee, 85, 93, 114, 127, 137, 138,
    213, 221, 250, 282, 296, 320,
    324
Colonial Office, 73, 75, 79, 87,
    255
Connaught, Duke of, 111, 249,
    324
Coryndon, Sir Robert, 81
Creswell, 159
cricket, 110, 113, 147, 190, 191,
    194, 196, 197, 199
Cunliffe-Lister, Sir Philip, 91
da Gama, Vasco, 25, 93, 134, 137,
    323
dak bungalow, 117, 118, 120, 141,
    224

Damji, Ludha, 31
Dar es Salaam, 20, 177, 229, 233,
    265, 302, 303, 306
Das, Ganesh, 150
Das, Lachman, 151
Dass, Isher, 85, 86, 88, 326
Dave, Pandit Keshav Lall, 150
Davies, Chief W.O., 285
de Souza, A.L.C., 85, 313, 326
debe, 139, 153, 166, 170, 174, 191
Delamare, Lady Gwladys, 253
Delamare, Lord (Third Baron
    Hugh Chalmondley), 71, 72,
    75, 82, 103, 104, 105, 107
Delamare, Tom (Fourth Baron),
    106
Desai, M.A., 77, 78, 79, 82, 83,
    84, 85, 249, 325
dhows, 20, 32, 93, 135, 157
Dhupa, Dev, 117
Dhupa, Dhruv Vrat, 228, 229
Dhupa, Durga Dass, 178, 220, 228
Dhupa, Lila Vati, 189
Din Muhamed, 228
Dinesen, Isak, 114, 115
Diwan Chaman Lal, 284, 285
Dixit, Ravi Dutt, 145
Dual Policy, 82, 85, 86
dudus (giggers), 47
dukanwallas, 175, 257
Duke of Edinburgh, 281
Duke of Gloucester School, 209
Dyan Chand, 192
East African Standard, 89, 108,
    267, 277
Eburu, 94
Eldoret, 289, 325
Elgin, Victor Alexander Bruce 9th
    Earl of, 71, 72
Eliot, Sir Charles, 62, 70, 71, 142,
    156, 157, 248, 249, 255, 324
Elkington, Jim, 250
Ellis, corporal George, 182
Elmenteita Station, 65, 94, 104,
    107
English Point, Mombassa, 29
Entebbe, 49
Ethiopia, S.S., 44

332

Europeans, 20, 25, 26, 31, 33, 35, 36, 37, 40, 65, 68, 69, 70, 71, 72, 73, 75, 77, 78, 79, 80, 81, 82, 83, 85, 87, 89, 90, 91, 92, 98, 105, 106, 116, 117, 119, 120, 121, 127, 139, 141, 142, 148, 159, 164, 183, 194, 195, 197, 254, 257, 258, 264, 278, 279, 280, 282, 285, 289, 291, 293, 300, 308, 312, 324

Ewbank, R.B., 81, 83

Fairplay, 85

falahin, 94

Farquhar, C. Kenya Police, 71

Felling, Christian, 161

fighting mamas, 214

Finch Hatton, Dennis, 114, 253

Flit, 117

Foran, Robert, 256, 257

Fort Jesus, 26, 27, 136, 138, 194, 323

Frere, Sir Bartle, 30, 35, 36

fundis, 200

Gajree, Sham Lall, 219

Gandhi, Mohan Dass Karam Chand, 78, 79, 82, 83, 89, 92, 131, 217, 218, 250, 268, 269, 314, 326

Gariama, 138

German East Africa, 76, 325

Ghadar, publication in Punjabi, 150

ghee, 20, 140, 170, 187

Girouard, Sir Percy, 76

Gohill, 272

Gondor, fortress of, 267, 326

Government Road, Nairobi, 212, 282, 293, 298

Great Train Robbery, 112

Grigg, Sir Edward, 85, 86, 87, 89

Grogan, Ewart S., 72, 91, 105

Gulam - engine driver, 124

Gurdial Singh, 158, 230, 231, 232, 233, 234, 235

Gwalior, Maharaja of, 247

Hamerton, Capt. Atkins, 35

harambee, 245, 289

Harcourt, Lewis, 76

Hassan, Yusef bin (Don Geronimo), 27

Hays Sadler, Sir James, 71

Heera Singh, 56

Highlands (Kenya), 59, 156, 289

Hilton Young, Sir Edward, 87

Hindus, 19, 31, 33, 88, 94, 99, 130, 131, 136, 140, 142, 147, 163, 217, 220, 248, 256, 257, 261, 279

Hiran Village, 129, 131, 159, 168

Hitler, Adolf, 264, 273, 278, 279

Hobley, C.W., 141, 328

Hockey teams, 108, 110, 120, 147, 191, 192, 203, 230

Huebner, 51, 258

human runners, 48

Huxley, Elspeth, 70, 120

Ibrahim Karimbux, 272

Imperial British East Africa Company (IBEA), 40, 324

India, 19, 20, 21, 22, 23, 24, 25, 26, 27, 28, 30, 33, 35, 37, 41, 44, 46, 49, 55, 56, 70, 71, 72, 73, 75, 76, 77, 78, 79, 80, 81, 82, 83, 84, 87, 89, 90, 92, 93, 94, 96, 97, 99, 100, 113, 115, 117, 127, 128, 129, 134, 135, 136, 139, 142, 143, 144, 147, 148, 149, 150, 151, 152, 154, 155, 156, 157, 158, 159, 163, 175, 183, 187, 190, 193, 194, 196, 199, 206, 207, 208, 214, 215, 217, 224, 228, 233, 243, 246, 248, 252, 261, 268, 269, 279, 280, 285, 286, 303, 316, 323, 326, 328, 329

Indians, 19, 20, 22, 23, 24, 25, 30, 31, 33, 34, 35, 36, 37, 40, 44, 47, 54, 61, 62, 63, 68, 70, 71, 72, 73, 74, 75, 76, 77, 78, 79, 80, 81, 82, 83, 84, 85, 86, 87, 88, 89, 90, 91, 92, 97, 98, 104, 106, 107, 113, 116, 120, 121, 129, 135, 137, 139, 140, 141, 142, 143, 146, 149, 152, 156, 157, 159, 164, 165, 189, 190, 192, 193, 195, 199, 200, 207, 211, 212, 217, 219, 226, 227, 249, 254, 256, 257, 258, 259, 261, 268, 271, 272, 275, 276, 278, 280, 287, 293, 300, 303, 304, 305, 306, 312, 323, 324, 325, 326

infertility, 211

Islam, 20, 23, 93, 99, 147, 208

Ismailis, 31, 37, 78, 122, 208, 211, 241, 305, 307

Italians, 126, 265, 266, 267, 275, 276, 280

Ithanasaris, 195

ivory
hunters, 246, 247, 248, 249
poachers, 256
traders, 20, 24, 29, 32, 36, 43, 317

Jackson, Sir Frederick, 66, 71, 72, 76, 108, 156, 248

Jadu:See Magic

Jaluo (Luo), 140, 149, 150, 156, 158, 169, 298, 300, 317

Jeevanjee, A.M., 73, 75, 79, 249

Jeevanjee, T.M., 73, 76, 151

Jinja, 49, 94, 108, 192

Johnstone, Sir Harry, 156

Joint Committee, 89, 90, 91

Kabaka, 237

Kake
Nakuru, 279

KANU (Kenya African National Union), 289

Kapila, Mathra Dass, 140, 147

Karen, area of Nairoibi, 115

Kariuki, J.M., 318, 319, 320

KAU (Kenya African Union), 282

Kaze (Tabora), 30, 32

Kazkazi (Trade Winds), 21

Kenya, Mount (Kere Niaga), 38, 247, 251, 276, 277, 285, 323, 329

Kenyatta, Jomo (Johnstone), 86, 89, 222, 281, 282, 283, 284, 285, 286, 287, 288, 289, 290, 291, 293, 294, 298, 299, 300, 301, 308, 309, 313, 314, 317, 318, 319, 320, 321, 322, 326, 327, 329

Khan, A.M., 125

Khan, Afzal (Simba Tatu), 102

Khan, Yakub, 195, 197

khat, 24, 138

Kibigori station, 67, 119, 159, 171

Kibos, 67, 97, 102, 153, 154, 157, 158, 159, 160, 166, 167, 170, 171, 187, 324

Kilimanjaro, Mount, 38, 99, 251, 302, 323

Kilwa, 20, 24, 25, 26, 32, 36, 323

Kima station, 51, 258

Kimathi, General Dedan Wachiuri, 281, 285, 294, 326

King's African Rifles (KAR), 157, 254, 265, 266, 283, 325

Kipandi(identification cards), 90

Kisumu (Port Florence), 48, 49, 97, 98, 103, 108, 109, 115, 117, 118, 119, 120, 121, 122, 124, 140, 141, 142, 144, 145, 146, 147, 151, 152, 153, 154, 155, 157, 159, 162, 163, 165, 168, 171, 174, 175, 176, 190, 192, 195, 206, 212, 215, 217, 226, 243, 298, 300, 324, 326

Kraff, Johann Ludwig, 323

Kuzi(Trade Winds), 21

laibon, 255

Lake
Bangweulu, 36
Elmenteita, 65
Naivasha, 63, 65
Nakuru, 65
Nyasa, 32
Tanganyika, 32, 36
Victoria, 44, 93, 140, 144, 160

Lancaster, Sir James, 26

landi, 102, 127, 145, 167, 182, 190, 191, 200, 210, 212, 214, 217, 236, 279

landiwallas, 106, 175, 186, 189, 202, 230, 245, 268, 269, 275, 278

Legislative Council (Kenya), 71, 75, 76, 78, 80, 84, 86, 88, 90, 142, 222

lions
  Kima station, 52
  Simba station, 59
  Tsavo, 51, 58

Livingstone, Dr David, 31, 32, 35, 36

Lobo, Emedio, 108, 109

Longonot, Mount, 63

Lorimer, Norma, 103

Ludhiana, 129, 131, 132, 144, 226

Luganda., language, 237

Lugard, Lord Frederick, 32

Lumbwa
  station, 117, 120
  tribe, 66

mabati, corrugated iron sheets, 136, 139

MacDonald, Capt. J.R.L., 43, 45, 105, 289

MacKinnon, Sir William, 41, 42

MacStead, Captain, 149

Madagascar, 19, 268

Madura, S.S., 43

Maini, Sir Amarnath, 231

Maji Mazuri Station, 141

Maji Ya Chumvi Station, 141

Makerere University, 229, 233

malaria, 29, 59, 67, 141, 160, 161, 163, 173

Malindi, 25, 134, 135, 191, 291, 323

Mamsa, 207

Mandal, Dev Raj, 154

Marco Polo, 25

Masai
  sleeping, 65
  tribe, 48, 60, 66, 104, 182, 249, 250

Masansa, 30

matama, 159, 169

Mayor
  Bauji, 160
  Dharam Dev, 98, 118, 226, 243
  Fakir Chand, 118, 129, 144, 145, 151, 158, 175, 183, 195, 212
  Ram Karan, 97, 154, 226, 243
  Shivan, 160

Mboijana, Chris, 232

Mboya, Tom, 298, 299, 300, 319, 320, 322, 326, 328, 329, 330

Mbulamuti Station, 230

McKinnon Road Station, 98

McMillan, Harold, 288

McMillan, Sir Northrup, 114, 297

Mehta, Seth Nanji Kalidas, 108, 147, 227

Meinertzhagen, Richard, 247, 250, 254, 255, 256, 329

Molesworth, Sir Gilford, 43

Molo station, 117, 122, 227

Moman, Kuldip, 121, 261, 276

Mombasa, 20, 21, 24, 25, 26, 27, 28, 29, 30, 40, 41, 43, 44, 45, 48, 49, 55, 56, 61, 66, 68, 70, 71, 73, 74, 76, 82, 84, 85, 88, 92, 93, 97, 98, 99, 101, 102, 103, 108, 110, 111, 114, 118, 120, 121, 124, 127, 129, 134, 136, 137, 139, 147, 148, 149, 150, 151, 182, 193, 195, 196, 199, 200, 201, 203, 208, 212, 215, 229, 243, 247, 249, 252, 258, 267, 271, 272, 323, 324, 325, 329

Monkey Stone - Nandi Hills, 153

Moshi, 302

Motabhoy, Darabshaw, 110

Moyale, 217, 265, 266

Mteita, 66

Muhindi, 169, 300, 315

Muhoroni station, 66, 67, 117, 120, 159, 174, 250

Murchison Falls, 125

Muscat, 27, 28, 30, 32, 137, 323

Muslims, 20, 23, 31, 33, 82, 88, 99, 130, 131, 136, 144, 195, 208, 218, 256, 257

Mussolini, 265, 326

335

Mzrui, 27, 28, 29
Naidu, Sarojini, 84
Nairobi, 51, 61, 62, 63, 64, 71, 72,
    73, 76, 78, 79, 82, 86, 87, 88,
    89, 91, 93, 97, 98, 99, 101,
    102, 103, 104, 107, 108, 109,
    111, 113, 114, 115, 116, 119,
    120, 121, 122, 124, 125, 127,
    132, 140, 147, 149, 150, 151,
    153, 154, 163, 182, 191, 192,
    193, 195, 196, 197, 199, 200,
    201, 202, 203, 208, 211, 212,
    213, 219, 220, 223, 225, 226,
    227, 228, 230, 243, 249, 250,
    251, 254, 256, 257, 258, 262,
    270, 276, 282, 283, 285, 287,
    290, 293, 294, 297, 298, 299,
    300, 301, 302, 305, 309, 311,
    313, 318, 322, 324, 325, 326,
    329
nakhoda, 36
Nakusontelon, 60
Nandi
    hills, 66, 94, 153, 158, 178
    tribe, 66, 67, 153, 158, 173,
        255
Nehru, Jawaharlal, 89, 217, 218,
    269
Nesbitt, 67
Neumann, Arthur - hunter, 247
New Stanley Hotel, 294, 295
Nile river, 31, 32, 42, 94, 252, 323,
    329
Njoro station, 122, 157, 227, 324
Norfolk Hotel, 107
Northey, Sir Edward, 77, 78, 79,
    81
Nowrojee, Pherozeshaw, 110, 111,
    112, 197
Nyanza Farmers Association, 167
Nyerere, Julius, 233, 303, 304,
    305, 308
O'Hara, 51
Obote, Apollo Milton, 231, 232,
    233, 234, 237, 238
Odinga, Oginga, 290, 300, 329
Oman, 24, 27, 28, 29, 303, 323
Onama, Felix, 231
Ormsby-Gore, William, 81, 84

Owen, Captain William, 28
Paice, Arnold, 105
Paice, Frank, 105
Pakistan, 193, 214, 218, 316
Pandya, J.B., 88
Parenti - Italian Vice-Consul, 51,
    52, 258
Pate, 25, 27
Patel, A.B., 88, 89, 92
Patel, Ambu, 287
Patel, C.D., 147
Patel, Dr Muljibhai, 231
Patel, Narshibhai, 152
Patel, Ravjibhai, 110
Patterson, Lt. Col. J.H., 53, 54, 55,
    56, 57, 58, 60, 62, 324
Pemba Island, 23, 24, 26, 29, 304
Periplus of the Erythraen Sea, The,
    20, 323
Phakey, Shadi Ram, 109, 124
Phillips, George, 29
pied-crested cuckoo (monsoon
    bird), 21
Pinto, N., 110
Pinto, P., 313
Pliny, 20
Polak, Henery S.L., 79, 81, 82, 83
Portuguese, 25, 26, 27, 134, 136,
    323
posho (white maize flour), 158,
    168, 313
Prasad, Lala, 148
Preston, Florence, 68
Preston, Ronald, 51, 54, 60, 63,
    64, 65, 67, 124, 137
Prinja, Ram Nath, 151
Pritt, D.N., 285, 286
prostitution
    Swahili, Coast of Kenya, 139
Punjab, 19, 47, 95, 102, 129, 130,
    131, 142, 143, 145, 147, 151,
    157, 159, 160, 166, 168, 171,
    175, 177, 180, 183, 187, 206,
    213, 215, 218, 226, 243, 259,
    329
Puri, D.D., 151
Purmar, Purhotam Hurjee, 58
Race Week, Nairobi, 270, 293
Railway Police, 51, 182, 257

336

Ram, Dhani, 110
Ram, Sita, 150, 151
Ramanand, Bhodraj and Company,
    149, 150
Rebmann, Johann, 38, 323
Reitz, Lt. John James, 28
Rhodes, Sir Godfrey, 164
Ribeiro, Dr. Rosendo Ayres, 224,
    225
Rift Valley, 63, 65, 94, 276
Rigby, General, 30, 31, 34, 35
Rodwell, Edward, 108
Roosevelt, Frankin D., 268
Roosevelt, Kermit, 252
Roosevelt, Theodore, 107, 252
Roshan - epic poem, 58
Royal Engineers, 182
rupee, 30, 77, 224
Ryall, Charles H., 51, 52, 257
Sagala Mission Station, 182
Salisbury Bridge, 46, 98
Salisbury, Lord, 43
Savle, L.M., 73, 150, 151
Sewji, Jairam, 31, 156
Seyyid Said - Sultan of Oman, 28,
    29, 303, 323
Shapley, 150
Sharma, B.R., 151
Sharma, Jiti, 113
Sharma, Lall Chand, 176
Sikhs, 21, 99, 127, 142, 208, 226,
    257, 329
Simba Mbili, 101, 102
Simba station, 59, 100, 251
Simpson, Mrs Wallis, 254
Singh, Baldev, 193
Singh, Bishen, 149, 150, 151, 257,
    258
Singh, Chain, 228, 230
Singh, Chanan, 219, 220, 221,
    222, 226
Singh, Dr Sirmukh, 216
Singh, Dyal, 177
Singh, Inder, 108, 144, 171, 192,
    223, 226, 227, 228, 316
Singh, Jagat, 158
Singh, Jaswant, 197, 285
Singh, Makhan - Trade Unionist,
    221, 286, 308

Singh, Nahar, 226, 228
Singh, Surjit, 193
Singh, Ungan, 54
slavery, 28, 31, 33, 34, 36, 37,
    142, 323, 324
slaves, 23, 24, 32, 33, 34, 35, 36,
    37, 38, 304
Smuts, General, 83, 250, 325
Soares, Eddie, 203, 204
Somalia, 20, 289
Soodanwalla (Kisumu), 146, 166
Soods, 143, 147, 155, 165, 195,
    210
Speke, John Hanning, 31, 35, 36,
    94, 125, 272, 323, 329
Stag's Head Hotel, 273
sugar cane, 119, 131, 154, 160,
    166, 167, 170, 179, 180, 213,
    291
Suswa, Mount, 63
Swahili - language, 21, 38, 45, 47,
    79, 93, 98, 113, 119, 135, 136,
    167, 214, 247, 287, 291, 312
Swahili - people, 22, 25, 31, 33,
    58, 98, 135, 138, 139, 214,
    247, 297, 309
Tanganyika, 30, 85, 88, 114, 148,
    229, 253, 264, 265, 277, 303,
    304
Tanzania, 229, 233, 301, 304, 306,
    307
Taru, 50, 93
Tarya Topan
    financeer - Livingston, 31
    financeer - slavers, 31
    first hospital in Zanzibar, 31
    first school in Zanzibar, 31
Terrazzo, 276
Thaker, Judge R.S. Q.C., 285
Thuku, Harry, 78, 79, 249, 282,
    325
Thuwain, Sultan, 303
Tippu Sultan, 28
Tippu Tib, 31, 36
totos, 106, 174, 189, 190, 195,
    280, 310
Tsavo, 38, 50, 51, 54, 55, 56, 58,
    59, 62, 101, 149, 262
tsetse fly, 49

337

turbans, 44, 50, 130, 135, 156, 168, 227
Turner, Mr, 67
Uasin Gishu, 191, 256, 289, 324
Uaso Nairobi, 60
ugali, 59, 169
Uganda Railway, 40, 44, 111, 124, 143, 148, 273
Ujiji, 30, 32, 36
Ukerewe:*See* Lake Victoria
unga gano, 287
Varma, B.S., 78, 79, 82, 88
Victoria, Queen, 249
Virjee, Suleman, 194, 256
Visram, Abdul Rasul, 151
Visram, Seth Allidina, 31, 73, 200, 236, 256, 324, 325
Visram, Sugrabai, 241
Voi station, 49, 51, 150
von Lettow-Vorbeck, Paul, 148, 325
Wales, Prince of, 96, 114, 162, 213, 253, 326
Waller, D.D., 157
Ward, Freda Dudley, 254
water trains, 49

Watkins, Frank, 78
Webb, Sidney (Lord Passfield), 87
Wedgewood, Colonel, 79
Whitehouse Bakery, 224
Whitehouse, George - Chief Engineer, 44, 60, 61, 63, 124, 193
Wilford, Francis, 19, 94
Wilkinson, Q.C., 232
Wilson Report, 88
Wilson, Sir Samuel, 87
World War
    First, 58, 159, 221, 264, 297
    Second, 70, 92, 125, 128, 191, 192, 221
Yokohama mammas (Japanese Legation), 293
Zanj, 19, 22, 25, 27, 147
Zanzibar, 19, 20, 22, 23, 26, 29, 30, 31, 33, 34, 35, 37, 70, 82, 135, 156, 194, 247, 256, 294, 303, 304, 306, 323, 324
zebra, 59, 65, 224, 225
Zinj:*See* Zanj
Zionists, 324